The Critics Savor Michael Smith's
The Afternoon Tea Book

"Now that afternoon tea is back in vogue, those who wish to partake and those who wish to serve it can have no better reference than *The Afternoon Tea Book* by Michael Smith, a noted British tea authority. It has wonderful recipes, some dating to the 1800s, along with its delightful history of tea-drinking from the 17th century to the present. And its descriptions of various teas makes it **a pleasure to read as well as use**."
— *Chicago Sun-Times*

"**Written with the authority only an Englishman has, [*The Afternoon Tea Book*] is brimming with tips and how-tos.** Michael Smith assures us that this ancient custom is enjoying a revival both in his country and in the States. He shares—along with some folklore and nostalgia—recipes for such teatime goodies as fruit butters, jams, scones, crumpets and sundry savories. **This one makes a delightful present.**"
— *Bon Appétit*

"**And for anyone serious about tea, Michael Smith's *The Afternoon Tea Book* is a must.**"
— *New York Daily News*

"*The Afternoon Tea Book* by Michael Smith reminds one why Henry James once wrote that 'there are few hours in life more agreeable than the hours devoted to the ceremony known as afternoon tea.' This, too, is a most agreeable book, covering every aspect of the ceremony from its origins to its utensils. **It should appeal alike to the romantic, the cook, the historian, the china collector, and, of course, those who enjoy 'a nice cuppa.'** It's charmingly made and illustrated, too."
— *Seattle Post-Intelligencer*

"***The Afternoon Tea Book* clearly wins the 'charming' award for the year.** It is as civilized and enjoyable as the repast it details. . . . Even if you never serve or go to tea, here's a delightful book for a rainy afternoon."
— *Baltimore Evening Sun*

The Afternoon Tea Book

Books by MICHAEL SMITH

The Afternoon Tea Book (1986)
New English Cookery (1985)
A Cook's Tour of Britain (1984)
The Homes and Gardens Cook Book (1983)
Amazing Grace and Flavour (1983)
Naughty but Nice (1983)
*The Collected Recipes of Michael Smith
from Pebble Mill* (1982)
Just Desserts (1982)
Cooking with Michael Smith (1981)
A Fine Kettle of Fish (1981)
The Saucy Cookbook (1980)
The Book of Sandwiches (1979)
Grace and Flavour à la Mode (1978)
More Grace and Flavour (1977)
Grace and Flavour (1976)
Best of British Cookware (1975)
Fine English Cookery (1973)

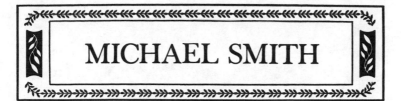

MICHAEL SMITH

THE AFTERNOON TEA BOOK

ILLUSTRATIONS BY
Michael R. P. Bartlett

COLLIER BOOKS
Macmillan Publishing Company
New York

Collier Books
Macmillan Publishing Company
866 Third Avenue, New York, NY 10022
Collier Macmillan Canada, Inc.

Library of Congress Cataloging-in-Publication Data
Smith, Michael, 1927–
The afternoon tea book/Michael Smith; illustrations by Michael
R. P. Bartlett.—1st Collier Books ed.
p.   cm.
Includes index.
ISBN 0-02-010351-4
1. Afternoon teas. 2. Tea. I. Title.
[TX736.S65   1989]
641.5′3—dc19   88-13835   CIP

Originally published in hardcover by Atheneum, 1986
First Collier Books Edition 1989

Macmillan books are available at special discounts for bulk purchases
for sales promotions, premiums, fund-raising, or educational use. For
details, contact:

Special Sales Director
Macmillan Publishing Company
866 Third Avenue
New York, NY 10022

Designed by Cathryn S. Aison

Cover art © 1986 by Gloria Adelson

10 9 8 7

PRINTED IN THE UNITED STATES OF AMERICA

For all my American friends

Note

As you read this book, more than *20 million* cups of tea will be drunk in London alone—TODAY!

Even so, that does not place Great Britain at the top of the tea drinkers' league (we're second). That honor goes to the Republic of Eire.

Third place goes to Tunisia, with New Zealand and Australia bringing up the rear!

Acknowledgments

I would like to thank the following people for their invaluable help in the preparation of this book.

Mrs. Pat Brayne, my secretary in London, for typing and patiently retyping the endless pages of manuscript.

Mrs. Elisabeth Smith, for reading the manuscript and suggesting some excellent improvements.

Mr. Sam Twining, for answering all my questions about tea and for willingly lending me his only surviving copy of *Twining's History of Tea*.

Mrs. Caroline Young, for translating many of my recipes into Americanese and for suggesting certain compromises.

Judith Kern, my editor at Atheneum for her patience in translating my English into . . . English!

A special thanks to Pat Knopf at Atheneum and to my American agent, Claire Smith.

Contents

I am of a generation old enough to remember *afternoon tea* being served in my family home, a handsome house in a thriving, industrial town set against the backdrop of the Pennine Chain in Yorkshire, one of England's most beautiful counties. It is up in the North and halfway between London and Edinburgh: land of the Brontës, "Last of the Summer Wine," J. B. Priestley, and *All Creatures Great and Small*. The youngest of six children, I was born into a vast Methodist family (over sixty-one cousins at one count!). My parents were middling-well-off, which is a Yorkshire expression for middle-middle-class! My father was a textile manufacturer, dyeing and spinning carpet yarns and knitting wools and such-like.

The household consisted of my mother and father, two brothers and three sisters, two live-in maids, a nanny, a charlady, and a general factotum—none of whom were the luxury they may sound in 1986, but a necessity in a household where every stitch of linen was laundered and ironed by the maids and my sisters and every loaf of bread, every cake and biscuit, pie, pound of jam and marmalade was made by my mother and her helpers. Guests were entertained at our table and not, as is fashionable today, in a neighborhood restaurant. We all lived in the mill house, a sturdy, square structure built of huge blocks of cream Yorkshire stone: nothing too fancy in style, for that went against the Methodist (and industrial northern) ethic, though certainly not against the general Victorian ethic with its tendency to be overopulent and somewhat frilly at the edges.

My parents were of course Victorians, in every sense. We children were well brought up by today's standards, with a strict discipline and an ingrained sense of guilt! Strange rules pertained in that home. We were never permitted to be idle; we always had to be doing something, or we were found jobs to do by my mother. We had to walk, never run; talk quietly, never shout; and—worst of all—we were permitted only one piece of cake at teatime, never two! That was considered greedy, as were two boiled eggs, yet three used in an omelet was permissible!

("If you boys are hungry, there is plenty of bread and butter in the kitchen!"—my mother's voice echoes in my ears now as I write this preface).

She was a kindly woman, an excellent raconteuse, almost to the point of hyperbole, and possessed a chuckling sense of humor, yet we children were constantly being warned not to be "excessive" as we told her of some experience or other that had happened during the day at school or while we were out playing.

I well recall the time I went to my mother after having just seen a catfight in the garden of our house (even my own children use this story against me to this day; it was no doubt told them by their aunts (my sisters,) who are wont to bring up embarrassing tales of my past).

"Mother, there's hundreds of cats fighting outside!" I exclaimed in great excitement (so they say).

"How many did you say?" my mother questioned.

"Well—dozens," I replied hesitatingly.

"How many are there *exactly*?" she asked again, determined to pin me down to fact and quell my overexcitement and my fast-growing tendency to exaggerate a story.

"Well," I said, now somewhat deflated, "there's our cat and another!"

"That's better" she exclaimed. "There's no need to exaggerate."

But there is, there is. Even if there were only *two* cats in that garden it *sounded* like hundreds, as anyone who has ever been near a catfight will bear out, and anyway two cats don't make for good telling or for a good fight!

What has all this to do with afternoon tea, you may now rightly be asking. Not a lot, I'll admit. It is simply to make the point that I was never allowed to be abundant! Nor was anything ever "abundant" at Bruntcliffe House. "Enough," yes, and "nice"—*nice*? You see, nothing was ever declared to be "wonderful" or "fantastic" or even "great." The most excessive compliment I ever heard my Yorkshire mamma pay was "That was *quite* nice, dear."

At the other extreme, it has to be said that words such as *awful, ghastly, terrible,* or even in modern-day parlance *the pits*, never passed our lips. Things were just "*not* very nice, dear."

I first learned to be abundant when, as a callow youth of seventeen, I left battle-scarred Britain after the Second World War and headed for the International Hotel School in Lausanne, Switzerland, to start out on my chosen career as an hotelier. There I saw, for the first time, neon lights. (While Bradford had the odd cinema sign in traditional red neon tubing, my village of Bruntcliffe did not even sport a modest floodlight. The gas lamps in the square were as modern as we got.)

This international Swiss city with its nightlife, its elite, its chic, its color, its shops, its demimonde, shocked my mother and father when they visited me. It was all too "excessive" for them by far, and they feared for their son's moral well-being. They need not have worried—my Yorkshire Methodist upbringing was having the very stabilizing influence they had intended it should have, except in one area—*cakes*! Almost within hours of arrival in Lausanne I had discovered Mutrux on the Grand Rue (or was it the Avenue de Chênes? I almost forget now).

Mutrux was the choicest tearoom in town. A far cry from Betty's in Harrogate in the Yorkshire Dales, or Fuller's Tea Rooms in Bradford and Leeds whose iced walnut cake was renowned throughout the county and the prime reason for everyone's patronage.

"Le five-o'clock tea" was *de rigueur* for the elegant Lausanneoise. Fashionable ladies would teeter into the pretty tea *salon*, cocooned against the icy Swiss weather in black ermine wraps and ocelot muffs, white-fox hoods and cashmere stoles— a far cry from the sturdy, heavy worsteds and woolens of functional, wholesome Yorkshire society, and excessive to boot, many a Northern English woman would have thought!

I well recall the tearoom's interior, decorated in shades of café au lait, with a frescoed ceiling, pink quilted cushions on gilt chairs, rosebud china, *and*—shock and horror—tea in glasses! I'd never seen *that* before, nor had I seen tea in individual metal infusers, nor had I seen tea served so *weak*! I made a mental note of it all, for this couldn't be right; perhaps for "foreigners" but not for us Brits.

There were cakes with rich frangipane fillings, fondant-iced tops, and edges coated in crushed pistachio nuts of the palest green. Excess in miniature. But it was not *real* afternoon tea, for where was the toast? Where were the muffins and crum-

pets? Where were the scones with rich yellow cream and strawberry jam? And, what's more, where, yes *where*, were the
potted-meat sandwiches!

American visitors to Europe will find many such famous
tearooms: Sacher's in Vienna, Rumpelmayer's in Paris, Cova
in Milan, the Angleterre in Copenhagen, Florians in Venice,
and the exceptionally beautiful Café Luitpol in Munich. All
still there to be enjoyed (at a price!).

These tearooms are each of the most elegant order, visited
only by the crème de la crème of society, as Jean Brodie "in her
prime" would say of Mackie's or Jenners in Edinburgh, and are
certainly not places where you would get afternoon tea, or "Le
five-o'clock tea," as they call it, in the English manner (and
anyway we have tea at four o'clock!)—their chic is something
quite different.

England, and London, has always had this strange division
between what the "county" and aristocracy do and what the
newly rich prefer. Somehow, on the Continent of Europe these
two groups blend almost imperceptibly—not so with us. It is to
the Yorkshire spa town of Harrogate that we all go—for tea
at Betty's.

It was to be five years before I encountered my first *London*
tearoom (or café, as they were contrarily called, for one never
drank coffee there, certainly not in the afternoon).

I became engaged to my wife-to-be at Gunther's in Curzon
Street, right in the middle of London's fashionable Mayfair
(my Yorkshire Methodist guilt was already beginning to fade
somewhat). Here was elegance in my home country, for Gunther's, along with Fortnum and Mason, the Ritz, Richoux,
Floris, and many others, was where the British upper crust
took afternoon tea—with sandwiches, hot buttered toast and
scones with jam and clotted cream, and cakes. A much better
state of affairs than in that Alpine land, I can assure you.

Right through the swinging, never-had-it-so-good 1960s,
under Prime Minister Macmillan, these institutions continued
to flourish. But all that was to go, as the makeup of British
society changed—many would say for the better, but that is
open to conjecture. Elegant tearooms, tea shops and cafés were
all to disappear, as fast foods and a help-yourself style of service made inroads into our lives, ridding us of that wonderful
institution—and a leisurely, glamorous one at that—of "taking"
tea, together with its waitresses in black frocks and white or-

gandie caps and aprons, and of course the inevitable string
quartet playing Johann Strauss and Franz Lehár!

But things have a way of righting themselves. Everyone
likes a bit of nostalgia, as witnessed by the huge success on
both sides of the Atlantic of such British television dramas as
*Upstairs, Downstairs, The Duchess of Duke Street, By the
Sword Divided*, and *Edward and Mrs. Simpson*, to name but
a few. Through the small screen, we have enjoyed, even if
vicariously, a taste of the past. People who, unlike me, don't
have firsthand experience of some of that past seem to want a
taste of it, and so we now, rightly and in a timely way, have a
whole new fashion starting, nay, started: a trip down memory
lane in search of times past. Afternoon tea is an essential part
of any such trip, and this book is intended to help you to make
such a journey in your own home.

Tea at the Ritz is back; the Waldorf runs a tea dance; The
Inn on the Park, the Inter-Continental, and the Dorchester
are all on the tea wagon in 1986. It is also now becoming fash-

ionable again to give tea parties in the home, and to meet people for afternoon tea in town. Afternoon wedding receptions are also becoming stylish, and this year this author is taking an afternoon-tea picnic in Glyndebourne, England's famous country opera house set in a Sussex hayfield, shunning dinner during the interval. It will be elaborate and somewhat extended in content, I admit; there will be foie gras sandwiches, smoked-salmon scones, caviar on wafer-thin brown bread, and a scintillating champagne cup. Excessive! I can hear my mother saying from her cloud up in the great beyond. Yes—but fantastic!

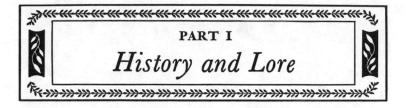

PART I

History and Lore

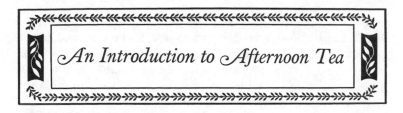

Had Anna, seventh duchess of Bedford (1783 to 1857) in the very early years of the nineteenth century, not been incredibly greedy, afternoon tea as we knew it in England, and to some extent as we still know it today, might never have become our national habit.

Legend has it that as the time between breakfast and dinner lengthened in the lighter months of the summer, this august lady, unable to await the immense repast she would surely have enjoyed at her laden dinner table, took to her boudoir midafternoon and demanded of her servants slivers of bread spread with "good sweet butter," on which, together with "mackeroons," cheesecakes, tarts, biscuits, small cakes, and other niceties, she secretly gorged.

It did not take long for her secret to be exposed, and far from ridiculing her—as might well have happened in back-biting eighteenth-century English society—other ladies who also might have enjoyed a clandestine indulgence joined her in the habit. Concealing screens were cast aside, and teapot and caddy, muffineer and cakestand, were revealed for all to enjoy. And so, Afternoon Tea became not only acceptable but a most fashionable thing of which to partake if you were to remain a lady of status.

But, before examining the more appetizing side of our afternoon indulgence—for indulgence it is—we must take a brief look at the history of tea drinking in Britain.

When this new drink first reached England, following its fashionable debut in Holland, it was called *cha*, which was Cantonese slang for tea. However, when the British moved their Chinese trading base from Canton to Amoy, the name changed to the one given in that region to the fragrant leaf, *t'e*. So, by the end of the seventeenth century the drink was already more popularly known in England as *tay* or *tee*.

It is interesting to note that in the north of England, tea is still referred to in local slang as *char*, and the English word for your daily cleaning lady was until quite recently (and in many places still is) *charlady*.

Following its initial introduction into Britain as a drink, there was a good deal of debate as to whether tea was harmful or beneficial. The Germans banned it, believing tea to be the principal cause of the "shriveled" appearance of the Oriental!

But tea, slowly but surely, was becoming a nationwide habit, starting as a social nicety for the rich (and in the early days men only, to boot) and rising to become, for many years, Britain's most popular beverage. (Note: Like so many of our feeding habits, the popularity of foreign travel has helped to alter this tradition, and coffee has now become the more popular drink.) For those interested in facts and figures, it is perhaps worth mentioning that in this land of 56 million people over 20 million cups of tea are drunk daily in London alone. But coffee came first.

The notion that in the seventeenth century a Cretan should come to study at Oxford University might strike one as odd, but one Nathaniel Conopios did, in fact, appear at Balliol College in 1637 and (apparently) introduced coffee drinking to his fellow students. Before long England's first coffeehouse was to open in that "City of Spires" and not, as might be expected, in the capital, London. London's first real coffeehouse opened in 1652, when Daniel Edwards, a much-traveled merchant, brought back coffee beans from Smyrna and trained his servant to pound and brew an aromatic drink that was so popular with his city colleagues that it soon became obvious there was an excellent commercial idea to be exploited. Edwards financed his servant, Pasqua Rosee, in setting up the first recorded coffeehouse in London, in St. Michael's Alley. However, there were to be problems, and Rosee's coffee shop was not to enjoy a long life.

Let me explain why. For a gentleman to open and run a business—or "go into trade"—in London at that time, he had to be a "Freeman" of the City of London, a Freeman being one who possessed the freedom of a city, borough, or livery company. Today this is an honor bestowed upon a citizen who has contributed significantly to a city's life.

There are some sixty-four livery companies today, with their roots planted deep in British history, and with such names as Haberdashers, Leatherworkers, Goldsmiths, Butchers, Cooks, Bookbinders, Fanmakers and Mercers. Stemming from the Latin *liberame*, when used in the sense of *distributing*, the companies are an extension of the ancient Guild system. Falling into the two categories, craft and merchant, guilds were formed to protect trade and to encourage and endow apprenticeship. The oldest, the Weavers Guild, dates back to 1130 and was the first recorded guild. As might be expected, in the days of horse transport, the Saddlers Guild came ten years later. My own father was a Liveryman of the Dyers Company, and therefore a Freeman of the City of London.

In smaller cities, one Guildhall suffices, whereas in London each Guild or Company had its own hall, often with an attendant chapel. Many of the original halls were lost in the Great Fire of London in 1666, their replacement buildings forming an important part of London's seventeenth and eighteenth century architecture. Quite a few of these were in turn bombed in the Second World War, and many of the buildings you see now are excellent restorations; so, when looking at our wonderful architecture, be sure to establish its true age!

The term livery is also applied to the distinctive apparel worn not only by members of Livery companies at civic events, but also to the uniforms worn by naval, military, and civil

officials as servants of State. Nowhere is pageantry manifested better than in London, when livery is seen in full splendour on many of our great state occasions.

In the twentieth century Livery companies are still involved in the "making" or electing of the Lord Mayor, a position which has always been honorary. In far-off days a member of a Livery company was entitled to vote, exempt from paying tolls, and enjoyed a share in the revenues accruing from his particular Livery company's property.

Imagine how seductive the aroma of roasting coffee beans must have been in those narrow City streets and alleys, overcoming, without doubt, those less-pleasant smells emanating from the open sewers bordering every London street, alley, and close. So seductive was it that Pasqua's coffee shop was packed all day long. But the sweet smell of success, while the best public-relations gambit anyone could wish for, was not pleasing to the owners of the numerouse taverns and alehouses in the "square mile." They rebelled, complaining to the Lord Mayor—head of all the guilds and the city in general—that as Pasqua was *not* a freeman, he was in no position to run a coffeehouse. Daniel Edwards had, however, married well: to the daughter of coffee-drinking Alderman Hodges of the City. Strings were pulled, and a partner was found for Pasqua in the person of Hodges's servant, Bowman. Bowman being of an entrepreneurial nature soon outwitted Pasqua, opening his own establishment. Pasqua's shop collapsed, or "went under," as the English saying goes, but by the time all this happened, coffee drinking had established itself as a City habit enjoyed by all. (Still men only, that is, for no self-respecting lady would be found in such a place.)

Male society used the London coffee and chocolate houses as centers for political, social, and cultural activity. They were, in due course, to become the foundation for the London clubs of today—White's, St. James's, Brook's, Boodle's, and so on.

Rumor has it that by the mid seventeenth century well over two thousand coffee houses existed in London alone. York, Norwich, Bristol, and other major guild cities of the day had a goodly choice of their own. So popular had the coffee-drinking habit become that in 1660 the Treasury levied a four old pence tax on every gallon of coffee brewed, though one wonders just how the authorities were able to keep track of how much was actually sold. The four-pence tax was followed in 1663 by a five-pound fee for a license to run a coffeehouse. Coffee in those days cost two old pence a "dish" and was served in a "can"— a straight-sided cup—and poured into the dish, or saucer, for drinking. A tip—*To Insure Promptness*—was put in a box, thus starting a habit unpopular the world over to this day.

A good deal of business was transacted in these city coffee-houses if the notices of meetings that ran in the *London Gazette* of those days are any indication. One of them, Edward Lloyd's, in the area of Cornhill, was to become the most famous, for it was at his coffeehouse in Tower Street, around 1688—twenty-two years after the Great Fire—that Lloyd prepared "ships' lists" for the benefit of seafaring men, ships' captains, merchants, underwriters, and the like, and thus built the foundation for what is now the greatest firm of underwriters in the world, Lloyd's of London.

Later on, in 1706, one Thomas Twining, then thirty years old, started his own venture by purchasing Tom's Coffee House in Deveraux Court, hard by St. Clement Danes' Church in the Strand and right in the heart of London's legal land of Temple, Temple Bar, New Court, and Inner Temple—all of which lay between the Strand and the north bank of the river Thames.

Twining had chosen his location well. Barristers and their clients, physicians, the literati, and men of importance in politics and other fields frequented his establishment in Deveraux Court. There is evidence of Thomas Twining's signature as witness to the signing of important documents drawn up by these lawyers and their clients while partaking of his *coffee*.

Not tea—yet!

No reference to tea appears in European literature before 1588, which is one hundred years before Thomas Twining opened his coffeehouse. Although the Portuguese must have come across it in their trading with China during the early part of the sixteenth century, they did little about it: Maybe they didn't like it! It was only after the Dutch made their forays into China—and Bantam in particular—in the seventeenth century that we begin to hear about tea, and it was they who introduced the tea-drinking habit to seventeenth-century Europe. The first teas used in England, however, appear to have come directly from Java.

The Gazette, for Tuesday, 2 September 1658, carried the announcement of the death of Oliver Cromwell (head of Britain's Commonwealth, 1649–60). There also appeared what is now known to be the earliest advertisement for *tea*, in a promotion for "The Sultaness Head, Cophee House, in Sweetings Rents near the Royal Exchange."

There is, however, an even earlier reference to *coffee* in *The Publick Advisor* for May 19, 1657, in which broadsheet we read what this drink will do for you!

In Bartholomew Lane on the backside of the Old Exchange, the drink called *coffee*, which is a very wholesom and physical drink, having many excellent vertues, closes the orifice of the stomack, fortifies the heat within, helpeth digestion, quickneth the spirits, maketh the heart lightsom, is good against eye-sores, coughs, or colds, rhumes, consumptions, headach, dropsie, gout, scurvy, king's evil, and many others, is to be sold both in the morning, and at three of the clock in the afternoon.

And there's no answer to that!

By 1660 China tea was being sold at prices ranging from 15 to 40 shillings for a pound (in today's terms, £812 to £1,900 or $1,150 to $2,600), so it was by no means cheap, and this price did not include Parliament's duty of eight pence levied on every gallon brewed (again, as with coffee, just how this was measured is difficult to establish).

Nine years later, in 1669, the East India Company brought back tea in their cargo for the first time. This was from Bantam, and the lonely two canisters carried were treated as a novelty by the directorate of the company. It was to be another nine years before serious importation of tea became a regular branch of that company's trading, and even then tea drinking was not fashionable. In fact it was seen by many to be a filthy habit, not to be encouraged.

All that was to change, of course, and what started off in a somewhat lethargic fashion soon began to gallop.

In Twining's coffeehouse, tea drinking was rapidly gaining in popularity, so much so that by 1717 Twining had opened a second house to cope with the increase in trade. This, too, was in Deveraux Court, and it took the name of the Golden Lion, rather in the same way pubs are called after heraldic beasts. At that time houses were not numbered—at least not accurately— and the public relied on such landmarks and signs as "Near the sign of the Golden Lyon."

While most purchases, particularly for refreshment, were paid for in good solid gold, there is nevertheless recorded in Twinings ledgers the names of some 355 customers who were given credit for the purchase of coffee, chocolate, sago, snuff, spa waters, and . . . tea. Oranges, tincture of rhubarb, lemons, and candles were also sold at coffeehouses—and even handmade writing paper.

The sale of tea at Twining's soon exceeded the sale of coffee, and we now have early reference to particular types of tea—though in 1715 the records still refer only to teas from China, including those bearing such renowned names as Bohea, pekoe, imperial, congou, green, gunpowder, and hyson.

In the twentieth century it is the grocer, the specialty

shop, or, more commonly, the supermarket that purvey tea and coffee, and already packaged to boot; but it is amusing to recall that in those days these two beverages, enjoyed as much for their stimulating effect as for their taste, also had a sales outlet through such extraordinary channels as milliners and jewelers! It is an amazing thought that tiaras and tea might well have been purchased together!

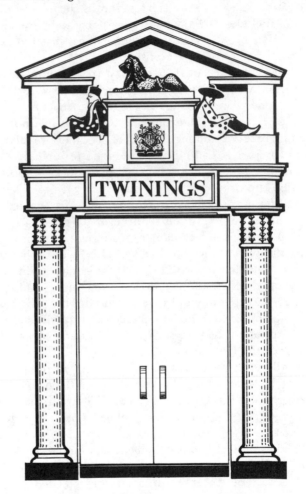

It can be fairly stated that the history of tea and coffee drinking in England, unbroken through twelve reigns, is directly linked to the history of the Twining family, existent today in the name of Sam Twining, director of R. Twining and Company Limited, and a ninth generation of that family. (Any

reader whose interest leads him to look for more profound information would do well to get sight of the book *Twinings:
Two Hundred and Fifty Years of Tea and Coffee, (1706–1956)*,
by Stephen Twining.) It may also interest readers to know that,
upon application, it is possible to look at the ledgers, bills, and
names of customers of this famous firm through the centuries.

By the middle of the eighteenth century Twinings teas
were being sold abroad: to the governor in Barbados, to the
consul in Leghorn, to customers in Cádiz and Lisbon, to the
British army and navy in those days based in Minorca in the
Balearic Islands, to customers in Aix-en-Provence, and Rotter-
dam, and to Governor the Honorable William Shirley in Boston, Massachusetts, a client of the firm from 1741 to 1756.

In 1773 three ships in Boston harbor holding cargoes of
tea valued at eighteen thousand pounds ($238 million in to-
day's terms) were raided by men masquerading as Indians,
who proceeded to empty those cargoes into the sea (*not* Twining's it must be added)! The Boston Tea Party was a protest
against the massive taxation of the thirteen colonies, and one
of the main reasons why America became a coffee-drinking nation was the vetoing, by the American housewife, of tea drinking in support of her husband's discontent with the British.

Wounds were to be healed when, in 1796, Thomas Twining (son of the first Richard Twining, 1783–1818), while returning to England during his time with the East India Company's Bengal service, paid a courtesy visit to General George Washington at his presidential home, a modest red-brick house on High Street in Philadelphia. And so we directly link the early days of tea drinking in England with those of colonial America.

TEA GARDENS

The second half of the eighteenth century saw the rise of the pleasure gardens and tea gardens, such as Vauxhall, Ranelagh, and Marylebone, where fashionable society could go to see and be seen.

On payment of a fixed entry fee, the customer could drink as much tea and consume as much bread and butter as he or she liked. At the same time he could be entertained by musicians (Handel himself frequently led his "band" at Vauxhall), jugglers, acrobats, and even firework displays.

As tea drinking became more of a ceremony, it began to accumulate a whole range of special manners and arts (and affectations!). For wealthy gentlemen, evening tea would be specially prepared and served in the tea gardens or the tearooms and clubs, by attractive young wenches known as tea blenders, who often "got to know" their employer and his friends in more than one sense! Emma Hamilton (later Lady Hamilton), the mistress of Admiral Lord Nelson, once worked as a blender for King George III, who enjoyed tea immensely and whose elder son, the Prince Regent (later George IV), was one of the first collectors of teapots.

THE RISE OF AFTERNOON TEA
IN NINETEENTH-CENTURY ENGLAND

In contrast to the elegance, orderliness, and symmetry of eighteenth-century Britain, Victorian England was opulent and extravagant almost to the point of vulgarity.

In their efforts to dispose of their accumulating industrial wealth, the newly rich Victorians commissioned everything from china, glass, silver, furniture, paintings, and especially music, to the imposing town halls such as you will see in the great industrial cities of Manchester, Leeds, Sheffield, Newcastle, and Birmingham, and the now much-admired Victorian Gothic churches, public libraries, and art galleries, and, as in America each city vying with the next for something bigger, better, and more elaborate.

Luncheon as the midday meal had by now gained full popularity and had become an important time for ladies and gentlemen to entertain members of their own sex; the gentlemen in their clubs, the ladies in the comfort of the home, attended by fleets of servants—yet a further indication to the world that the middle classes could afford things.

Dinner in the grander houses was often served as late as 9:00 P.M., though 8:30 was a more popular time, and the gap between luncheon and dinner had widened (as indeed it had done between breakfast and dinner in the previous century, leading to the introduction of luncheon—and so the Duchess of Bedford's secret munchings began!). There was therefore ample time for ladies to create a whole new social rigmarole—the "At Home."

Even today, in the late 1980s, this somewhat strange form of entertaining is still enjoyed in grander circles. A simple white "At Home" card, stating that "Mrs. John Smith will be At Home" on a particular date, is issued. The time of day, what to expect (afternoon tea, cocktails, champagne, dancing, or whatever) and the mode of dress are always printed in the right-hand corner, and in the case of a ball the line "Carriages [sic] at ——— o'clock" is the rather amusing way of indicating at what time the guests are expected to leave.

In England we don't subscribe to the American practice of "refusals" or "regrets only." It is an obligation to reply formally, either accepting or declining an invitation and, in the case of a regret, giving a brief reason why.

So, afternoon tea was fast becoming a fashionable social occasion to be enjoyed, usually by ladies, although men were often "in attendance," helping to pass food or glasses of wine cup.

It was a ritual that provided the upper-middle classes and the middle classes with an enjoyable way of passing—or wasting—time as they entertained each other on an almost daily basis. Inevitably, the ritual became more and more elaborate

as such items as delicate finger sandwiches, sausage rolls, patties, "fancies" (small iced cakes or pastries) and cutting cakes were to be added to the former, somewhat simpler menu.

Mrs. Beeton, in her *Book of Household Management*, gives an excellent record of how society set about creating social rules for itself. After luncheon was over, calls and visits were made and received, and I can think of no better way of describing the complete and complex procedure than to quote exact extracts from her tome on social etiquette in the Victorian/ Edwardian period known as the Gay Nineties.

Visiting

After luncheon, morning calls and visits may be made and received. These may be divided under three heads: those of ceremony, those of friendship, and those of congratulation and condolence. Visits of ceremony or courtesy, which sometimes merge into those of friendship, are to be paid under various circumstances. Thus, they are uniformly required after dining at a friend's house, or after a ball, picnic, or other party. These visits should be short, a stay of from fifteen to twenty minutes being sufficient.

When other visitors are announced, it is well to leave as soon as possible, taking care not to give the impression that your departure has been hastened by the arrival of the new guests. When the newcomers are quietly seated, and the bustle of their entrance is over, rise from your chair, taking leave of the hostess, and bowing politely to her guests. Should you have called at an inconvenient time, not having ascertained the luncheon hour, or from other inadvertence, retire as soon as possible, without, however, showing that you feel an intruder. It is not difficult to make suitable excuses, and a promise can be made to call again, if it appears to be regretted that circumstances have caused you to shorten your visit.

Visits of Friendship are, of course, far less formal, depending upon your degree of intimacy. Take care, however, to call at suitable times, and avoid staying long if your friend is engaged. Courtesy and consideration for others are safe rules in these everyday matters. During visits manners should be easy and unstrained, conversation

natural and unforced. Do not, unless invited, take pet dogs into another house; there are people who have a great aversion to animals, and there is always a chance of the animal breaking something. Moreover, the people themselves may have a dog—and anything may happen! Except in the case of close friends, or by special invitation, little children should not accompany a lady who is making morning calls.

It is a frequent practice for the mistress of a house to set aside a day every week, fortnight, or month, as the case may be, on which to receive callers. Wherever this is known to be the case, casual and non-intimate visitors should make it a rule to call on that day. It is hardly necessary to add that the mistress must make it a point of honour always to be prepared for guests on such "At Home" days. If circumstances will oblige her to be from home, she should strive to let the fact become known to her acquaintances, that they may be spared a fruitless journey.

When an 'At Home' day has been fixed and cards issued as, for example:

Mrs. A——— At Home Wednesdays, 4–7 p.m.

Afternoon Tea should be provided, fresh supplies, with thin bread-and-butter, fancy pastries, cakes, etc., being brought in as other guests arrive.

Morning Calls demand good but fairly plain attire; a costume much more elaborate than that you generally wear would be out of keeping. As a general rule, on this and other occasions, the fault of under-dressing is more likely to be condoned than that of over-dressing.

Accounts should be kept of ceremonial visits, and notice taken how soon your calls are returned. An opinion may thus be formed as to whether frequent visits are, or are not, desired. There are, naturally, instances in which old age, ill-health, or other circumstances, preclude the return of a call; when this is the case, it should not interrupt the discharge of the duty by those who have no excuses to make.

Visits of Condolence, except among close friends, generally take the form of card-leaving, the words "with kind inquiries" being written in. In due course the bereaved family issue cards returning thanks for the sympathy displayed, after which they are understood to be ready again to receive visitors. When paying visits of condolence, sympathy with the family is expressed by dressing very quietly. The calls are never protracted.

Receiving Morning Calls. The etiquette to be observed in paying calls will apply to receiving them. Generally speaking, all occupations should be suspended on the entrance of morning visitors, but a lady engaged with light needlework may continue it quietly during conversation, particularly if the visit be protracted. When visitors prepare to leave, the hostess should rise, shake hands, or bow, and summon a servant to open the door.

Weddings, "At Home,"
High and Family Teas

Wedding teas are very much the same thing as 'At Home' teas, but are, as a rule, more crowded and less factory than the latter. People ask so many more to a tea than they would think of inviting to the now old-fashioned wedding breakfast, and the visitors all come together, as the bride has, as a rule, but a very short time to stay. She cuts the cake, or rather makes the first incision, as at a wedding breakfast, but there are no speeches and but little ceremony.

'At Home' teas. Some entertainment is generally provided, usually music, professional singers and pianists being sometimes engaged. When this is the case, the lady of the house does not often ask her amateur friends to give their services; but sometimes these friends contribute the music, and it is well to make a little plan or programme beforehand, arranging who shall be asked to perform, and appraising them of the fact so that they may come prepared. The hostess, even if she be herself musical, has her time taken up very fully with receiving and looking after her guests, and unless she sings the first song, or plays the first piece, should leave herself free to devote herself to her guests. The instrumental pieces chosen on these occasions should not be long ones, and a good break should be made between each song, solo or recitation, for conversation, people going more to these entertainments to meet their friends and have a chat than for the sake of the music. Introductions are not the rule at "At Homes", but they can be made when there is any necessity. The tea is not served in the drawing-room as at smaller "at homes", but at a buffet in the dining-room, where people go during the afternoon, or sometimes as they leave, to partake of the light refreshments provided.

Servants usually do all the work of pouring out tea or handing sandwiches, fruit, ices, etc., unless gentlemen bring refreshments for ladies to where they are seated. At the buffet, people may help themselves, or be helped by gentlemen if there are not sufficient attendants.

A weekly 'At Home' tea is served upon small tables, the servant, before bringing it in, seeing that one is

placed conveniently near his mistress, who generally dispenses the tea. No plates are given for a tea of this kind, and the servant, after seeing that all is in readiness, leaves the room, the gentlemen of the party doing all the waiting that is necessary.

The tea equipage is usually placed upon a silver-salver, the hot water is in a small silver or china kettle on a stand, and the cups are small. Thin bread and butter, cake, petits-fours and sometimes fresh fruit are all the eatables given. These are daintily arranged on plates, spread with lace doilies, and placed in a cakestand or on a convenient table.

High Tea. In some houses this is a permanent institution, quite taking the place of late dinner, and to many it is a most enjoyable meal, young people preferring it to dinner, it being a movable feast that can be partaken of at hours which will not interfere with tennis, boating, or other amusements. At the usual High Tea there are probably to be found one or two small hot dishes, cold chickens, or game, tongue or ham, salad, cakes of various kinds, sometimes cold fruit tarts with cream or custard,

and fresh fruit. Any supper dish, however, can be introduced, and much more elaborate meals be served, while
sometimes the tea and coffee are relegated to the side-
board. In summer it is not unusual to have everything
cold at a High Tea.

At *Family Teas*, cake, jam, sardines, potted meats,
buttered toast, tea cakes and fruit are often provided, in

addition to the tea, coffee, and bread and butter. Watercress and radishes are nice accompaniments in summer.

The hours for family teas may vary in many households, but are generally governed by the time of the dinner
that has preceded them, and the kind of supper partaken
of afterwards. Where this is of a very high character, such
as a glass of wine and a slice of cake, or the more homely
glass of beer and bread and cheese, a 6 to 7 o'clock tea
would not be late, and a few savouries or eggs would be
needed in addition to the bread and butter and cake so
generally found; but where a substantial supper is to follow the tea the latter would be of a light description, and
should be served about 5 o'clock, or earlier.

Bridge Teas afford a very pleasant afternoon. These
generally commence about 3.30 p.m. Punctuality is naturally most essential.

Tennis Teas are customary at many houses during
summer.

The meal is informal, and usually served out of doors.
Iced tea, coffee, claret cup etc. are served, with sandwiches, pastry, cakes and other light viands. The tables
are set under shady trees, and members of the family or
servants are in attendance at them, the visitors themselves
going to the tables for what they want.

THÉ DANSANT—THE TEA DANCE

My first encounter with the tea dance came when as a
youth I attended afternoon dances in our local town hall in
Yorkshire. Evening dances were avoided, particularly in the
winter months, because of the ever-present danger of Nazi
air raids at night, making the journey home—always on foot—
hazardous, certainly in the industrial areas. Gasoline was rationed, and only to be used for essential journeys. These tea
dances were friendly affairs. People would take their own little
packs of sandwiches, made from meager wartime rations, and
pool them together for all to enjoy a taste of something different. A sense of fair play pervaded, preventing any greedy person from taking more than their share. Often the dances were
charity affairs to raise funds for blankets, bandages, and food
parcels for troops, or for other good causes created when a
country is under siege, as Britain surely was. The organizers

would provide a cup of gray, wartime tea with a splash of reconstituted dried milk and a saccharine tablet for the sweet tooth.

Those who know only the ear-blasting music of present-day disco dancing have missed one of life's greatest pleasures, for the most exhilarating experiences of those far-off days was dancing to the sound of the big bands. Such names as the great legendary Victor Silvester (whose ballroom-dancing academy was already on the way to huge success before the Second World War) took their bands on the road to uplift the spirits

and boost the morale of soldiers, sailors, airmen, and common folk. Wherever room could be made on factory floors, in canteens, air-raid shelters, or church halls, people would gather to forget the horrors of war and dance to the sound of such masters of the baton as Joe Loss, Felix Mendellsohn and his Hawaiian Serenaders (!), and Ivy Benson and her all-ladies' orchestra, or to the magnificent band of the Royal Air Force, the Squadronaires. The great bands of America, too—Tommy Dorsey, Benny Goodman, and the never-to-be-forgotten Glenn Miller—made frequent and dangerous trips across the Atlantic to raise the morale of troops and civilians alike. Woman danced with woman with never an eyebrow raised; you made your own fun as and when you could and out of what was available—and young men were not! Not exactly the sort of tea dance we think of in our more romantic minds today, you might say, but I doubt if we will ever again dance to such wonderful sounds and melodies as those produced by the big bands.

Documentation is meager as to where exactly the tea dance began on a more elegant social level. There is evidence in the *Oxford English Dictionary* supplement, under *dansant*, that as early as 1819 there was a *danceant* at "old Prince Ester-hazy's" in Vienna. Dancing on ice was featured on a winter's afternoon in the film *Mayerling* and in *Punch* magazine of 26 July 1841, there is reference to a tea dance in London. So Queen Victoria might well have tripped the light fantastic on occasion in the early part of her reign (1837–1901), though I somehow doubt it! But for a more positive and well-documented reference we can turn to one Gladys Beattie Crozier, who in 1913 published *The Tango and How To Dance It*. While it can be assumed that the *thé dansant* was already well established on the continent of Europe, it did not cross the Channel as the fashionable thing to do until just before the First World War.

Edward VII, while still Prince of Wales (and particularly after Queen Victoria retired from public life to become the Widow of Windsor, with only the odd sortie in the summer to Osborne House on the Isle of Wight), led fashionable society in London. The Edwardian period, as we know it, started in the Gay Nineties, before the Queen's death and Edward's succession to the throne. Dancing-tea, dinner and supper clubs, where dancing was the chief attraction of the afternoon and evening's entertainment, abounded in London in those Edwardian heydays. Mrs. Crozier tells us that the revival of the *thé dansant* was received with much enthusiasm at Biarritz and all along the Riviera, where British and continental members of the *haut monde* met to dance every single afternoon. French phrases illuminated the talk of the English upper classes of the day, and two of the dances that were *de rigueur* were the one-step and the outrageous tango. So popular was this second dance to become, that tea dances were often called tango teas, and, according to Mrs. Crozier, tango masters made their fortunes.

Soon the *thé dansant*—along with the new dances—slipped across the Channel and was received with such enthusiasm by hostesses in London and in the counties that it was to become *the* form of winter entertainment for both the elite and the not-so-elite. It had everything to recommend it: What could have been pleasanter on a dull wintry afternoon at five o'clock or so, when calls or shopping were over, than to drop in to one of the cheery little *thé dansant* clubs that had sprung up all over the West End and throughout the land? Quite one of the most exclusive clubs met at the Carlton Hotel, organized by Mrs. Carl Leyel and a Mrs. Fagan. The Four Hundred Club met at a venue in Bond Street and the Public Schools and Universities Dance Club at the Savoy Hotel. The Waldorf, the Boston Club, and dozens of other centers in London were also extremely well patronized, even though subscriptions were high.

"*Thé* tangos" abounded as specialist occasions from Lon-

don's Hotel Cecil to Jenners shop in Edinburgh's fashionable
Princes Street, from the Grand Hotel in the elegant spa town
of Scarborough to Tilley's Rooms in industrial Newcastle. Ac-

cording to the knowledgeable Mrs. Crozier, the latter was one
of the finest galleries for dancing in the whole of the north
of England.

    In London's exclusive society it was an achievement to
get into the club at the Carlton Hotel. Membership was strictly
limited to one hundred, we read, subscriptions were high—
often as high as five guineas—and election to membership was
difficult. No young girl was admitted without a chaperone, and
guests' names had to be submitted to a committee (usually
composed of people from a military or county family) by the
member introducing them, and the members had in turn to be
present to receive their guests on arrival in the ballroom and

to sign them in. Inside the rigidly guarded portals of these emporia, there were tiny tables crowding the borders of the dance floor. These were "set forth" with pretty gold-and-white china, and "within a moment of one's arrival" a most elaborate and delicious tea was served while the assembled company danced to the haunting airs of the tango or a lively ragtime melody, a "Boston" or even a modest waltz. An hour or two whisked magically by until, at about 6:30, it was time to return home to change and sally forth yet again to the Royal Opera, a dinner, the theater, or perhaps an evening at the musical comedy, which was tremendously popular at the time.

It is interesting to note that cigarettes were allowed in the ballroom after tea, and at the most exclusive venues, the famous French tango dancers, Les Almanos, hot from Paris, would visit and demonstrate their latest variations of the Parisian tango. All very heady stuff when you read that "their dancing was the most graceful, gay, infectious thing imaginable, and an absolute revelation of the possibilities of the tango . . . for their movements were the very poetry of motion, and no step seems ever to be repeated twice."

If you have ever toiled over the mysteries of the breakdance, I suppose you can imagine yourself trying with the utmost seriousness to master the intricacies of the latest tango variation, the *Maxixe Brésilienne*—"delicate, spirited and graceful," to music that was "ravishing, alluring and gay!" This sort of descriptive writing makes today's life seem somewhat pale by comparison! It is not difficult to see why the tea dance, and the tango tea in particular, was so popular for *le monde qui s'amuse*. What could be more agreeable than dancing in a pleasant bohemian atmosphere starred with fellow guests who might include royalty, an English duke or two, a clutch of well-known peers, and some of the best-known and brightest lights of London's musical-comedy stage?

The Great War saw the end of this national frenzy, though the tea dance returned in the Roaring Twenties, when "flappers" danced the Charleston and the sensuous tango slipped in the popularity ratings. Fox-trots and the newer quickstep became the rage and, with the arrival of the great American musical films, Carmen Miranda with her rhumbas and sambas. Then Bill Haley and his Comets replaced the big-band sound, and we let go of our partners to gyrate alone to the jive, the bop, the twist, and the locomotion.

Will we ever hold our partners again, I ask? One does wonder. But perhaps some of us will with the rebirth of the tea dance, for it *is* a pleasant and elegant way of passing an afternoon, and it's an excellent and novel idea for a party in the home—even though your band may be courtesy of the stereo.

NURSERY TEA

The popular television series *Upstairs, Downstairs*, put out by London Weekend Television and seen worldwide on the small screen, did a great deal to pull back the curtains, so to speak, on life in a typical upper-class household at the turn of the century in Edwardian London. Depicted in each episode was the life-style of the master and servant classes during the

heyday of the British empire, when school atlases showed over a third of the world's surface hatched in red. The series also showed the well-defined lines laid down by society between the ruling establishment and the servant classes. The great wealth earned and enjoyed by the British beginning with the Industrial Revolution led to a way of living unknown before in the history of the country, or the world for that matter; it also led to the founding of the middle and upper-middle classes, whose newly made money came from industry, and to the creation of more wealth for people coming in contact with them, particularly the professional classes and people in "trade." We had, of course, become a nation of shopkeepers.

India, under the raj, was responsible in no small way for a system of education that was unique and remains almost unique to this day, the public school. Children of aristocratic, "county," and other well-to-do-families, particularly those involved in the ruling of India and many of the colonies, were sent off to private schools and traveled home only for holidays. It was thought that this type of spartan schooling built "character" and made a child "independent" and ready to face life alone or fit into the ranks of the military. As young as eight years old, boys and girls alike, these children were pushed out of the nest of the nursery, out from the comforting wings of their nanny, to face the world alone. And life was never the same again, for child grew away from parent, the more so when three or four years of university followed school.

Up to leaving for school a child lived a life again peculiar to the British, a life where Nanny and not Mummy was the authority. From birth, the children of well-off parents were handed to a nurse, to be returned to the parents only briefly, at specific times during each day. One of those occasions was teatime in the nursery, or children's hour. Otherwise Nanny presided virtually unhampered over the early years of her charges. It is interesting to note that even today many grown men, captains of industry, cabinet ministers, or dukes of the realm will refer with more affection to "what Nanny said" than to any memories of their father or mother.

The road to becoming a nanny was well defined. A young girl of respectable family would start life as a nursemaid. According to Isabella Beeton, she should be "patient and good-tempered, truthful with a purity of manner, minute in cleanliness, docile and obedient." Her responsibilities, when she rose in rank to upper nursemaid, would start the instant the children were weaned. She would wash, dress, and feed them, take walks with them, supply and regulate all their wants, and also "be acquainted with the art of ironing and be handy with her needle." The nursemaid was also heavily involved with children's moral welfare. Mrs. Beeton laid down that "kindness, perseverence and patience are of the utmost importance," as the offspring were persuaded not to suck their thumb, not to throw their toys down "in mere wanton-ness," and to eradicate any "evil propensities." To indulge or flatter a child was considered "extremely foolish," and nursemaids were encouraged to report to the parents "faithfully and accurately" any defects they had observed in the disposition of their charges. With these heavy responsibilities on her young and uneducated shoulders, the nursemaid needed help, so the under-nursemaid was employed to see to such chores as the lighting of fires, sweeping, scouring, dusting, making beds, washing, mending, dressing the children, emptying "slops," carrying water up to the nursery (always at the top of the house), and bringing the nursery meals upstairs. The nursemaids took their meals together in the nursery, after the children of the family had finished. Social proprieties were observed, even in the nursery.

As to the nursery tea, this was a simple affair and would consist of such sandwiches as potted meat or fish paste, jam, mashed banana, grated chocolate, a simple spreading of honey or a smear of Marmite or Bovril or some other vegetable extract peculiar to the British. A fruit jelly might also make an appearance, wobbling tantalizingly until each sandwich crust had been swallowed. Crusts were *never* cut off nursery sandwiches and were the cause of more disciplinary action by Nanny than any other misdemeanor. Children made strenuous efforts not to eat them, and the crusts were pushed to the side of the plate, hidden inside clothing, and even thrown over the fender into the nursery fire. On Sundays a concoction of milk, gelatin, food coloring, and some synthetic essence might appear as a treat in the form of a "shape" or "mold." Other occasions might see a lightly boiled egg with its attendant toast "soldiers" as a supplement to the nursery diet; and a good, plain "cutting cake" would be there at all teatimes. Coconut kisses, jam tarts, and buns were considered luxuries to be kept for high days and holidays. With the exception being freshly made lemonade as a celebratory drink, milk was the only drink considered fit for children at teatime.

To those of us brought up in a very different world, such a childhood seems to have underlying hints of near deprivation, overdiscipline, and penury, yet most British people who survived this time in our history think back to nursery days with affection and to nursery tea as their happiest hour.

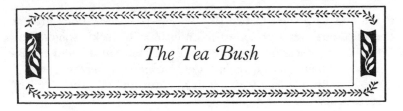

Camellia sinensis, a cousin, though perhaps a distant one, of the garden variety Camellia japonica, is an evergreen tropical bush, originally (from the British point of view) found growing wild in Assam, India, by eighteenth-century British botanists sent by the Royal Horticultural Society of London. Commercially grown to approximately five feet in height (left wild it has been known to surpass twenty feet), and kept at this height by regular pruning, the bushes are nurtured for five years before they are ready to yield their first pickings. The tea bush enjoys growing, as does the vine, on a hillside, its feet in loamy, dry earth. Like the camellia, it prefers the protection of tall trees from the scorching sun, and can produce a good crop from near sea level up to six to seven thousand feet. It likes a lot of rain, but at the right time.

The higher the plantation, the better the quality of the leaf because in the cooler air it is slower to mature. "High-grown" teas are the best and most expensive used for blending; they are much sought after by those tea merchants in Britain who still prefer to mix their own particular blends for individual clients.

The actual gathering, or plucking, of the leaves—or rather,

the bud with the top two tiny leaves—is a continuous process carried out over a period of six months at biweekly stages. The first or "new season's tippings" are the best. Subsequent pluckings are then referred to in a descending scale as "first flush," "second flush," "quality," "rains," "autumnal," and "end of season" leaves.

The native gatherers of the crop are paid pro rata by weight, and their baskets are dispatched as soon as they are filled to the nearby tea factories, where the leaves are processed into either black or green teas. Black tea is preferred by most Westerners and Americans. Green tea is nowadays used for consumption in China, Japan, and other Eastern countries and also to an extent in North Africa, though there has been a renaissance of green-tea consumption in newly health-conscious Britain.

GREEN AND BLACK TEAS

In America, black tea is tea without milk. In Britain it is taken for granted that you will be given milk in your (Indian) tea. If you prefer tea "black"—in this sense—then you ask for "tea without milk." All of which has nothing to do with what really constitutes black tea!

The manufacturing of tea begins when the freshly gathered green leaves are shriveled in dry, warm air. They are withered just sufficiently to leave them soft and limp, or "pliable," as it is known in the tea-making trade.

At this stage they are ready for rolling, a mechanical process that releases the unwanted sap or juice. After the rolling process the leaf can remain as green tea—the word *green* meaning fresh, or young, as well as referring to the somewhat dingy green color of the leaf—or it can be fermented (oxydized). This fermenting or oxydizing process is done on bamboo tables in a humid atmosphere, where, within a period of a few short hours, the leaves turn from green to a bright rust or copper color. At this stage of partial fermentation the tea is called *Oolong* and is used in blending. The bulk of it, however, goes through a third stage of fully fermenting the leaves by "firing." This is done by passing trays of the copper-colored leaves through "ovens," or hot-air chambers, for drying out. The leaf then becomes the "black" leaf known to most of us as regular Indian (or Ceylon or China) tea.

Then follows the more complicated process of grading. An earlier process called cutting, tearing, and curling is now followed by sifting the dried tea through a series of graded meshes. After sifting, the tea leaf emerges in sizes known as *leaf, broken leaf, fannings,* and *dust.*

Leaf—the first quality—is then categorized into four grades ready for blending: *flowery orange pekoe, orange pekoe, pekoe,* and *Souchong.* Broken leaf and fannings are also graded in parallel descending orders of quality, but the dust has only two grades, referred to simply as *one* and *two!* Dust, contrary to what you might expect, is the smallest leaf designated for the cheapest packet of tea and is not the sweepings from the floor. That said, it can also be the dust of an expensive, high-quality tea and is frequently designated for better drinking!

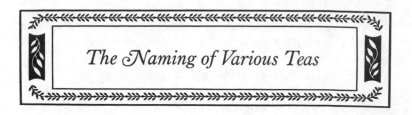

The Naming of Various Teas

The naming of teas is a somewhat complex subject, which even the experts seem unable to unravel completely. The British, in their attempts to anglicize Chinese words, have managed to confuse names of towns and districts with types of tea bushes and leaf sizes. India, on the other hand, is not so complex because the British were in there from the start and did not have to rely on or untangle complex local names as they did in China.

Most people put teas into categories: China tea and Indian tea. The latter includes teas from India, Ceylon, Africa, Indonesia, and Malaya, which are grown from Assam (north Indian) seed. The former includes Keemuns, Lapsang souchongs, and the various exotic teas, such as gunpowder (so called because sailors thought it resembled gunshot), Formosa oolong, Formosa jasmine tea, and scented orange pekoe, which are grown from China seed.

North Indian teas come from the districts of Assam, Dooars, Cachar, Darjeeling, and Sylhet (now part of Pakistan) and can be roughly divided into two classes:

«← Orthodox manufacture teas—the type of teas that have been seen for most of the present century up to the end of the last war. These have well-made black leaves, which sometimes contain golden leaf tips. This type of tea needs a full five or six minutes to infuse in order to obtain its full strength and quality.

«← Those with a very attractive golden brown color in the cup when milk is added. These teas are smaller and browner in leaf than orthodox teas and their quick infusing also makes them especially valuable for commercial blends. They have a wonderful muscatel flavor but are rarely strong or colorful.

Darjeeling tea has for many years been regarded throughout the world as a tea of outstanding quality in this category and one for which the connoisseur is willing to pay an extremely high price in order to obtain the very best.

South Indian teas are grown in the states of Kerala, Orissa,

34

and Mysore and are somewhat similar in character to Ceylon teas, but seldom equal them in either quality or leaf appearance.

Ceylon teas are of orthodox manufacture but are mostly smaller in leaf than north India teas. They vary in flavor and strength according to the district and the elevation in which they are grown. Teas grown high up in the districts of Dimbula, Dikoya, and Nuwara Eliya have a very attractive flavor, especially during the two quality periods of spring and autumn. Autumn teas from the Badulla district (Uva) also have a very distinctive flavor, as well as good strength and color. Teas from the lower altitudes have a very good color and strength but are mostly lacking in real flavor. Except for teas from Dimbula and Nuwara Eliya, Ceylon teas, especially fannings, infuse quickly but not as quickly as Assam tea.

Keemun-type teas, which include true Keemuns and other China black teas of similar character, have a well-made black leaf and a distinctive flavor, with, according to the Chinese, "the fragrance of an orchid."

Lapsang souchongs have a bolder and more brittle leaf. The true Lapsangs come from a particular district in the province of Fukien and have a very distinctive tar-like character.

Green tea is the preponderant product of China, Formosa, and Japan and is distinguished from black tea by its green-gray color, which, as we have seen, results from the fact that this tea is not subjected to fermentation. When it has been picked, the leaf is not withered but is at once strongly heated in a large "steamer" and becomes soft and pliable, so that it is in a fit state to be rolled. While still in its green condition it is fired in precisely the same manner as black tea. The best-known kinds of green tea are gunpowders, Chun Mees, and Sow Mees, which are consumed principally in North Africa and the United States. In some parts of China and Japan, green tea is still manufactured by hand, though the methods used are essentially those already described.

Oolong tea is manufactured exclusively in China and Formosa—by far the greater part of it in Formosa—and it is in reality a cross between green tea and black tea, since it is only partially fermented. Oolong teas, which are principally in demand in the United States, have a very delicate, but nonetheless fine, aroma.

All these traditional China teas need a full five to six minutes infusion time.

Scented orange pekoes, which have a jasmine flavor, are, like gunpowders, seldom sold direct to the consumer, but, like oolongs they are always found in Earl Grey tea.

Jasmine teas are sold with the dried jasmine flower in the tea and have only recently been permitted importation into the United Kingdom. These teas are popular in the United States and some European countries because of their exotic flavor.

China Tea

Legend has it that the tea leaf was discovered in China almost three thousand years ago, when Emperor Shen-Nung, in 2737 B.C., was boiling his drinking water to purify it and leaves from the nearby branch of a tea plant were blown into the cauldron, imparting a delicate flavor the emperor found to his liking.

Farfetched? Perhaps. But then most legends are farfetched, their shining core of truth having acquired centuries of clinging barnacles. To check the whole truth of the legend would turn this book into an academic exercise. Nevertheless, it is fascinating to know that there had been centuries of tea drinking going on in China (as there had been of noodle making and ice-cream eating) long before the first pound of tea reached the shores of England in 1645.

No one knew who actually grew and manufactured Chinese teas until one Robert Fortune, a collector of plants for the Royal Horticultural Society in London, managed, in 1842 and 1848, to penetrate into the tea-growing areas of mainland China. Until that time buyers had been kept at arm's length in the township of Canton, dealing only with the merchants.

His second visit to the tea plantations of the She-hsien (formerly Hweichow) area inland from Shanghai shows again how difficult it was for any foreigner to penetrate mainland China, for it is recorded that he had to adopt a disguise (presumably coloring his skin and wearing a wig complete with pigtail!). However, he must have endeared himself to the Chinese tea farmers, for he managed to collect vast quantities of seedlings, which he skillfully packed and shipped off to the East India Company's plantations in the Himalayas.

Eventually, Fortune ceased to work for the British and went on to collect plants for the United States government—probably a wise and financially fruitful move. In his book *Two Visits to the Tea Countries of China* (published by Murray in London, 1857), he describes his journeys and also tells how the

Chinese, in their numerous crudely constructed cottages in the tea hills, produced tea for their own families, selling the surplus to the merchants to earn them some extra money (as used to happen in the wine-growing countries of Europe). He also tells how they grew, gathered, and dried the leaves in iron drying pans set into brick-built furnaces before hand-rolling them on split bamboo benches or tables. The moisture emitted during this rolling process, he tells us, was of a greenish hue and apparently went to waste. There then followed a second drying process. This time the pliant leaves were exposed to the open air before yet a further session in the iron pans, when the tea was redried and ready for packing.

Tea (in China as well as in Europe) was drunk initially as a medicine and stimulant. One might say that it still is, if you agree that "the cup that cheers" is relaxing for the nerves if only because it stops you in your tracks for a moment or two from your daily toils and traumas—or perhaps it is the caffeine it contains that, though a modest 2 percent, stimulates you to further activity! In strife-torn Britain a "nice cup of tea" is the first thing proffered following bomb disasters, car crashes, bereavements, layoffs, and the other hazards of stressful living in the twentieth century.

It was around A.D. 620 that tea began to be enjoyed simply as a pleasant drink. Its popularity in China is indicated by an informative treatise on the subject of tea growing and drinking. *Cha Ching*, which in the Mandarin language means *Tea Classic*, gives us the first written account of the methods of gathering, bruising and drying, roasting, and packing the fragrant leaves of the tea plant. It is also an early reference to other fragrances being added to the prepared leaves, for Lu Yu, the author of *Cha Ching*, refers to ginger, orange, peppermint, and even onion being used, though I suppose originally these additions were employed to buck up some particularly weak crop.

It is interesting to note that in 1886 the United Kingdom's consumption of China tea was recorded as 170 *million* pounds. This figure dropped dramatically over the next fourteen years to a mere 13 million pounds, recorded in 1900, representing but 7 percent of the total consumption of black tea. Presumably loyalties to Empire were of paramount importance.

China-tea drinking in England is on the increase again, and it is now enjoyed by a much broader cross section of the population. Thanks to foreign travel Britons have developed a more sophisticated palate, they read more about food and drink, and tea without milk has gained popularity with the diet-conscious—which means drinking the more delicate China teas.

The importation of tea followed the natural progress of all things from ancient China to Europe, a procession starting, in rough terms, with the Turkish caravans trading on the northern borders of China in and around the fifth century A.D., progressing through Asia, Arabia, Persia, Greece, Italy, and southern France and Germany, then fanning outward to include central Europe, Scandinavia, and eventually Great Britain.

From our school days we know that it was not until 1497, when the Portuguese mariner Vasco da Gama sailed around the Cape of Good Hope into the Indian Ocean, that trade with the East began to take on any significance. And even then there was little interest in tea, and that interest limited mostly to verbal reports of the tea habit in China. There was more fascination shown in these Eastern men "sitting at floor level" at individual tables drinking rice wine and eating with "two pieces of wood" (chopsticks) than there was with their drinking "cha."

Only when the Portuguese closed their ports to the Dutch in the late sixteenth century did the latter begin to show a serious interest in importing tea. They began to ship the first significant cargoes of (green) tea from Bantam in Java, reverting to using it as a medicine and acclaiming its laxative powers. From the Netherlands, the Dutch traded with France and Italy, where apothecaries also used the beverage for its strong medicinal qualities.

The link with England began when Catherine of Braganza was betrothed and wed to Charles II in 1662. The young infanta sipped tea in her drawing room at St. James's Palace, which naturally popularized it with the ladies and other members of the court circles.

Russia was also by now well into the tea-drinking habit, being able to trade by land through the back door to China, and the Chinese encouraged their interest by sending gifts of tea to the czar. Controlled by the Russian czarist government, tea caravans traveled a mind boggling eleven thousand miles, taking up to a year and a half to get from the Chinese border

back to Western Russia. It is worth remarking here that the
schooners of the East India Company—known as East India-
men—took as long as four years to complete the round trip by
sea from England to China and back. As with the race for

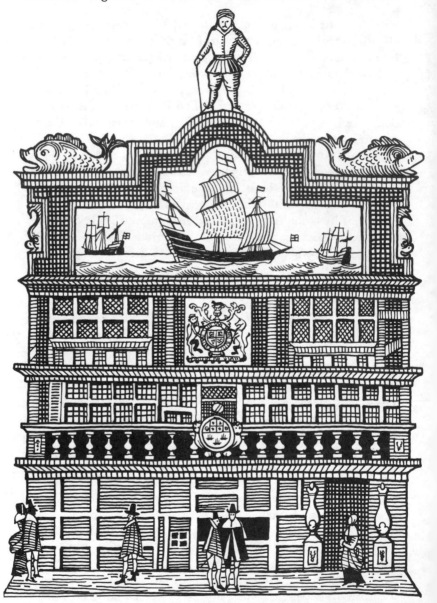

THE OLD EAST INDIA HOUSE IN LEADENHALL STREET 1648 TO 1726

Beaujolais Nouveau of today, races and betting took place between these tea clippers, and often the price of tea was affected as one company's boat beat that of another back to London, enabling them to auction their cargo earlier.

The opium clippers, built with money made from the lucrative opium trade, were to improve on that time, making the return journey from Foochow to London in ninety-nine days, or just over three months.

By the late eighteenth century, Britain—in the reign of George III—was to attempt to form an official relationship with China. His Majesty chose an Irishman, Lord Macartney, to make this approach. Ireland (or Eire, as it is called since becoming a republic) was then in the Union, and Macartney was an experienced diplomat, having been for more than two decades ambassador at the court of Catherine the Great of Russia. But friendly though the Chinese were, they were also very guarded, and he was unable to find a way around the restrictive practices in force at the port of Canton, not to mention the language barrier and the fact that foreigners were not allowed to live on mainland China but had to stay in Macao.

What he *was* able to do, however, was to collect seeds from the tea plants, which were eventually cultivated and made to thrive in the botanical gardens in Calcutta. While the Calcutta plants did not yield the quality and quantity of leaves necessary to produce a good tea, they did kindle the notion that colonial India might be the right place to develop tea plantations.

India and Ceylon Teas

When the British government abolished the East India Company's China tea monopoly in 1833, they asked the then governor general of India, Lord Bentinck, to investigate and put forward proposals to start a tea-planting industry. Botanists in the eighteenth century had established that the climate and terrain in Assam, and therefore probably elsewhere in India, was propitious. Five years later, the first Indian teas were sold in the auction rooms in Mincing Lane, London. Twining, Horniman, Lipton and other well-known names of today were in there bidding.

However, Britain had to do some political sorting out. The Americans had become very competitive since British ports were closed to them following the American Revolution, and even though British ships were considered the fastest afloat, American skippers were now using new, sleeker, and faster vessels in their endeavors to increase their trade with China. They had developed the French designed "clipper," a slimly built boat with three or four sloping masts and new concave waterlines. Keels were deepened and hulls slimmed down to help counteract the vast expanses of canvas needed to catch every gust of wind.

THE CLIPPER JOURNEY

As long as the East India Company enjoyed a trading monopoly, there was no real concern to get shipments of tea back to England quickly, but after the repeal of the Navigation Acts in 1849, an American clipper, the *Oriental*, entered West India Docks in London only ninety-five days after leaving Hong Kong! This was a real shock to the British, and something had to be done to speed things up. So began the legendary clipper races, of which the most famous occurred in 1866, with eleven clippers taking part. Having loaded their cargoes at Foochow on 28 May of that year, four of these clippers, the

Ariel, *Fiery Cross*, *Taeping*, and *Serica*, were already passing the Western Isles by 29 August. *Ariel*'s Captain Keay was a shrewd navigator and, we are told by observers on land, cleverly blocked the *Taeping*'s attempt to hire the first pilot at Dungeness Roads, thus taking the lead up the mouth of the Thames estuary. *Ariel* was still in the lead on 7 September.

However, *Taeping*'s captain was the first to spot a tug, thereby beating *Ariel* to Gravesend. The outcome was a win for *Taeping* by only twenty minutes as she landed at London Docks, earning a bonus for her crew of some ten shillings a ton. (A clipper could carry 1 million pounds of tea, which is in the region of five hundred tons! So it was some bonus.) The clippers were eventually superseded in 1869, when steam took over from sail and the Suez Canal was opened, cutting the distance by several thousand miles.

Back in Assam, tea growing was burgeoning, though the imported China tea plants had been abandoned in favor of developing the wild bushes native to India.

While India tea had a flavor totally different from the delicate China teas enjoyed during the previous century, it was soon to become attractive to the English palate, particularly because of its more robust flavor, so much so that it became India's largest export, from which it, and Ceylon, still benefit to this day.

The Chinese had ever been secretive about their tea-growing techniques, but not so the Indians, or the Sinhalese. Of course the reasons for this are obvious. Britain was from the start the sole investor in the Indian development and could therefore call the tune and control the quality of the product. They could also eliminate adulteration of shipments, which had been a growing problem in the China trade.

Victorian England was running at a "high," the population was growing, industry was booming, the tea break had begun in the mills and factories of the provinces, and tea drinking had become universal. By the Edwardian period—or at least the 1890s—Britain was to import only one-third of its tea from China. The remainder came from India and Ceylon.

Sri Lanka, or Ceylon, as it was known in the days of the British empire, might never have become a tea-growing country had not their coffee crops been struck by a killer fungus (*Hemileia vastatrix*) in 1869. In their efforts to combat almost certain ruin and possible nationwide deprivation, the coffee planters turned their minds to cultivating the tea plant. This was to be their salvation.

D. M. Forrest, in his book *100 Years of Ceylon Tea* (1967) refers briefly to Scottish-born James Taylor, whose pioneering work with tea "gardens" was to be the savior of the Sinhalese people. Taylor, having arrived in Ceylon as a coffee-estate manager in 1852, had already been experimenting with tea growing and introduced new technologies, such as machinery for rolling and generally processing the leaves, as well as establishing and building proper factories for this purpose.

The typical Ceylon tea is a small, black, delicately flavored leaf of the Assam variety, and because the island has two monsoon seasons a continuous crop can be grown, one side of the island being harvested while the opposite side is under monsoon. The tea-growing area is in the hills some thirty miles south of the ancient capital of Kandy. Nuwara Eliya, Ceylon, Lady Londonderry (a blend), Dikoya (a blender tea), and Dimbula are the best known names.

Here again, high-grown teas—that is, high up in the hills— are usually considered by tea drinkers to be among the best, and those from Ceylon in particular. "Self-drinkers" are those with a strong, full taste. Others, known as blenders, are those with a more pungent flavor that need to be mixed with the more delicate varieties.

Blended Teas

The bulk of tea drunk in Britain today is blended. In the eighteenth century, the hostess would blend her own balance of green and black teas, taking them from her caddy and measuring them with her silver caddy spoon into a crystal mixing bowl. Realizing the value of a good sales point, the local grocer often adopted the blend of the lady of the manor for others to enjoy. The merchants also created their own blends, which at first were regional if not local, but today are national and even international. It is doubtful that a packet of Earl Grey purchased from your nearest supermarket would bear any resemblance to His Lordship's original mix, but the romantic idea that it does is still an excellent sales point, for we all hanker after a taste of the past.

It is said that the secret of this delicately bergomot-scented blend was passed by a Chinese Mandarin about 125 years ago to Earl Grey, who used it in his own household and eventually had it made up for him by a London tea merchant, who was in turn allowed to sell it to selected purchasers. It is still a special blend of fine China and other exotic oriental teas, which can be blended with a China Keemun or good-quality Darjeeling if the consumer requires the scent to be less strong.

Other fashionable people whose names live on to this day as blends of tea are Queen Mary, Lady Londonderry, and the Marquis of Queensbury of Oscar Wilde fame.

When next in England, if you care to search around, there remain a few specialist blenders who will make up and hold a recipe peculiar to your particular taste. On the other hand, you could purchase a handsome caddy, buy a variety of green and black teas, settle yourself on a Chippendale chair, summon the butler to bring a kettle of boiling water, and enjoy a unique journey into the past as you personally mix and pour, infuse and sip, from a shallow baroque Rockingham cup!

THE TASTE OF TEA

Many years ago at my public school we boisterous lads were asked by a somewhat effete English master to write an essay entitled "The Flavor of a Strawberry, as Described to One Who Has Never Tasted the Fruit." No doubt he saw this as a good exercise in the use of our mother tongue in its written form!

An impossible task, as it is with wine. Yet there are tomes written on the subject of enology, and to some extent it *is* possible to convey what an imbiber might expect from a particular wine produced in a particular area.

To write about tea and not attempt to give the reader some guide as to what to expect from the different leaves and blends would be to evade the issue. I can, however, only attempt to convey to you in the very broadest of terms what characteristics to expect. Thus, I have divided teas into the following categories.

English Breakfast Tea

A blend of Ceylon and Indian teas, this is a "brisk" tea with a full-bodied, astringent flavor, ideal as a "wakeup" tea. Is there anywhere in the world other than England where a chambermaid will creep into your bedroom at the crack of dawn and slide a tray of tea on to your bedside table, then open the curtains and allow a blinding light to flood the room, thus rudely awakening you from a soothing night's sleep? This ritual is often accompanied by the whispered words "Good morning, sir (or madam), it is seven o'clock, drizzling lightly, though the sun might soon break through. The prime minister has increased the tax on petrol. Oh! and could you please vacate your room by noon?"

This blend of tea is also the one to be served when you finally arrive in the Breakfast Room. It has a good restorative quality about it, leaving you ready to face the day.

It is with this first cup of the day that the "rich tea biscuit" appears alongside the teacup and sitting, alone, on a tiny plate. *Rich* is a misnomer, if ever there was one, for this ubiquitous English biscuit is as plain as they come! Welcomed in the morning as not too challenging, and good, I am assured, for ladies "in waiting."

Russian Caravan Tea

Don't be put off by its name, which sounds like a blend made for Gypsies!

This finely blended tea [originally brought to Russia by the long "caravan" route] was established by the Empress Elizabeth of Russia in 1735, is excellent for afternoon drinking.

Yunnan Tea

The sweetly flavored deep-toned and golden-hued tea from the western province of Yunnan in China became my favorite during the extensive tasting I did for the writing of this book.

Delicately scented, it is ideal for iced tea, and for the lighter tea punches.

Jasmine Tea

As the name implies, these China tea leaves are scented with jasmine petals. It should be drunk weak, with a slice of lemon in each cup, and is good as a refreshing drink in the afternoon or for a late-night soothing beverage.

Darjeeling Tea

Probably the most popular tea at the top end of the market. It is the blend most favored in the exclusive clubs of London's St. James', and the India tea most likely to be offered to you in an English country home. It has a delicate yet positive flavor and is India tea at its best!

Pure Darjeeling tea is the most cosly of the India teas and good enough to be drunk unblended (a self-drinker, as they call it in the tea trade), though it is customary to purchase it ready-blended. I find its flavor not unlike muscatel in character, and its color a most satisfying deep-toned reddish brown.

Serve it with milk or, for the more adventurous, light cream, which gives it a very rich, smooth taste.

Earl Grey Tea

The name of Charles, the second Earl Grey (1764–1845), prime minister of England during the reign of William IV, is probably the best known in the world when it comes to tea.

Legend has it that the recipe for this unique and exquisite blend of China teas was presented to "The Right Honorable

Gentleman" by one of His Majesty's envoys on returning from a tour of duty in the East. Twining continued to make up this special blend for the earl, but sadly for them, they never had the name copyrighted. As a result, many tea merchants today use the name Earl Grey tea—though I consider Twinings' particular blend, with its almost colognelike scent derived from the oil of bergamot used in the blending, to be the best for afternoon drinking and a singularly refreshing beverage on a warm summer's day.

Drink it with a slice of lemon, although I often take a weak infusion with the merest drop of milk.

Orange Pekoe Tea

This smooth-flavored blend of specially selected Ceylon teas is excellent for afternoon tea and is a name well known

throughout the tea-drinking world. The word *orange* refers
to the color of the leaf, not the flavor.

Lapsang Souchong

The tea with the most distinctive flavor of all. Recognizable the instant the first cup is poured, not only by its light
grayish green color, but more particularly by the pungent
smoky aroma.

Souchong is the generic name of the large leaf of most
congou teas. Chinese souchong teas are "positive," rich (too
rich for some), and almost syrupy. It is never drunk with milk,
always with lemon, or unadulterated by either of these addi-
tives.

I consider its exotic smoky flavor too overpowering for
making tea punches, and prefer a less scented blend for this
purpose.

Black Currant Tea

It would be illogical to dismiss this tea as a gimmick, for
to introduce the black currant flavor (a natural essence),
which marries so well with tea, is no more a gimmick than to
add jasmine, gardenia, or bergamot to other blends of tea.

Ideal as an iced tea to be drunk at poolside on a hot summer's day or hot after a brisk walk on a crisp winter afternoon.

Keemun

A North China congou tea with a smooth, somewhat sweet
taste. Many consider this, along with the slightly smoky
I-Chang and Formosa oolong, to be among the best connoisseur
teas in the world.

As with wine tasting, once you leave the broad boundaries
of these teas with their distinctive flavors and characteristics,
you enter the world of connoisseurship, which demands years
of concentration and making notes on the blending, tasting, and
savoring of tea: a world full of interest, though perhaps not
for the general public, who are looking, on the whole, simply
for "the cup that cheers."

Other green teas of China and Japan are not for inclusion
here. Any reader wishing to take up tea testing seriously would
be well counseled to search out a copy of W. H. Ukers's *All
About Tea,* though this may prove a difficult search, since it

was published back in 1935. Another, more readily available book would be *Tea for the British* by Denys Forrest, published by Chatto and Windus in 1973. Even so, some of the larger reference libraries may well have a copy in their archives.

How is tea blended, and what is its path to your pantry shelf?

On leaving the plantation, whether in India, Sri Lanka (Ceylon), or China, tea is packed into plywood chests lined with aluminum foil to keep it dry and fresh. Each chest is branded or marked with all the information the British merchants will require when it arrives in dock, such as the estate name, the grade of leaf, the year it was plucked and fired, weight of contents, and any other relevant data. Chests containing one particular make and from one particular grower are known as "breaks."

On arrival in the United Kingdom the tea is first stored in warehouses in or around the docks of the port of landing, which could be London, Manchester, Avonmouth, or elsewhere. Here samples from each "break" are taken and distributed for examination by the various tea brokers who are going to buy at auction and resell the tea to packers and other merchants. The brokers are known as selling or buying brokers. Catalogues are compiled by the selling brokers giving details of the types and qualities of tea on sale and stating the available quantity of each tea or blend of tea, and where it is warehoused.

The smaller buying broker will draw his samples from the selling broker so that he in turn can advise his clients, the packers and distributors, and he can also assess to a fairly accurate degree the probable price each tea will fetch at auction. All this has to be done through the Tea Clearing House, which deals with the complicated Documents of Title, and the organizing of samples of tea to be collected by buyers. Today all this is done by computer.

Up to 1833 the East India Company held the monopoly on tea shipping, at least from China, and on the tea auctions.

While the East India Company was first chartered by Queen Elizabeth I in 1600, it was to be some time before its ships brought the leaf back to England; though it had enjoyed exclusive rights of Eastern trade for two and a half centuries, for obscure reasons teas were never a part of the cargo. Each time the charter came up for renewal, varying independent

merchants opposed its granting, but to no avail: the East India
Company continued to enjoy its monopoly. There was a break-
through in 1813, when certain commerce with India was permitted for British ships only, but tea was excluded. It appears
that the government of the day would or could not believe that
individual merchants were competent to deal with the wily
Chinese at Canton, preferring to leave the tea monopoly with
the East India Company, even though at the Whampoa anchor-
age in Canton other nations' ships appeared to have little difficulty in bartering with the local merchants. Quarterly auctions
went on at East India House, headquarters of the Company in
Leadenhall Street.

We first hear of Mincing Lane, the street so much associated with tea, when the new auction rooms opened there
in 1834.

The system of a tea auction is too complicated to enter into
in a book of this nature. Suffice it to say that bids are made and
the tea bought by both buying and selling brokers at the top
price bidden and accepted by the auctioneer. When bids have
been accepted and the various teas bought it is the turn of the
manufacturer to make up, or blend, his own brand product for
the retail market. This all-important blending is the responsi-
bility of the specialist tea taster, whose job it is to select a
variety of teas from those bought at auction and mix these to
the public taste. As many as twenty or thirty different teas can
be used to make a popular blend. The taster's blend has to
match up with previous blends in order to arrive at a contin-
uity of flavor, almost in the way a blended wine has to have no
recognizable difference from its predecessor. Copious notes are
made as the taster works, sipping, smelling, gargling and spit-
ting in order to prepare a final sheet listing the different teas.
This is then sent off to a factory, which will draw the requisite
teas from the warehouse where they have been stored. At the
packer's factory the bulk blending is done in large automatic
revolving drums before finally being filled and sealed into the
packet we all recognize.

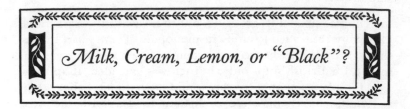

Milk, Cream, Lemon, or "Black"?

There is probably more debate as to whether the addition of milk, cream, or lemon makes the best cup of tea, than there is on any other food subject in England. Those who spurn the addition of milk or cream must be reminded that the Chinese themselves originally made their infusion by adding boiled milk to their tea, so the argument that the Chinese always drink it in its natural water infusion falls apart!

The addition of lemon started as an affectation in the Victorian era. Queen Victoria, as is well known, was the "great-grandmother of all Europe," her many children and grandchildren being conveniently married off—to the other families' advantage—to most of the crowned heads of European countries. Her eldest daughter, the princess royal, was the consort of the emperor of Prussia, where they made tea differently (in fact, it was drunk from a glass, in the Russian manner, and served from a samovar, not a teapot). Russians were to be seen sucking it through sugar lumps and even stirring in jam! Dear God! how the British reacted against this notion! However, the slice of lemon, as served at the Russian court, came to England following a short visit by the queen to her daughter's adoptive country, as did *"service à la Russe,"* where courses at dinner were, for the first time, served consecutively rather than being placed on the dinner table all at once, a habit that still persists in many parts of provincial and industrial England, where high tea or supper is still the main evening meal.

High tea, as opposed to afternoon tea, is an assembly of breads, cakes, scones, and preserves supplemented by one simple cooked dish, which is invariably "something-on-toast" or "something-and-chips" (which are fried potatoes and not to be confused with American "chips," which in England are called "crisps") and of course pints of good strong tea laced with milk and (too much!) sugar.

In the two major northern counties of Yorkshire and Lancashire, the pint pot—which in Britain means twenty fluid

ounces, not the American sixteen fluid ounces—is an essential feature for the man of the house. These straight-sided "mugs," or "pots," are very individually decorated and sometimes carry mottoes or proverbs. The author of this book—a Yorkshire man first, Englishman second—uses for his daily morning Sanka just such a pot, which bears an old Yorkshire proverb in the words of a man's advice to his son:

> Hear all, see all, say n'owt
> Eat all, supp all, pay n'owt
> And if ever tha does owt for n'owt
> Allus do it for thee sen.

which, roughly translated, means:

> Hear everything, see everything
> Say nothing
> Eat all, drink all, pay nothing
> And if ever you do anything for nothing,
> Always do it for yourself!

It is generally accepted in today's England that it is permissible, nay usual, to add milk or cream to black teas, but it would be tantamount to sacrilege to desecrate green or oolong teas with anything—not even lemon and certainly not whisky, which is often added as a comforter to black tea on a winter's eve in Ulster and Scotland!

Sam Twining, director of R. Twining and Company and a ninth-generation descendant of that important tea-blending family, has this to say on the subject:

There is no doubt tea is, on the whole, improved by milk. It smooths the taste, and is often referred to as "creaming," giving a more pleasant, gentler, softer result. Teas like *Gunpowder, Green* and *Jasmine* however are *not* good with milk. Assam type teas cannot be drunk without it.

Now, whether the milk goes in first or last is a matter for conjecture. Put in first, it can be seen as a cautionary measure against the cracking of fine china cups, yet fine bone china is very heat-resistant. Putting it in after the tea has been poured means that each individual can control the amount of milk or cream to his or her taste.

In those days the captains and ships' officers of the East India Company were allowed perks in that they were permitted to ship anything for their own profit as long as it traveled in the bilges! We know that the first chinaware entered the country this way.

In the early days of tea drinking in England, mugs of silver, pewter, or just plain earthenware were used, the same mugs that had hitherto been used for the drinking of ale and porter. Totally ignorant, the Brits thought that pouring scalding-hot tea into the newfangled Chinese tea *bowls* would crack the delicate porcelain, so they put the milk in first!

The first European account of milk being used in tea occurred around 1655, when the Dutch ambassador described being given milk with his tea when he first arrived in Canton. There are also references around that same time to Parisian society taking milk in their tea.

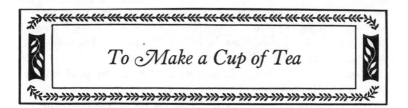

To Make a Cup of Tea

While the verb may change, the traditional way of making, infusing, brewing, drawing, or mashing tea ought not to. The method is as follows:

≪ Use the finest tea you can afford.

≪ Warm the teapot either by standing it near the fire or by rinsing with boiling water.

≪ Use one teaspoonful per person, plus "one for the pot."

≪ Bring freshly drawn water to the boil. Do not allow it to rattle once it boils, as this rids the water of air.

≪ Take the pot to the kettle and pour in the boiling water.

≪ While the "one-for-the-pot" rule is a habit in every house in the land, nowhere are you told how much water to add! You assess this for yourself over the years. I suggest you start off with 1¼ pints of boiling water to each ounce of tea (more water for China tea).

≪ Stir the mixture well, replace the lid, and allow the tea to infuse, brew, mash, or draw (depending on where you live) for five minutes.

≪ Pour into warm cups and add milk and sugar to taste.

A ceramic pot is best, as it retains the heat well.

Aluminum should never be used for a teapot, strainer, or tea ball infuser. It turns the tea black.

Isabella Mary Beeton (1836–1864), with her *Book of Household Management,* was to the English housewife what Fannie Farmer and her *Boston Cooking School Cookbook* was to the American woman. Only a modest generation divided them. They both dealt with domestic life at the end of the nineteenth century and influenced generations up to the beginning of the Second World War. Mrs. Beeton gives in her tome what is the best, and only, advice this author has ever seen in print on the making of a pot of tea. How often is the first cup perfect, but later cups taste stewed and bitter as the pot is left standing, sometimes complete with tea cozy to aid and abet the crime? Her answer—and a brilliant one at that, used by professional tea tasters the world over—is to use *two* pots!

The tea is made as instructed and is fused for five minutes. (Why don't we use this expression: "Infuse a pot of tea," for that is exactly what we are doing? Yet we persist with our *brewing, mashing,* and *drawing!*)

She then instructs her readers to decant off the freshly made tea through a tea strainer into a second warm teapot. And presto! There you have it. The perfect "cuppa" to the last drop.

CLEANING TEAPOTS

Contrary to many old wives' tales, a teapot that is "lined" with tannin does not make a good cup of tea; it can and does make the infusion bitter.

The pot should be meticulously cleaned, and where a coating of tannin is present, this must be removed, either by prolonged soaking or by the use of a cleansing powder, in which case the pot must be well rinsed.

The Impedimenta

The most elegant setting for afternoon tea has always been the drawing (from the word *withdrawing*) room. In medieval times, when a "progress" was made and people were received formally by the king or queen Regnant, it was to the "withdrawing room" that the procession meandered after the reception. In less imposing aristocratic houses, the smaller room off the main center of social concourse was the withdrawing room. Life-styles and customs evolved, and later the drawing room became the room to which ladies withdrew to chat of trivia and scandal while the gentlemen passed the port after dinner. Today this room, if not called the drawing room, may, in smaller homes, be called a sitting room or even a lounge.

To this author, a fireplace is an essential factor for an elegant afternoon tea, for where else would you toast muffins, crumpets, pikelets, or just plain bread? "In a mechanical toaster," you'll say, but that cuts out the romance of the occasion. Comfortable chairs and plenty of small tables are then all that is needed to create the cozy *mise en scène* necessary for this social ritual to begin.

An elegant Georgian tea table should be covered with a fine lace or embroidered tea cloth and set out with the tea-

cups and saucers, each standing on a tea plate with an embroidered organdie tea napkin between plate and saucer. An adequate space must be left for a handsome oblong or oval silver galleried tea tray, which in turn will be the resting-place for an elegant silver teakettle complete with spirit burner, a sugar basket with its blue Bristol-glass liner, a helmet-shaped creamer, a hot-water jug, strainer, and the all-important "slop" bowl, into which dregs can be poured from each guest's cup before a second cup is proferred.

For those households that possess a teapoy (*q.v.*) this will take the place of a tea caddy (*q.v.*) or canister.

A silver muffin dish with a hot-water liner and high-domed lid will be needed to hold freshly toasted *hot* muffins or crumpets dripping with good sweet butter sent up by the cook from the nether regions, and a jam dish and spoon to hold homemade preserves.

A muffineer, not unlike a domed pepper dredger—in fact, by some people often mistaken for one—will contain cinnamon, sugar, or even salt for gourmets to sprinkle on their muffins.

For those huddled on the floor by the fireside, an expanding toasting fork will be provided so that each guest may make his own hot toast; the gentlemen spreading theirs with butter and Gentleman's Relish (a type of strong pâté of anchovies), the ladies with pieces of honeycomb from the local hives or homemade preserves or fruit "butters."

TEA CADDIES AND CADDY SPOONS

Tea caddies became objects to which master craftsmen and silversmiths could apply their skills.

The word *caddy* derives from the Malay word *kati*, meaning "one pound." The term applied to the small box containing about a pound (in fact, 1.2 pounds) in which tea was packed for importing into England.

Canisters, as they were first known, or caddies, were unknown in seventeenth-century England, but in the first half of the eighteenth century they soon became part of the silver tea service so loved (as a status symbol) by the British until this day (though a solid silver service today would cost thousands of dollars.)

Caddies come in all sorts of shapes and sizes, plain and elegant, or elaborate and ornate, some in silver, most in unusual and pretty inlaid and polished woods. Whatever it was made of, the caddy would be provided with a lock and key to prevent servants from removing any of the expensive leaf.

Glass canisters were also fairly popular in England from about 1750 until 1820. Known as tea bottles, they were commonly made of "Bristol blue" glass, opaque white glass, or clear glass, gilded or enameled with elaborate designs and often bearing the name of the type of tea they contained. They were usually made in pairs to hold green and black teas. Most had hinged metal lids, some were made with ground glass stoppers, and the more exotic ones might well have had silver or ormulu mounts.

When the hostess did not reign or preside at her own tea table, the necessary measure and mixture would be handed to the servants in the mixing glass, and the caddy would then be locked again. (Ironically, caddies often had sliding bottoms for ease of filling!)

Controversy still reigns as to whether—in the larger three-sectioned caddies—the center compartment was intended for lump sugar or to contain the cut-glass mixing bowl. Usually there is an obvious solution, for often, where a mixing glass is a composite part of the caddy (and the glasses are frequently missing from antique caddies, as they were easily broken) there is a suitably shaped aperture cut out to hold it. Where the center compartment is a simpler and broader version of its two neighbors, it was perhaps for sugar, and the mixing glass or bowl would have been a separate affair, either with a silver holder or just on its own, depending on the wealth and status of the family.

Wooden caddies often bore inlaid designs of Chinese scenes and characters reflecting the origin of tea. And there were, of course, single caddies for the less well-to-do.

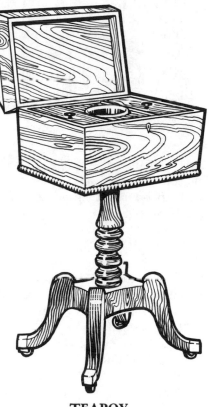

TEAPOY

The teapoy is a small pedestal or three-legged table fitted with tea containers or canisters and mixing bowls. The word derives from an Indian word meaning "three feet."

CADDY SPOONS

The first silver caddy spoons were fashioned in the shape of a shell. Probably this pattern was chosen because the Chinese used to include a natural scallop shell for scooping out the tea in each box they shipped.

Eighteenth-century silversmiths let their imagination run wild, creating short-handled spoons to fit inside the caddy when the lid closed, forged in every possible shape, from the

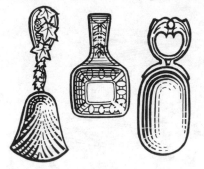

traditional bowl to hands, leaves, paws, and fruits. Many people have fine collections of caddy spoons.

A pretty caddy spoon makes an ideal gift for a christening, coming-of-age, or barmitzvah.

THE MOTE SPOON AND TEA STRAINER

The rolling, drying, and packing of teas in the eighteenth century, while remarkably sophisticated even when compared with twentieth-century methods, nevertheless had a few problems, one being that "bastard" leaves and other debris would sometimes escape the eagle eye of the blenders and selectors and mar the clear golden liquid.

But as usual the ever-resourceful British had an answer to this problem of unwanted "floaters" on the top of a filled cup.

If these stray leaves escaped first the filter in the teapot (if it was fitted with such a device) or perhaps overflowed the silver strainer placed across the mouth of each cup as it was poured, a mote spoon would be used to scoop up and catch any wayward specks of tea dust.

These spoons, whose name is taken from the Old English word *mot,* which came from the Dutch word of the same spelling meaning "dust" (we still talk of a "mote" in the eye), were beautifully wrought and pierced by the various and many-talented silversmiths in a variety of delightful patterns.

THE TEA URN

The tea urn, often mistakenly referred to as a samovar, which is its Russian cousin—or fountain, as it was sometimes

called—first appeared in mid-eighteenth century England to replace the teakettle. It could be taken as a good sign that tea
drinking was on the increase, as an urn holds considerably
more water than a kettle. Invariably made of Sheffield plate
or japanned metal (sterling would be prohibitive in price,
though fine examples do exist), they have a bellied pear- or
round-shaped body standing on four feet or curved spindle legs.
Others have a square base with four feet, with a spigot and
tap at the bottom from which to fill the teapot, two handles
for ease of handling, and a domed lid with finial. Inside there
is usually a fixed, hollow, cylindrical compartment, so wrought
to receive a thick 1½-inch diameter red-hot iron rod to keep the
water hot.

THE TEAKETTLE

Teakettles came in different forms. In the early part of
the eighteenth century there are examples of teapots themselves being used as kettles, set over small wick holders. Usually
fashioned with a side handle and a tiny hinged lid on the
curved spout itself, in addition to the main lid, these could

be taken as a sign that some few people made their tea differently—by putting the tea leaves in the kettle!

Not much later, there appeared the kettle as we think of
it, of which there are many examples in the antique shops
throughout Britain today, and they are considered to be an

excellent investment. (The author purchased an early nine-teenth-century kettle and lamp in 1969 for twenty-two pounds. Today's value is in the region of eight hundred pounds—an increase of nearly 360 percent—in sixteen years!).

The teakettle could be made from sterling silver, Sheffield plate, or electroplate. As with a teapot, the fixed handle, or bail, had an ivory or ebony inset, which acted as an insulator. The kettle could be freestanding on its trivet and spirit lamp or the kettle could be hinged to the tripod, so that all the hostess had to do was tip it forward in order to fill her teapot, thus minimizing the risk of accidents.

Eighteenth-century carpenters cashed in on the fashion for teakettles and created teakettle stands, which are sometimes taken to be plant or candle stands, for they, too, are small and round, with three claw feet, but are obviously lower in height than the other two pieces of furniture.

THE TEA TRAY

This large oval or oblong tray was made of sterling silver, Sheffield plate, or electroplate, and was used in eighteenth-century Britain and Europe for serving tea. Four-footed, with two handles for ease of carrying, tea trays could be up to twenty-two inches long. Their edges were molded or swept in the rococo fashion, with the elegant oval ones having a vertical pierced gallery and a slot at each end to act as a handhold in place of the more usual extending handles. The center of the tray would have an engraved shield or family monogram. It is said there are more Sheffield plate tea trays made than any other item in this medium.

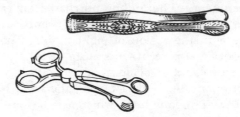

The tea tray was designed to hold a kettle—where a separate kettle stand was not in use—and a pot, sugar canister and tongs, spoon tray, caddies, and milk or cream jug (though a matching jug was not considered necessary until later in the eighteenth century—a helmet jug or creamer of a different design sufficed). The teacups, saucers, and spoons were set out on the tea table, not on the tray.

THE TEA TABLE

This was an occasional table with a carved rim that was sometimes made of pierced metal to prevent the cups and saucers from sliding off. Later, when afternoon tea was in full flight, extra tables, often in the form of a nest of tables, or a folding table, were needed. The late Victorian period also saw the advent of portable freestanding, three-tiered cakestands, a piece of furniture considered very useful when a variety of cakes and biscuits was to be offered.

THE TEACUP AND TEAPOT

It is not without reason that china is so called.

During the T'ang Dynasty (A.D. 620–964) the Chinese were fast developing their love for tea drinking. At the same time they were making a type of pottery vastly superior to any seen before, certainly in Europe.

This pottery became known in England as china, and it was the Dutch and Portuguese who first introduced it to Europe. What they brought back were often pieces used in tea-making ceremonies in China. Earlier imports were made of stoneware and were in fact wine jars, the urn-shape of which was eventually to form the basis of the teapot we still know to this day.

Likewise the teacup. The Chinese and Japanese drank their tea from small bowls. These bowls were to become the basic shape for the European teacup, though the handle wasn't added until the mid eighteenth century, probably because

English and European ladies found it uncomfortable to hold the (hot) handleless cup with the forefinger on the top rim, the thumb forming the base of a pincerlike grip by supporting the bottom "under rim" of the bowl. It is said, and not without logic, that this method of holding the tea "can" or cup gave rise to the "refained" upward soaring of the little finger to make the grip look elegant. It must also have been more comfortable when fingers were jewel-laden!

The first ceramic teacups did not differentiate between coffee and chocolate cups. The former eventually became straight-sided with one handle and known as a coffee can, whereas the latter was given two handles and a lid and was used for chocolate only. The "trembleuse saucer" or teacup stand, the deep recess or raised rim of which was designed to prevent the cup from sliding about—or "trembling"—was a

French notion that came in later in the eighteenth century and, with some potteries—Hilditch for one—as late as the early nineteenth century.

For a time the teacup remained a shallow cup without the single handle that was added in the mid eighteenth century. It also had a shallow, rimless saucer, and it was considered quite polite to pour into and drink your tea from the saucer, a habit still in evidence among elderly people in some parts of Britain to this day. My mother and aunts always took their tea from the saucer, the tea "can" held in one hand, the saucer in the other, with much sipping and elegant blowing to cool the liquid. When it became the fashion to have cups with handles, the "cans" fell into disuse, although many examples appear in antique shops throughout the land.

My mother had a penchant for collecting tea services. If my memory serves me well, she had some ten or twelve different sets of a dozen. A very pretty one from Minton was her favorite, with garlands of miniature rosebuds around the gilt rims. Then there was another delicate fluted white one with simple gold handles from the Belleek factory in County Fermanagh, and a third, early-nineteenth-century set of handleless tea "cans" and rimless saucers from the Hilditch Pottery (which only existed for about fifteen years between 1815 and 1830), which I now possess. My favorite, as a boy, and the one I always put out if it was my turn to "lay" the teatable, was a service from the Royal Worcester Pottery given to her by someone or other as a wedding gift in 1908. Its pattern was typical of that period when Art Nouveau was all the rage. The wide, shallow cups were in a bright butter-yellow with a deep black band at the rim, on which there was a further embellishment of full-blown pink roses.

There was also an "untouchable" set in a delicate pale blue, rose pink, and gold pattern, complete with lidded sugar bowl, milk jug, and teapot; each of its four cups was footed in a rather fragile shape. This was a gift my father brought back from the Noritake porcelain factory in Japan, after a business trip he had made to the East. Yet another pattern was from Meissen, but the most valuable of all, with four painted panels of figures and flower garlands on each cup, was from the Sèvres factory in Paris. These last three were my mother's pride and joy and were hardly ever used. The exception was when my grandmamma made an appearance, demanding the finest china cup for her tea.

More mundane services, used on weekends and for more "ordinary" "At Homes" or to eke out the numbers of cups required when she took it upon herself to entertain large numbers or, to be more precise, when she wanted to show off to the entire neighborhood (her attitude to our neighbors was not unlike that of Lucia in E. F. Benson's Mapp and Lucia books), were from potteries with such names as Copeland, Mason, Denby, or Johnson (I recall a rather tedious blue and white printed one). Then there was an ugly "green dragon" pattern. Almost every household had that one, if not in green then in blue. There was also a "modern" pink set with brown polka dots from the hands of the designer Susie Cooper in Staffordshire. (Very, very collectable in 1986: though no one would have thought so in 1956!)

When my mother died, well into her eighties and having led a *very* full life indeed, my sisters, as is the wont of sisters, gathered and divided these spoils, thinking (in all honesty) that my brothers and I, "mere men" (sic), would not want such domestic trivia. Trivia! to *me*? Ah well, I did get the Hilditch, which I treasure, along with a very odd silver tea service fashioned from what was at one time known as Indian silver (I think it is now more commonly called Britannia metal!). It is certainly a curvaceous riot, rococo in style, with bas-relief panels, cabriole feet, and asymmetrical knobs and handles; it is also very difficult to clean!

Her "best" Georgian silver—from my grandmother's family—went to my eldest sister, who has never drunk a cup of tea, or had a tea party, in her life.

However, there came a time in my life when, between 1955 and 1964, I was to mastermind a series of banquets, buffets, and "At Homes" at Harewood House, near Leeds. Harewood was the country home of the (late) Princess Royal, Countess of Harewood. She was the sister of King George VI and aunt to Her Majesty, Queen Elizabeth II.

In this unbelievably handsome Adam mansion, I was to enjoy the total freedom of taking from the silver vaults any pieces I chose to use when working in the house.

Fashioned by such masters of their craft as Hesther Bateman, Paul de Lamerie, and Paul Storr, to name but three. There were vast tea trays, almost too heavy to carry, teakettles, urns, creamers, teapots, strainers, sugar canisters, and caddies, each and every one wrought by one or other of England's famous silversmiths, the choice of which would make Shreve Crump & Low, or even Tiffany turn green with envy!

It was the luxury of working at Harewood House and later at St. James's Palace that kindled in me the urge to delve more deeply into the history of English food and domestic life and —in no small way—was to lead to my writing this book on the history of afternoon tea and its impedimenta.

That said, it now occurs to me that my mater's abundance of tea services was never, in her eyes, considered "excessive" in the way that other luxuries were. I think, as with bricks and mortar, they were perhaps seen even then, certainly by my father, as an investment, though if I am to be kind and honest, I think she liked them intrinsically.

Mind you, "the boys"—my brothers and I, that is—were never allowed to drink from any of this exquisite china. We were (and rightly, too) considered too clumsy by far, so we each had our own mug on the side, so to speak.

It is well to recall here that after a tea party, my mother followed the well-established habit of having two bowls of water sent to the drawing room, one soapy, the other for rinsing, along with a fine linen cloth, where she washed the cups and saucers herself. This, of course, was exactly what the mistresses of the household did in seventeenth- and eighteenth-century England. China and porcelain of this fine quality were considered far too valuable for the servants to handle, and that is probably why so much of it survives to this day.

With the advent of the Second World War everything was

packed away in crates for safety from the devastating Nazi bombs, and disappeared from our lives, along with the habit of "taking tea," only now rearing its head as something to be enjoyed again, though the fine china tea services are now too valuable to be used except on "high days" and holidays.

TEAPOTS

Early British-made teapots were always wrought and forged from sterling silver or Sheffield plate and were similar in shape to the coffeepot, with a tapering cylindrical body, a straight, forty-five-degree-angled spout, and an ebony or fruit-wood handle set at right angles to the spout. The cover, or lid, was dome-shaped, with a handsome finial as a knob. Later, the pineapple, a traditional British symbol of hospitality, was to be a frequent motif for the knobs or finials of teapots.

Very early silver teapots were made by cutting down the taller existing coffee and chocolate pots, and examples of this thrift—and one can only imagine it was just that—are in the archives of the Goldsmiths Hall in London. There is no logical reason why a teapot should not have been tall, but it did not take long before such eminent silversmiths as Paul de Lamerie, Paul Storr, and Hesther Bateman began to modify this shape using round, polygonal, and pear-shaped forms with a molded foot, the handle and spout (now curvaceous and with a filter set in where it was welded to the body of the pot) sometimes at right angles to each other, but more usually at opposite sides.

Toward the last quarter of the eighteenth century the drum-shaped teapot with a straight spout and flat lid was to become very fashionable. This was then followed in social desirability by the oval, rectangular, and multifaceted boat-shaped pot. Often made with flat bottoms, these pots had matching stands to protect the top of the tea table. Stands were often forged as an "extra" for existing teapots and could well be by a different maker, yet another sign of wealth in eighteenth- and nineteenth-century Britain.

By the time tea drinking became a national habit in the nineteenth century, pots were being made for the common man. These were of pottery and china, the designs for which were originally based on the silver pots of the gentry rather than upon the Chinese wine jug. While many of them were plain in design, more were lavishly ornamented and sculpted in every conceivable form: cauliflowers, rabbits, cottages, human forms, top hats, some with two spouts even. In fact, anything that could be made to hold the golden liquid—tea—was thrown, cast, or wrought.

Today these pots, for years considered vulgar by the middle and upper classes, are collectors' items of great value, as well as being an excellent social record of times past, as the tea bag

and instant tea make inroads into our busy, servantless lives.

The growth in popularity of tea drinking and its eventual availability to the middle and lower classes created a whole new business for the pottery industry at Stoke-on-Trent in Staffordshire and at nearby Derby. Josiah Wedgwood (1730–1795), one of the better known names in the pottery world, was quick off the mark in introducing machinery to his factory at Burslem.

Wedgwood is perhaps best known for his development of a cream-colored earthenware that was refined into what is still known today as Queensware, named after patroness Queen Charlotte, consort of King George III. At the bottom end of the trade, so to speak, and alongside his fine china, Wedgwood worked heavily with transferwork as a means of keeping costs down by not having to pay for hand painting.

In about 1767 he developed black basalt, an unglazed black stoneware made from native clay, ironstone, manganese, and ochre. Basalt was suitable for polishing and engine-turning and was the basis for the famous Wedgwood vases, busts, and relief "tablets" as well as teapots.

His partnership with T. Bentley in 1768 led to the opening of their well-known Etruria Works in 1769. At first they produced only high-quality ornamental ware, but soon the demand for domestic ware made great inroads into their production line at both ends of the scale, for Wedgwood didn't forsake the making of exquisite china.

Alongside all this, other potteries at Chelsea, Bow, Worcester, and Derby, to name but a few, were jumping on the bandwagon and fashioning tea services—or tea "sets," as they were often known—at first using the designs of the exquisitely wrought silver services as patterns. Soft-paste porcelain (as opposed to the Continental hard-paste porcelain of Meissen in Germany and Sèvres in France) was soon being used to produce the better-quality porcelain tea services that were—and still are—greatly sought after by antique collectors as well as first-time buyers.

Spode, another well-known name, and Josiah Spode II to boot (1754–1827), went even further in the nineteenth century, making porcelain from natural feldspar, a crystalline white mineral. Spode is also credited with the discovery of the formula for "bone" china, in which bone ash is combined with china clay. Much of England's finest and most delicate china is made from this. Rockingham, Coalport, Copeland, and Minton were other names to reckon with, all equally well known and vying for position as Britain's finest makers of china.

China itself—through tea drinking—influenced all these potters in their designs, for many years giving us the lovely blue and white ware known as delft, which was in itself the Dutch potters' attempt to copy, in tin-glaze earthenware, the Chinese porcelain imported by the Dutch East India Company into seventeenth-century Holland. The eighteenth-century Famille Rose of the Ch'ung period and the Imari designs from Japan are without doubt the most famous patterns.

Although tea sets, comprising teapot, sugar bowl, and cream jug, were probably made before the middle of the eighteenth century, they very rarely date earlier than the time of George III.

In the eighteenth century, a tea service from China would comprise twelve small handleless teacups, twelve rimless saucers, and six small coffee cans, the saucers doubling for both cups. A small teapot (for teas were still expensive), milk jug, and sugar and tea canisters completed the set.

It wasn't until the nineteenth century that the hot-water jug became part of the service, along with the slop basin. This slop basin, or slop bowl, appears to have been necessary, as silver strainers were a luxury and stray leaves often arrived inadvertently in the cup. Mind you, this gave way to the hobby of "reading the tea leaves," which superstition prevails to this day.

The large ten-inch bread-and-butter plate was included in early nineteenth-century services, but the small tea plate was not to appear until mid-Victorian times, when a separate utensil for everything was to become the order of the day. Tea knives and cake or pastry forks also made their appearance around this time.

And so we get nearer to the whole rigmarole of afternoon tea as all the necessary impedimenta became available.

THE POURING
AND PASSING AROUND OF TEA

It was always usual at breakfast for the lady of the household to sit at one end of the table and supervise the pouring of tea. The eldest daughter, or the mistress of the household's companion, took up a different position, where she was in charge of the serving of coffee and chocolate. Many single ladies, or spinsters as they were so harshly called, and older ones when widowed or past their prime, would engage a companion, often a relative in a similar state, to combat any possible loneliness and, in some cases, to act as a general dog's body. Remembering that there was neither television nor radio to occupy the long solitary hours, this seems to have been a good idea. Card and other board games, embroidery, particularly of tea cloths, puttering in the garden, walking, music, in the form of duet playing and singing, and many other occupations were more pleasant when two took part.

In grander households, a footman or maidservant would carry and pass the filled cup on a small silver salver to the member of the family or the house guest who was to receive it. In smaller households, it was passed down the table as we would today. At an afternoon-tea party the hostess would sit at her tea table (as in fact she would do today), mixing and infusing the tea. She would then ask whether her guests would take milk or lemon, sugar or not, before passing the filled cup.

In households where there were many retainers, the "black" tea would be carried on a small tray or salver alongside which would be a small creamer, sugar basin, and tongs for each guest to help himself. Younger members of the family would also fulfill this function when on vacation from their public school.

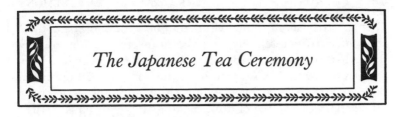

The Japanese Tea Ceremony

It is impossible to exclude Japan from any book on tea drinking, not least because most people, when they think of the tea ceremony, think of this Japanese ritual rather than the social "carry-on" of the British gentry.

A.D. 815 was the year the Emperor Saga issued a royal edict that tea should be grown in Japan. But for almost two hundred years thereafter, tea growing languished while the country was engaged in prolonged civil war.

As elsewhere, tea in Japan was originally seen more as a medicine—or a sacred remedy—than as a beverage to be enjoyed for its own savor. Witness the cure of the Shogun Sanetomo (A.D. 1203–1219): One Yeisai, a Buddhist monk who had been in no small way responsible for the reintroduction of tea to Japan following their period of unrest, was called upon to attend the sick shogun. Whatever his illness, apparently the cure was miraculous, and tea drinking, understandably, gained in reputation.

Parlor games were not unknown in those far-off days, and Tocha—or tea tasting—was a popular one introduced from China. Participants were asked to identify the best tea and say whence it came. Prizes were given, and a cult was started. Sixteenth-century Zen Buddhists claimed to be responsible for the elaborate tea ceremony, which eventually grew out of this early approach to drinking tea.

Special wooden buildings or teahouses (*sukiya*) are constructed in the corner of a garden for the tea ceremony, which is overseen by a tea master, often, but not always, the host himself. A wealthy host will often employ a tea master to perform the ritual for him.

To arrive in the *sukiya*, guests must tread a special path (*roji*) to the door or entrance of the waiting room (*yoritsuk*). Meanwhile, in the preparation room (*mizh-ya*) the tea master assembles all the impedimenta needed to perform this four-hour-long, spiritually cleansing and socially important ritual.

Guests, rarely more than five in number, must prepare their thoughts for the ceremony by walking reverently—and soberly dressed—through the garden to the waiting room. Here they are greeted by their host, who leads them to the tearoom itself. The room is entered by crawling through a low doorway, a ritual seen as a leveling of rank, making all people equal. Much attention is also paid to admiring the *ikebana*, or meaningful flower arrangements, and the specially painted scroll hanging in a place of prominence. Other observances, such as admiring the quality of the china, vary from ceremony to ceremony.

First of all a light meal (*kaiseki*) is offered, after which the invited guests repair to the garden or waiting room. At the tone of a gong they are signaled to return to the tearoom, where the scroll has been replaced in position of importance by a vase of flowers arranged in one of the traditional Japanese manners. (Each arrangement has some special significance to the occasion.)

A fire is now burning in a low stove, alongside which are set a tea caddy (*cha-ire*), a bamboo tea whisk (*cha-sen*), a tea bowl (*cha-wan*) and a scoop (*cha-shakm*), kettle, and ladle. (You will notice that the Japanese word for tea, as in China, is *cha*.)

A kettle of water is simmering by the fire. Having cleansed and rinsed all the utensils, in a way Westerners might observe at a Catholic Mass, the tea master puts three scoopsful of green tea (*matcha*) into the bowl and ladles over hot water from the kettle in a specific amount, handling the ladle in a very precise way.

This thick tea is whisked and is now ready. The guest of honor then shuffles forward on his knees and takes the bowl into the palm of his left hand while supporting it with the fingers of his right. He sips, praises the flavor, then takes two further sips, before wiping the rim and passing it to the next guest, who, after partaking, also wipes the rim with a small paper napkin (*kaishi*), which he will have brought with him along with his or her fan.

The host or tea master then makes a second infusion of thin tea (*usucha*), which is served in individual tea bowls.

Following this cleansing ritual the host or tea master leaves the tearoom, taking all the utensils with him, and the guests either depart or stay on for more social chitchat and local gossip, as they choose.

While there are many subtle variations of the tea ceremony, such as the mysterious and complex ways of using the tea ladle, the ritual of taking thick and then thin tea, is invariable.

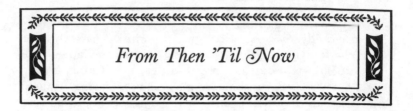

From Then 'Til Now

So there we have it—the exciting, not to say intriguing, history of the art of taking tea. We have glimpsed its beginning in seventeenth-century Europe, learned a little about the blending of tea, and counted the innumerable legends and customs that have grown up around its drinking. We have learned the history of the teapot and teacup, not to mention all the other impedimenta of the tea party. Looking down from the pinnacle of the late 1980s across the broad sweep of history, it is fascinating to see how events move in broad "swells." Perhaps it is the birth of someone with an exceptional mind who influences thought or sets history off in a new direction, or perhaps a clutch of great artists or musicians appears on earth in different places, yet at the same time, and starts a renaissance of all things beautiful. Someone invents a machine, and suddenly an industrial revolution takes place. A new drug saves lives that hitherto had been lost in an untimely fashion. The history of food and drink, in the wake of these swells, also changes in the same way: Georgian cooking in Britain was refined and tasteful, as were Georgian architecture, music, and arts. Cooking in Victorian times was on the one hand lavish, but on the other rather coarse, reflecting an era when the rich were getting richer—particularly the industry-related rich— and the poor needed the suet, the flour-thickening of dishes, and the rice in the ubiquitous English pudding to sustain them for the cruelly long hours they worked and against the icy chill of winter in their spartan workmen's cottages.

I hope you will make all the traditional tea-party tidbits described in this book and be encouraged to collect the evocative and elegant treasures associated with afternoon tea. But history, as I have said, is a process of evolution. Should we not also build on the past? Learn to mix new blends of tea leaf? Find new uses for its infusion? Invent new foods to eat with it? Above all, patronize a brilliant new generation of designers and encourage them to produce fine ornaments for the table? France has the exquisite new Monet-inspired yellow and co-bolt-blue service, the original of which is there to be seen at the artist's home at Giverny (now a museum). We in England have skilled furniture makers, such as John Makepeace, men-tor of H.R.H. Princess Margaret's son, Viscount Linley, as well as inspired silversmiths, embroiderers, and lace makers whose work we should be collecting. Given the space-age devices that make food preparation so easy, we should be building on our knowledge and experience to create new recipes. The advent of the food processor should alter the look of the tea table with-out any doubt! Nuts ground in a second, added to butter whipped to a white, airy lightness, and eggs beaten to a foam in a trice, should mean new, light-as-air cakes. Sandwich fill-ings take on a new attraction when one can wave the wand of the blender to make fine purees of this and that for more elegant eating. Let us therefore use our knowledge to create a whole new era of teatime delights!

PART II

Recipes

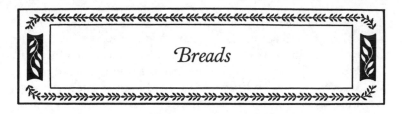

Breads

GUIDELINES TO
SUCCESSFUL BREAD MAKING

There is nothing more mouth-watering than the smell of freshly baked bread. To achieve a result that tastes and looks as good as it smells, here are a few points to remember:

« Yeast, the agent that makes the bread rise, can be bought both fresh—usually from a local bakery—or dried, in individual packets, at the supermarket.

« Fresh yeast should be a creamy color, smell sweet, and crumble easily between the fingers. It will keep in a plastic bag in the refrigerator for up to 1 month or in the freezer for 1 year. If freezing yeast, measure it out into recipe-sized portions before freezing.

« Fresh yeast can be added to the flour in any one of three ways: (a) blending it with the warm liquid, then adding it to the flour; (b) the batter method, in which one-third of the flour is mixed with the yeast liquid, left in a warm place for 20 minutes until frothy, then added to the rest of the flour; or (c) the yeast can be blended with part of the liquid, then added to the dry ingredients, and the remaining liquid.

« Dry yeast is equally as good as fresh, and often more easily obtainable. It will keep in an airtight container (or in its foil package) for 6 months. Dry yeast needs sugar and liquid to activate it. The proportion is 1 teaspoon sugar to 1 cup water, add the yeast and leave for 10 to 15 minutes. It is more concentrated than fresh yeast, so generally only half as much is needed.

« Using the correct flour is essential in bread making. Bread flours have a high gluten content, which helps in the raising of the bread, making it lighter, with a more open texture. Using whole wheat flour gives a closer texture and a stronger, more distinctive flavor. There are many different flours now on the market in addition to white and whole wheat —wheatmeal, stone-ground, "granary," and rye.

≪ Salt improves the flavor and also affects the gluten in the flour. Too much salt kills the yeast, making the bread heavy and uneven, while too little makes the dough rise too quickly. Accurate measuring is very important.

≪ The liquid can be water, which gives an even texture and crisp crust—most suitable for plain breads. A combination of milk and water, or milk alone, will give a softer texture, and the bread will stay fresh longer. The amount of liquid can depend on the absorbency of the flour and should be of a temperature that is hot to the hand to speed up the development of the gluten.

≪ The fat, which can be lard, butter, margarine, or oil, makes the dough softer. Plain mixtures rise faster than the richer ones that contain fat, sugar, fruit, and eggs.

There are a few basic steps that should be followed in bread making.

≪ If the ingredients and utensils are warm rather than chilled, the process of rising is speeded up somewhat.

≪ Measure all ingredients carefully.

≪ Kneading the dough is essential, as it releases the gluten in the flour, giving elasticity to the dough and allowing it to rise well and evenly. Knead for a good 10 minutes, or until the dough is firm, smooth, and no longer sticky.

≪ The dough must rise in a warm place, in a greased or oiled plastic bag to prevent a skin forming. Extreme heat kills the yeast, and extreme cold retards its growth. Dough will rise in a refrigerator overnight, or for up to 24 hours. The risen dough should spring back when pressed gently with a floured finger.

≪ The second kneading, known as knocking back, gives the dough a good texture. Knead for 2 to 3 minutes to knock out any air bubbles.

≪ Shape and leave the dough in well-greased pans or baking sheets, covered with oiled plastic, to rise a second time. Fill the pans only halfway.

≪ Proving, the second rising stage, is always done in a warm place until the dough rises to the top of the pans or has doubled in size. (To keep the top of the loaves flat for making neat sandwiches, cover a baking sheet with lightly oiled foil.

Place this, oiled side down, on top of the dough in the pans before the second rising. Place ovenproof weights on top and bake as usual.)

« Glaze and bake in a preheated, very hot oven so that the extreme heat will kill the yeast.

« After its stated baking time, test for doneness by tapping the base of the baked loaf with your knuckle: it should sound hollow, and the loaf should be crisp and a good brown color. If the loaves are still soft and doughy, unmold and put upside down on a baking tray, and return to the oven for a further 10 minutes.

« The bread should be cooled on a wire rack so that air can circulate around it, otherwise any remaining moisture will make the crisp crust go soft.

« Bread is best eaten fresh, especially brown breads, but it can be refreshed in the oven, wrapped in foil and reheated at 450°F/230°C for 5 to 10 minutes. Let the bread cool before removing the foil. For a more crusty loaf, reheat without foil.

The finishing touch:

« For a crusty top, brush before baking with 2 teaspoons salt dissolved in 2 tablespoons water.

« For a soft, shiny crust, brush before baking with beaten egg or a combination of egg and milk.

« For a floury crust, lightly sift a little flour over the top before baking.

« For a sticky, shiny glaze, use either honey, maple syrup, or 2 tablespoons sugar dissolved in 2 tablespoons water. Brush over the cooled, warm loaf after baking.

« For extra crunch, sprinkle before baking with sesame, poppy, caraway, celery, or fennel seeds when the flavor complements the recipe. Cracked wheat or crushed cereal may also be used.

WHITE BREAD

This basic white-bread dough makes one 2-pound and one 1-pound loaf. The large cottage loaf is the shape associated with a country-farmhouse tea; other shapes are known as plaits, bloomers, cobs, or crowns. The dough may also be shaped into

individual rolls—knots, plaits, and so forth—and will make
about 18. Sprinkle the rolls with sesame or poppy seeds, glaze
with egg for a shiny top or salt water for a crusty finish, or dust
with flour for a soft roll.

1 tablespoon active dry yeast	4¼ cups white bread flour
OR ½ ounce fresh	2 level teaspoons salt
¼ teaspoon superfine	2 teaspoons lard
granulated sugar	Salt water OR beaten egg and
2 cups warm water	milk, to glaze

Makes one 2-pound and one 1-pound loaf

Grease one 2-pound and one 1-pound loaf pan.

Mix the yeast, sugar, and water together in a small bowl
and leave in a warm place for 10 minutes, or until frothy.

Sift the flour and salt into a large bowl and rub in the
shortening with your fingertips.

Add the yeast liquid and blend together until a firm dough
is formed and the sides of the bowl are clean. Turn out onto a
lightly floured surface and knead for about 10 minutes, or until
the dough is smooth, shiny, and elastic.

Place the dough in a large oiled plastic bag and leave in
a warm place for about 1½ hours, or until doubled in volume.
Punch back, then knead again for 2 to 3 minutes to knock out
any air bubbles. Cut into two pieces, one twice the size of the
other. Shape and fit the dough into pans. Place the filled pans
back inside the oiled plastic bags and leave to rise again in a
warm place for 30 to 40 minutes, or until the dough has risen
to the top of the pans.

Meanwhile, preheat the oven to 450°F.

For a crusty top, brush with the salt water. For a shiny top,
brush with the beaten egg and milk.

Bake in the center of the oven for 35 to 40 minutes. The
loaves are done when the bottom of the loaf sounds hollow
when tapped. Let cool on a wire rack. For a really crusty loaf,
return the unmolded loaves, on a baking tray, to the oven for
a further 5 minutes. Let cool on a wire rack.

WHOLE WHEAT (BROWN) BREAD

This bread is either freshly baked or toasted.

1 ounce active dry yeast OR 2 ounces fresh	⅓ cup superfine granulated sugar
1 teaspoon sugar	⅓ cup salt
4 cups warm water	4 level tablespoons lard
10 cups whole wheat flour	Salt water, to glaze (optional)
	Cracked wheat (optional)

*Makes two 2-pound loaves, four 1-pound loaves, or one
2-pound plus two 1-pound loaves*

Grease the loaf pans you have chosen to use.

In a small bowl, mix the yeast and sugar with 1 cup of the warm water and leave in a warm place for 10 minutes or until frothy.

Sift the flour, sugar, and salt into a large bowl, and rub in the shortening with your fingertips.

Pour in the yeast liquid and the remaining water and mix to form a firm dough. Turn out onto a lightly floured surface and knead with the heel of your hand for 10 minutes.

Place in a large oiled plastic bag and leave in a warm place for 1 to 1½ hours, or until doubled in volume. Punch down and knead again for 5 minutes. Divide the dough into the desired sizes and place in the loaf pans. Place the filled tins inside the oiled plastic bags and leave in a warm place until the dough has almost risen to the top of the pans, about 30 to 40 minutes.

Meanwhile, preheat the oven to 450°F.

For a crusty top, brush with the salt water. Sprinkling cracked wheat on the top will add to the attractiveness of the loaves.

Bake in the center of the oven for 35 to 40-minutes. Test for doneness by knocking the base of the baked loaf with your knuckle; it should sound hollow. Turn out onto a wire rack to cool.

BRIDGE ROLLS

I have never had a hand in bridge, if you'll forgive the attempted pun; but it is for those enthusiasts who have (which in Britain is a considerable number) that the bridge roll was invented!

So loath are these cardplayers to leave their velvet-covered tables to partake of afternoon tea (as was the earl of Sandwich at the gaming tables) that a device in the form of a minuscule soft, semisweet bread roll was thought up to contain their favorite sandwich filling and assuage their hunger.

1 tablespoon active dry yeast	1 teaspoon salt
OR ½ ounce fresh	4 tablespoons (½ stick)
¼ teaspoon superfine	lightly salted butter
granulated sugar	1 egg, beaten
⅓ cup warm milk	Beaten egg, to glaze (optional)
1½ cups white bread flour	

Makes 18 rolls

Mix the yeast and sugar with the milk and leave in a warm place for about 10 minutes, or until frothy.

Sift the flour and salt into a large bowl and rub in the butter with your fingertips. Add the yeast mixture and egg and mix to form a soft dough. Turn out onto a lightly floured surface and knead for 10 minutes, or until smooth.

Place in a large oiled plastic bag and leave in a warm place for 1½ to 2 hours, or until the dough has doubled in volume. Punch back and knead again for 5 minutes, then cut into 18 equal pieces.

Shape each piece into a roll about 3 inches long. Place fairly close together in rows on a greased baking sheet. Slip the tray into the oiled plastic bag and leave to rise in a warm place for a further 20 to 30 minutes, or until the rolls have almost doubled in size.

Meanwhile, preheat the oven to 425° F.

For a glazed, shiny top, brush with a little beaten egg. Bake in the center of the oven for about 20 minutes. Let cool on a wire rack.

BRACKS AND BRITHS, MUFFINS, CRUMPETS, AND PIKELETS

The confusion!

It is in the field of baking that some of the Old English names are still used in the late twentieth century.

In Northern Ireland, and in the Republic, *brack* is the Celtic word for salt and is used to mean "bread." *Barm brack* is leavened bread, the word *barm* meaning yeast.

Barm cakes are still baked, sold, and eaten in the northern counties of England and are a flat bread "cake," usually split and filled with meat, cheese, or fish as workmen's midday meal. It is the richer type of these breads that have found their way onto the afternoon tea table.

In Wales spiced fruit breads were baked on a griddle and were known as pitchy bread—*bara pyglyd* or *bara picklet*, which name has survived with us as the *pikelet* in the Midlands, North, and in Wales. Today pikelets are made from a batter of yeast, milk, and flour and are cooked in metal rings on a griddle and cooled. They are always served toasted and buttered. In the south of England the pikelet is more commonly known as a *crumpet*, the name coming from the Middle English word *crompid*, meaning "to bend or curl up"—which in fact is what home-made crumpets do at the edges.

A *muffin* (hardly ever seen in England today, though they abound in America) was a more breadlike affair than its two aforementioned first cousins. The derivation of its name is more readily recognizable, as it stems from the Old French dialect word *moufflet*, meaning "soft bread."

A muffineer, by the way, is not the dome-lidded dish with its hot-water liner used to keep them warm. It is the small silver dredger with its pierced domed lid used in olden days for sprinkling muffins with salt or spices, a habit given over to jam and honey today.

BARA BRITH

This is a Welsh tea bread traditionally served at Christmastime. Cut it very thin and serve it buttered.

1 tablespoon active dry yeast
2 cups milk
1 teaspoon superfine
   granulated sugar
10 cups white bread flour
1 teaspoon salt
2¼ cups (4½ sticks) butter
   OR lard OR vegetable
   shortening

1¾ cups brown sugar
1¾ cups dried currants
¾ cup chopped candied citrus
   rind
2 teaspoons mixed spice (equal
   amounts of nutmeg,
   cinnamon, cloves,
   allspice, and/or mace)
3 eggs, beaten

Makes two 2-pound or four 1-pound loaves

Grease four 1-pound or two 2-pound loaf pans.

In a small bowl, combine the yeast, milk, and superfine sugar. Leave in a warm place for 10 minutes or until frothy.

Sift the flour and salt into a large bowl and rub in the butter or shortening. Stir in the brown sugar, currants, citrus rind, and spice. Make a well in the center and mix in the yeast liquid and eggs. Mix to a firm dough. Turn out onto a lightly floured surface and knead for 5 minutes. If kneading by hand, you may find it easier to do it in two batches.

Place in an oiled plastic bag and leave in a warm place for about 2 hours, or until almost doubled in size. Knead again for 5 minutes and divide into the proper number of portions for the pans to be used. Place in the pans and return to the oiled plastic bag for about 1 hour, or until the dough reaches the top of the pans. Meanwhile preheat the oven to 400°F.

Bake for about 1½ hours. Test for doneness by knocking the base of the baked loaf with your knuckle; it should sound hollow. Remove the pans and return the loaves to the oven on their sides for a further 10 minutes. Let cool on a wire rack.

IRISH TEA BRACK

This is an easy-to-make version of barm brack, which uses yeast.

2½ cups mixed dried fruit   cinnamon, cloves,
   (dried currants and dark   allspice, and/or mace)
   and golden raisins)   4 teaspoons marmalade
1 cup boiling black tea   1 heaping cup superfine
1 egg   granulated sugar
1 teaspoon mixed spice (equal   2⅓ cups self-rising flour
   amounts of nutmeg,

Makes one 2-pound loaf

Place the dried fruit in a bowl, cover with the hot tea and leave to soak overnight. The next day, add the remaining ingredients and mix well.

Preheat the oven to 375°F.

Pour the batter into a greased 7-inch square pan and bake in the center of the oven for 1½ hours. Let cool in the pan on a wire rack.

Slice and serve buttered. Store in an airtight container.

CRUMPETS

Crumpets may be eaten fresh and hot or, if made the day before, toasted with jam, honey, or a slice of cheese on top.

2¼ cups white bread flour	¾ cup milk
1 tablespoon active dry yeast	½ teaspoon baking soda
or ½ ounce fresh	1 teaspoon salt
½ teaspoon superfine	Oil or shortening to grease the
granulated sugar	griddle
1⅓ cups warm water	

Makes about 16 crumpets

Sift half the flour into a large bowl. Add the yeast, sugar, and water and blend until smooth. Leave in a warm place for about 20 minutes, or until frothy.

Add ½ cup of the milk and the remaining ingredients. Beat well, adding more milk if needed to make a batter of thick pouring consistency.

Grease a griddle or heavy frying pan and about 6 metal crumpet rings or plain cookie cutters, about 3 inches in diameter. Arrange the rings on the griddle and heat thoroughly. Pour about 2 tablespoons of batter into each ring and cook for about 10 minutes, or until they are set and the characteristic holes and bubbles appear.

Turn the crumpets over, removing the rings. Cook for a further 10 minutes.

Repeat with the remaining batter.

Eat freshly toasted and buttered, with any of the potted foods, page 244.

MUFFINS

Not to be confused with the medley of cakelike muffins available in the United States, this resembles what is known as an

English muffin, but is somewhat richer in texture. It is always eaten fork-split, toasted, and well buttered with jam or honey.

Flour OR fine semolina OR cornmeal

1 tablespoon active dry yeast OR ½ ounce fresh

1 teaspoon superfine granulated sugar

1⅓ cups warm water

3 cups white bread flour

1 teaspoon salt

Makes 10 to 12 muffins

Dust a baking sheet with the flour, semolina, or cornmeal.

Mix the yeast, sugar, and water in a small bowl and leave in a warm place for 10 minutes, or until frothy.

Sift the bread flour and salt into a large bowl. Add the yeast liquid and mix with a fork to form a soft dough. Turn out onto a lightly floured surface and knead for about 10 minutes, or until smooth.

Place the dough in a large oiled plastic bag and leave to rise in a warm place for 1 to 1½ hours, or until doubled in volume. Punch back and knead again for about 5 minutes, or until smooth and firm.

Roll out to ½ inch thick, cover with a tea towel, and leave to relax for a further 5 minutes. Cut into 10 to 12 rounds with a 3½-inch plain round cookie cutter.

Place on the prepared baking sheet and dust again with flour, semolina, or cornmeal. Slip the baking sheet back into the oiled plastic bag and leave to rise in a warm place for 25 to 40 minutes, or until doubled in volume.

Meanwhile, preheat the oven to 450°F.

Bake in the center of the oven for about 10 minutes, turning over carefully after 5 minutes. The muffins are done when they have risen and are golden brown and firm to the touch.

Let cool on a wire rack.

PIKELETS

The bakestone, girdle (griddle), or pan is the traditional place for cooking these pancakes.

1⅓ cups self-rising flour   ⅓ cup margarine or butter
½ cup sugar   ¼ teaspoon baking soda
1 egg, beaten   1 teaspoon vinegar
Milk, to mix

Makes 20 to 24 small pikelets

Sift the flour and add the sugar. Add the egg and just enough milk to make a thick batter.

Melt the margarine or butter, add the baking soda and vinegar, and mix into the batter.

Drop 2 teaspoons onto a hot greased bakestone or heavy-bottomed skillet. Cook until bubbles appear and the bottoms are brown, then turn and cook the other side (about 1 to 1½ minutes on each side).

Serve hot and well-buttered.

If made in advance, the pikelets are always toasted and served hot.

Sandwiches

A POTTED HISTORY OF THE SANDWICH IN BRITAIN

Although John Montagu, who lived in the eighteenth century and was the fourth Earl of Sandwich, did not actually invent the device whereby two pieces of bread enclose fillings varying from meat to cheese, it cannot be denied that he popularized and gave his name to it. Legend tells us that he was such an ardent gambler that he couldn't bear to leave the gaming tables long enough to partake of food in a proper manner, so he bade his servants put the meat between two slices of bread and bring it to his chair—thus starting a fashion in eating that has been increasingly popular ever since.

But what has happened to the sandwich since those far-off days? Up to the conclusion of the Second World War it was the way every workingman in Britain got his midday meal, as it was the only cheap and effective means of transporting his food to his place of employment, there being no employee cafeterias at that time. At the other end of the social scale, ladies and gentlemen of means nibbled their way through dainty finger sandwiches in their drawing rooms, in fashionable tea shops, and in the lounges of luxury hotels.

Today we meet sandwiches everywhere, usually in a modern, debased form—two slices of "plastic" bread with the insert of a sliver of "plastic" ham or "plastic" cheese, garnished, at best, with a slice of unskinned tomato and a lettuce leaf.

In this book we are concerned only with the delicate morsels that are deliciously filled and served on napkin-lined silver salvers at four o'clock in the afternoon or thereabouts.

AFTERNOON-TEA SANDWICHES

Many cookery writers today are bidding us use fresh, crisp, crusty breads of a French nature or, if not French, then made with gutsy whole wheat flour. All of which is fine if you're making lusty sandwiches for the children's lunch box, a husband's office snack, or a picnic. This kind of sturdy, wholesome bread is designed to contain with safety robust fillings with crisp lettuce leaves cascading out the sides and mayonnaise dripping appetizingly over the edges. It is not, however, made for the delicate mouth-watering finger sandwiches served at an "At Home" cocktail party or reception, when elegant presentation is called for.

For such morsels the English sandwich loaf was created: square, flat-topped, and with a soft, close-textured crumb.

Bread for sandwich-making is best when it is homemade and one day old. It helps to put the loaf into the freezer for an hour or two before cutting to firm up the crumb. It is also easier to cut if you use a knife with a long, sharp, serrated blade, or you might like to try experimenting with an electric carving knife (after a little practice this can produce excellent results).

It is always easier to work with butters and spreads that have been prepared in advance and are softened to room temperature. Spread the cut face of the loaf *before* slicing and decrusting; a flexible, small-bladed palette knife is a good implement for ease of spreading.

When making pinwheels or fluted, shaped, or rolled sandwiches, have a dampened kitchen towel ready. Take the bread from the freezer, cut off the crust and spread the cut face with butter. Then carefully cut the thinnest possible slice from the full *length* of the loaf. Done this way, it will not break up. If the next slice is too frozen, you will have to wait only a couple of minutes for it to be manageable. Lay the slices side by side on the damp towel to prevent the bread from drying and curling at the corners; this will also facilitate the rolling up. Fill the first slice and roll it up carefully but tightly. Put each roll into a suitable plastic bag to freeze or store. Cut while still frozen into delicate $\frac{1}{8}$-inch disks, which will thaw out in a matter of minutes and be absolutely fresh.

For elegant presentation, the sandwiches must be crusted before being cut into squares, fingers, triangles, or—when the occasion is special enough—with fancy cookie cutters into round, oval, diamond, or heart shapes. In order not to be too wasteful, the filling should be contained as nearly as is possible within the area of the shape. The scraps of buttered bread can then be toasted in the oven on a baking sheet and made into savory bread crumbs for use in some other dish.

To keep sandwiches moist, cover with a piece of wax paper that has been wetted and wrung out. Then cover with plastic wrap and refrigerate.

NOTES ON FREEZING

Ideally, sandwiches should not be kept in a freezer for more than 3 to 4 weeks. When packing them for freezing, protect them in a cardboard box lined with aluminum foil to prevent damage to the edges. Fill the sandwiches evenly to avoid misshaping and to help with even defrosting. Decrust the sandwiches for freezing, but do not cut them into serving sizes. Pinwheels and rolled sandwiches are better packed uncut in lidded foil boxes to avoid squashing. Wrap the sandwiches in plastic wrap first, then in freezer foil. Do not put different fillings into the same bag—the flavors may transfer on defrosting. Sandwiches made a day in advance, which you do not wish to freeze, should be packed in plastic bags to avoid contamination from other odors in your refrigerator.

THE PRESENTATION OF SANDWICHES

In England, crisply starched cotton-lace doilies or folded linen napkins are used to line plates and dishes. For homes not possessing these charming plate covers, attractively punched paper doilies or dish papers make a more than adequate substitute.

While it is the usual habit to serve piles of tiny sandwiches of one particular filling together on one plate, it is also quite acceptable to arrange sandwiches on silver trays or other attractive platters and baskets in rows or groups of complementary shapes, colors, and fillings.

For wedding teas, I have used little clusters of mixed sandwiches tied with ribbon bows for each guest to lift on to his or her tea plate, and of course, flower garlands and posies have a place here and can be arranged any way you like.

The following notion may sound messy, but if freshly made sandwiches are cut small enough, it is a novel and very tasty idea to dip the exposed cut edges in a little homemade mayonnaise and then in toasted finely crushed hazelnuts, freshly crushed pistachio nuts, or freshly chopped herbs, such as parsley, mint, or chives.

Another attractive way of presenting mini-sandwiches for a reception is to make a checkerboard: Having cut the sandwiches into even-sized squares, using both whole wheat and white breads, select a square tray or board and simply arrange them alternately to look like a checkerboard.

Yet another idea is to brush the top slice of bread with a thin coating of mayonnaise before cutting and crusting, then make mosaics using the sieved whites and yolks of hard-boiled eggs, chopped parsley, various crushed nuts, and mock caviar or paprika—all of which will give a variety of textures and colors.

A NOTE ON BREADS

In addition to white or brown (whole wheat) breads, any of the following fruit or tea breads can be used for sandwich making:

> Currant Bread (page 126)
> Saffron Cake (which is a bread!) (page 174)
> Sally Lunn Tea Cakes (page 124)
> Bara Brith (page 91)
> Date and Nut Loaf (page 130)
> Harvo Loaf (page 128)

A NOTE ON QUANTITIES

An average 2-pound loaf 4 by 4 inches square will yield 20 to 24 slices, depending on how deftly you cut the bread.

In turn, this will yield 10 to 12 sandwiches, which can be cut into 40 to 48 squares or triangles or 30 to 36 fingers.

To spread the bread slices fairly liberally and to the edges, you will require ¾ cup (1½ sticks) softened butter, creamed butter, or other soft spread, such as cream cheese.

Guidelines for Fillings

Soft, spreadable fillings such as a fine pâté, meat, fish, or cheese will require 1 to 1½ cups (8 to 10 ounces) to fill 10 to 12 sandwiches.

Fillings of a coarser nature, such as composite mixtures— crab mayonnaise, chopped chicken and flaked salmon, cheese and nuts or fruit, and so on—will require up to 2 cups of filling.

Allow 1 ounce sliced meats per sandwich, or up to ¾ pound for 10 sandwiches.

Allow 12 watercress leaves per sandwich or 1 small lettuce leaf, deveined, per sandwich.

Allow 2 teaspoons mayonnaise or other flowing spread per sandwich, or ¾ cup for 10 sandwiches.

A NOTE ON GARLIC AND SCALLIONS

At teatime, hostesses may prefer to omit garlic and scallions from their sandwich fillings. In Edwardian times, the abundant sprigs of parsley scattered, apparently at random, were in fact for guests to eat. The chlorophyll content of the parsley was said to sweeten the breath.

THE UBIQUITOUS ENGLISH NONSOGGY TOMATO OR CUCUMBER SANDWICH

There are two traditional English sandwiches that are really difficult to eat and guaranteed to mess up tie and blouse alike as their filling slithers out: They are the tomato sandwich and the cucumber sandwich. Yet they are the best, revealing the essential flavors of their respective fillings.

You will need 1½ cups softened creamed butter (see below) or other spread, such as cream cheese, or mayonnaise, to spread 10 sandwiches (20 slices of bread, to yield 30 fingers or 40 squares or quarters).

CREAMED BUTTER

1½ cups (3 sticks) sweet butter, softened	Tip of a teaspoon mild French mustard
2 tablespoons heavy cream	Juice of ½ lemon
	Salt and pepper

Blend all ingredients to a fine, soft, spreadable consistency.

TOMATO SANDWICHES

2 pounds tomatoes (of a size where you get 5 to the pound)	Salt and freshly ground pepper OR old-fashioned regular white pepper

With a small knife, make a small cross in the base of each tomato. Plunge the tomatoes into a pan of boiling water and count to 20. Remove them to a bowl of cold water, drain, and peel off the skins.

Now, this is where the mistake often happens. Most people slice them. I don't. I quarter the tomatoes, remove the seeds, press the petals flat, and lay them on the slice of buttered bread. If you attempt to use two layers of tomato, they will come unstuck. They will "slither," so to speak. So, one layer only. Then, after seasoning, on goes the top, which is pressed firmly home, and the sandwich is cut into appropriate shapes.

THE VICTORIAN CUCUMBER SANDWICH

One 12-inch cucumber	1 tablespoon lemon juice
Salt	Scant teaspoon sugar
1 tablespoon good olive oil	Freshly ground white pepper*

The cucumber must be cut as thin as possible, using a mandoline or a food processor fitted with a metal blade. Very lightly salt the slices and leave them to drain in a colander, lightly weighted with a plate, for 2 hours or so, pressing from time to time to get rid of the excess juices.

Combine the sliced and drained cucumber with the oil, lemon juice, sugar, and a dredge of freshly ground white pepper (no more salt). Spread thin slices of white or brown bread with creamed butter; fill in the usual way, but at the last possible moment, as this sandwich can become soggy.

* Freshly ground black pepper can, of course, be used; it just is a short move away from authenticity.

POTTED-MEAT SANDWICHES

(See also "Potted Meats and Fish," pages 244 to 248.)

1 pound beef shin	1 teaspoon freshly ground
½ cup medium-dry Madeira	pepper
OR sherry	½ cup clarified butter (page
1 teaspoon salt	224), cool but not set
1 teaspoon mace	

Makes 15 to 20 sandwiches

Trim the meat of all skin and fat. Cut into ½-inch cubes and put into a small casserole or bowl along with the wine and seasonings. Cover with a piece of foil and a lid.

Stand the container in a pan of water. Cover the pan as well and simmer at a very gentle roll for 2½ to 3 hours, topping up the pan with boiling water as necessary.

In a food processor, make a fine puree of the meat and its juices. Let cool for about 30 minutes. Start the machine again and dribble in three-fourths of the cool clarified butter. Run the machine until you have a smooth paste. Adjust the seasoning.

Transfer to one large or several individual pots or ramekins (approximately ⅓ cup in each). Spoon over a thin film of the remaining butter. Refrigerate. Allow to come to room temperature before serving with hot buttered toast or as a sandwich filling (use white bread as the base slice and brown bread as the top).

DEVILED-SALMON SANDWICHES

20 to 24 slices brown bread
Tomato Butter (page 228)

Lettuce leaves, dressed in a rich French dressing

FOR THE FILLING

2 cups flaked cooked salmon
1 tablespoon Worcestershire sauce
3 to 4 dashes of Tabasco

Squeeze of lemon juice
A little heavy cream, to bind
Salt and freshly ground pepper

Makes 10 to 12 sandwiches

Mix all the filling ingredients to a spreadable paste in a food processor or mash well with a fork.

Spread 10 to 12 slices of the bread with the Tomato Butter.

Lay a lettuce leaf on each buttered slice, then the filling, then the top piece of bread.

Crust and cut as desired.

CREAMY TOMATO AND ANCHOVY SANDWICHES

20 to 24 slices brown   1 cup Watercress Butter
   or white bread   (page 227)

FOR THE FILLING

About 1 cup heavy cream or   seeded, and chopped
   cream cheese, to mix to   ⅛ teaspoon cayenne
   a spreadable consistency   10 anchovy fillets, pounded
2 pounds tomatoes, skinned,   to a paste

Makes 10 to 12 sandwiches

Beat the cream cheese, if used, with a fork. Mix the heavy cream or beaten cream cheese with the chopped tomato. Season with cayenne. (Salt will not be necessary as the anchovies will be salty enough.)

Spread 10 to 12 slices of the bread first with a small amount of the anchovy paste, then with the Watercress Butter. Fork over the creamy tomato filling. Top with the second slice of bread.

Crust and cut as desired.

RUSSIAN SANDWICHES

These were very popular between the two World Wars.

20 to 24 slices brown bread   Paprika
1 cup Watercress Butter   ½ cup red caviar
   (page 227)   or lumpfish roe
Coarse-grained salt   Juice of ½ lemon, strained

Makes 10 to 12 sandwiches

Spread 10 to 12 slices of the bread with the Watercress Butter. Sprinkle with a little coarse-grained salt and a good smidge of paprika.

Cover with the red caviar or lumpfish roe. Add a squeeze of lemon juice. Top with the second slice of bread.

Make up at the last minute and keep refrigerated until ready to serve.

DELHI SANDWICHES

Straight from the days of the Raj is this one! Shades of *Jewel in the Crown* or *A Passage to India*. Reason enough to have a Raj tea party.

12 anchovy fillets	1½ level teaspoons mild
12 ounces skinless and	curry powder
boneless sardines	Salt (optional)
2 teaspoons mild chutney	4 to 6 dashes of Tabasco OR
1 large egg yolk	1 to 2 pinches of cayenne

Makes 10 to 12 sandwiches

In a blender, make a paste of all the ingredients and cook over low heat in a small pan until cohered. Allow to cool if this is to be used for spreading.

Serve hot, spread either on fingers of hot buttered toast or on split toasted muffins. Or allow to cool and use with brown bread as a sandwich filling.

CHICKEN AND ALMOND SANDWICHES

20 to 24 slices brown OR	Basil Butter (page 227)
white bread	

FOR THE FILLING

1 cup ground cooked chicken	½ cup heavy cream OR
breast	mayonnaise, to bind to
½ cup slivered almonds,	a spreadable consistency
lightly toasted	Salt and freshly ground
	pepper

Makes 10 to 12 sandwiches

Mix all the filling ingredients together. Spread 10 to 12 slices of the bread with the Basil Butter. Top with the filling and the second slice of bread. Crust and cut as desired.

DEVILED SANDWICHES

Perhaps these are more appropriate as aftertheater snacks or cocktail food than for afternoon tea; but no matter, they're unusual and very tasty.

20 to 24 slices brown or   Chive Butter (see page 227)
   white bread

FOR THE FILLING

1 cup ground smoked fish   2 tablespoons Worcestershire
   (such as haddock, kipper,   sauce
   mackerel)   3 to 4 dashes of Tabasco
½ cup mashed hard-boiled   Salt and freshly ground
   egg   pepper
¼ cup minced parsley   ½ cup heavy cream, to bind
¼ cup minced chives

Makes 10 to 12 sandwiches

Mix all the filling ingredients together to a textured paste. Spread 10 to 12 slices of the bread with the Chive Butter. Top with the filling and the second slice of bread. Crust and cut as desired.

LOBSTER SANDWICHES

20 to 24 slices brown bread   Watercress Butter (page 227)

FOR THE FILLING

1 cup roughly ground or   Salt and freshly ground
   chopped lobster meat   pepper
   (fresh, canned, or frozen)   A squeeze or two of lemon
¼ cup roughly chopped   juice
   watercress leaves   Heavy cream, to bind

Makes 10 to 12 sandwiches

Mix all the filling ingredients together. Spread 10 to 12 slices of the bread with the Watercress Butter. Top with the filling and the second slice of bread. Crust and cut into long fingers.

CHRISTMAS TURKEY SANDWICHES

Spread bread slices either with Lemon-and-Parsley Butter (page 225) to which has been added a modicum of ground sage, or Mustard Butter (page 228) to which sage has been added.

Cover with sliced turkey, top with a second slice of bread, and crust and shape as desired.

CHRISTMAS CHEESE SANDWICHES

| 20 to 24 slices fruit or brown bread | Walnut Butter (page 230) |

FOR THE FILLING

| 1½ cups grated Stilton cheese (not too much of the ripe blue part) | 2 to 3 tablespoons port ¼ cup heavy cream, to bind Freshly ground pepper |

Makes 10 to 12 sandwiches

In a blender, make a fine puree of the cheese, port, and cream. Season with ground pepper only.

Spread 10 to 12 slices of the bread with the Walnut Butter, then with the cheese mixture. Top with a second slice of bread. Crust and cut as desired.

WHITE CRAB SANDWICHES

| 20 to 24 slices white bread | Lemon-and-Parsley Butter (page 225) |

FOR THE FILLING

1½ cups finely chopped white crab meat*	4 scallions, very finely chopped
½ cup sieved hard-boiled egg yolks (approximately 4 yolks)	Salt and freshly ground pepper Lemon juice
Mayonnaise, to bind	

Makes 10 to 12 sandwiches

Mix all filling ingredients together. Spread 10 to 12 slices of the bread with the Lemon-and-Parsley Butter, then with filling. Top with a second slice of bread. Crust and cut as desired.

* These sandwiches should not be frozen if frozen fish has been used.

SARDINE SANDWICHES

20 to 24 slices bread   Mustard Butter (page 228)

FOR THE FILLING

Two 8-ounce cans skinless,   Salt and freshly ground
   boneless sardines in oil,   pepper
   drained, oil reserved   Lemon juice
Sieved yolks of 6 hard-boiled   2 to 3 dashes of Tabasco
   eggs

Makes 10 to 12 sandwiches

Mash the sardines to a paste along with the sieved egg yolks. Season with salt, pepper, lemon juice, and Tabasco. Moisten with a little of the reserved sardine oil.

Spread 10 to 12 slices of the bread with the Mustard Butter, then the sardine filling. Top with a second slice of bread. Crust and cut as desired.

LETTUCE SANDWICHES

These are known as honeymoon sandwiches because they have a filling of lettuce (let us) alone!

20 to 24 slices brown bread   10 inner lettuce leaves, finely
Mint Butter (page 226)   shredded

Makes 10 to 12 sandwiches

Spread 10 to 12 slices of the bread with the Mint Butter, then add the lettuce leaves. Cover with a second slice of bread. Crust and cut as desired.

LETTUCE SANDWICHES II

1½ cups finely chopped   Tartar sauce, to bind to a
   lettuce leaves   spreadable consistency
   (approximately 8 to   20 to 24 slices brown bread
   10 leaves)   Mustard Butter (page 228)

Makes 10 to 12 sandwiches

Mix the lettuce and tartar sauce together. Spread 10 to 12
slices of bread with the Mustard Butter, then with lettuce mixture. Top with a second slice of bread. Crust and cut as desired.

MOCK CRAB SANDWICHES

20 to 24 slices white bread   Sweet butter
                   FOR THE FILLING
⅔ cup grated Cheshire OR   ⅔ cup finely diced, skinned,
   Cheddar cheese   and seeded tomato
⅔ cup finely chopped hard-   Salad oil, lemon juice, salt,
   boiled egg (3 to 4 eggs)   pepper, and Tabasco

Makes 10 to 12 sandwiches

Mix the cheese, egg, and tomato together and moisten with
salad oil and a drop or two of lemon juice. Season well.
Spread 10 to 12 slices of the bread with the butter, then
with filling mixture. Top with a second slice of bread. Crust and
cut as desired.

CREAM CHEESE AND WALNUT SANDWICHES

20 to 24 slices bread   Honey Butter (page 230)
                FOR THE FILLING
1½ cups cream cheese, beaten   1 teaspoon light cream
½ cup crushed walnut halves   Salt and freshly ground
⅛ teaspoon nutmeg   pepper

Makes 10 to 12 sandwiches

Mix all the filling ingredients together, adding a spoonful of cream if the mixture is too stiff. Spread 10 to 12 slices of the bread with the Honey Butter, then with the filling. Top with a second slice of bread. Crust and cut as desired.

CREAM CHEESE AND PINEAPPLE SANDWICHES

20 to 24 slices brown or fruit bread

Cinnamon or Honey Butter (pages 229 and 230)

FOR THE FILLING

1 cup cream cheese, beaten
½ cup finely chopped fresh or canned pineapple

¼ cup slivered almonds
Salt and freshly ground pepper

Makes 10 to 12 sandwiches

Mix all the filling ingredients to a spreadable paste, using a fork. Spread 10 to 12 slices of the bread with the Cinnamon or Honey Butter, then with filling. Top with a second slice of bread. Crust and cut as desired.

CREAM CHEESE AND SHRIMP SANDWICHES

20 to 24 slices bread

Lemon-and-Parsley Butter (page 225)

FOR THE FILLING

1 cup cream cheese, beaten
1 cup small cooked shrimp, finely diced
1 small clove garlic, peeled and crushed

¼ cup finely minced chives or scallions
Salt and freshly ground pepper

Makes 10 to 12 sandwiches

Mix all the filling ingredients to a spreadable paste, using a fork. Spread 10 to 12 slices of the bread with the Lemon-and-

Parsley Butter, then with shrimp filling. Top with a second slice
of bread. Crust and cut as desired.

CREAM CHEESE, ORANGE, AND HAZELNUT SANDWICHES

20 to 24 slices bread

Tomato Curry and Orange
Butter OR Cinnamon
Butter (pages 225 and
229) (optional)

FOR THE FILLING

½ cup canned mandarin
orange segments, drained

1 cup cream cheese

½ cup roughly crushed
toasted hazelnuts

½ teaspoon cinnamon
(optional)

Salt and freshly ground
pepper (optional)

Makes 10 to 12 sandwiches

Squeeze some of the juice from the orange segments, or the
mixture will be too wet. Combine all the filling ingredients,
using a fork.

Season lightly with salt, pepper, and cinnamon *or* spread
10 to 12 slices of the bread with the Tomato Curry and Orange
Butter or the Cinnamon Butter. Spread with the filling and top
with a second slice of bread. Crust and cut as desired.

CREAM CHEESE, CHIVE, AND ALMOND SANDWICHES

20 to 24 slices white bread   Chive Butter (page 227)

FOR THE FILLING

1 cup cream cheese, beaten

½ cup slivered almonds

¼ cup finely chopped chives

Salt and freshly ground
pepper

Makes 10 to 12 sandwiches

Combine all the filling ingredients with a fork. Spread 10
to 12 slices of the bread with the Chive Butter, then with the
filling. Top with a second slice of bread. Crust and cut as desired.

CAVIAR SANDWICHES

20 to 24 slices (½ inch thick)
   white or brown bread,
   toasted
1 cup Lemon Butter (page
   225)

8 ounces caviar or lumpfish
   roe
Lemon juice
5 hard-boiled egg yolks, sieved
Heavy cream, to bind

Makes 10 to 12 sandwiches

Split the thick toasted bread slices and butter the crumb sides well with the Lemon Butter. Spread with a thin layer of caviar or lumpfish roe. Season with lemon juice and add a thin cushion of sieved hard-boiled egg yolk, seasoned and bound with a spoonful of heavy cream.

Add the tops, cut into bite-size pieces, and serve while the toast is still crisp.

TOASTED OATMEAL SANDWICHES

20 to 24 slices any of the fruit
   or tea breads (pages
   124–132)

Honey Butter (page 230)

FOR THE FILLING

1 cup coarse oatmeal, toasted
   in the oven to a golden
   brown

½ cup heavy cream, to bind
   to a spreadable paste
½ cup of honey

Makes 10 to 12 sandwiches

Spread 10 to 12 slices of the bread with the Honey Butter, then with the oatmeal filling. Top with a second slice of bread. Crust and cut as desired.

CELERY SANDWICHES

20 to 24 slices any fruit bread   Walnut Butter (page 230)

FOR THE FILLING

1 cup finely minced crisp
   celery
¼ cup heavy cream, to bind

Salt and freshly ground
   pepper

Makes 10 to 12 sandwiches

Spread any fruit bread with the Walnut Butter. Combine the celery, heavy cream, and salt and pepper in a bowl. Spread the celery over the butter and top with a second slice of bread. Crust and cut as desired.

QUEEN ALEXANDRA'S SANDWICHES

Alexandra was the queen consort of Edward VII, son of Queen Victoria and Queen Elizabeth II's great-grandfather.

20 to 24 slices brown bread	Mustard Butter (page 228)

FOR THE FILLING

1 cup ground cooked chicken breast	10 to 12 thin slices lamb's OR ox tongue
Mayonnaise, to bind to a spreadable paste	1 punnet of Mustard-and-Cress* OR picked
Salt and pepper	watercress leaves
2 drops of Tabasco	

Makes 10 to 12 sandwiches

Mix the chicken and mayonnaise to a spreadable paste with a fork. Season well. Spread 10 to 12 slices of the bread with the Mustard Butter. Lay on slices of the tongue, spread with the chicken mixture, then the cress. Top with a second slice of bread. Trim off the crusts and cut into dainty squares.

* Mustard-and-Cress is perhaps totally English. It is grown almost overnight from seed scattered over a piece of wet flannel. Picked leaves of watercress can be substituted.

QUEEN ADELAIDE'S SANDWICHES

This was said to be a favorite of King George IV (probably better known as the prince regent).

20 to 24 slices brown OR   Tomato Curry and Orange
     white bread   Butter (page 225)

FOR THE FILLING

1 cup ground cooked chicken   ½ cup heavy cream, to bind
     breast   1 scallion, finely minced
1 cup ground lean ham (not   Salt and freshly ground
     smoked)   pepper

Makes 10 to 12 sandwiches

Combine the chicken, ham and scallion in a bowl. Season with salt and pepper and bind with enough heavy cream to form a thick, spreadable paste.

Lightly butter 10 to 12 slices of the bread with the Curry Butter and spread with a layer of the chicken and ham filling. Top with a second slice of bread. Crust and cut as desired.

SMOKED HADDOCK SANDWICHES

20 to 24 slices white bread   Mayonnaise OR Watercress
                                    Butter (page 227)

FOR THE FILLING

1½ cups skinned, boned, and   ½ cup mayonnaise, to mash
     flaked cooked smoked   and bind to a thick,
     haddock OR other   spreadable paste
     smoked fish

Makes 10 to 12 sandwiches

Spread 10 to 12 slices of the bread with mayonnaise or, for added color, Watercress Butter. Spread with the prepared haddock filling. Top with a second slice of bread. Crust and cut as desired.

SALMON AND CUCUMBER SANDWICHES

This sandwich combines three of England's summer flavors.

20 to 24 slices brown bread   Mint Butter (page 226)
FOR THE FILLING

1½ cups flaked and mashed   Mayonnaise, to bind
   cold poached salmon   Salt, freshly ground pepper,
½ cup finely diced, peeled,   and lemon juice
   and seeded cucumber

Makes 10 to 12 sandwiches

Mix the filling ingredients to a spreadable paste with a fork. Spread 10 to 12 slices of the bread with the Mint Butter, then with the filling.

EGG AND CURRY SANDWICHES

20 to 24 slices brown OR white   Watercress Butter (page 227)
   bread
FOR THE FILLING

1 teaspoon curry paste OR   Heavy cream, to bind
   curry sauce   Salt and freshly ground
2 cups sieved hard-boiled egg   pepper
   (approximately 6 eggs)

Makes 10 to 12 sandwiches

Mix the curry paste or sauce with a little cream, then with the eggs. Season with salt and pepper.

Spread slices of the bread with the Watercress Butter, top with the filling. Crust and cut as desired.

ROLLED OR PINWHEEL SANDWICHES

ASPARAGUS ROLLS WITH HOLLANDAISE SAUCE

20 to 24 slices crusted brown   1 cup Hollandaise Sauce
    bread   12 asparagus spears, lightly
                cooked

Makes 20 to 24 rolls

Spread each of the slices of bread with some of the Hollandaise Sauce. Place one fat or two or three slim asparagus tips on the lead (front) edge of each slice and roll up tightly.

Cut into 2 pieces with a diagonal stroke of the knife to give an interesting pointed shape.

SMOKED-SALMON PINWHEELS

1 uncut brown or white loaf   ¾ pound smoked Scotch
1 cup Chive Butter or   salmon, thinly sliced
    Basil Butter (page 227)   Lemon juice
                Freshly ground black pepper

Makes approximately 40 pinwheels

Slice the loaf along its length. Cut off the crusts at this stage. Spread evenly with the Chive Butter or Basil Butter.

Cover with slivers of smoked salmon, leaving a ½-inch border uncovered on one long side.

Season with lemon juice and pepper.

Roll up *tightly* from the side opposite the ½-inch border. Wrap in wax paper and store, refrigerated, until ready for use.

To serve: Unwrap and cut into ¼-inch-thick pinwheels or disks.

ROLLED MUSCATEL AND RUM SANDWICHES

1 cup muscatel raisins
2 tablespoons dark rum
½ cup cream cheese, beaten

1 cup Cumberland Rum
    Butter (page 229)

Makes approximately 80 pinwheels

Soak the raisins for 2 hours in the dark rum. In a blender, make a rough puree of the cream cheese, raisins, and their liquor.

Slice any of the fruit breads (pages 124 to 132) or brown bread lengthwise. Take off the crusts at this stage. Spread with the Cumberland Rum Butter, then the filling.

Roll and slice as for Smoked-Salmon Pinwheels (page 114).

NURSERY TEA SANDWICHES

Nursery sandwiches, to be tempting, should be crusted and cut into tiny bite-size shapes.

EGG SANDWICHES

White or brown bread
Chive Butter (page 227)
1 cup sieved hard-boiled egg
    (approximately 3 eggs)

Salt and freshly ground
    pepper
Heavy cream, to bind

Makes 10 to 12 sandwiches

Spread the bread with the Chive Butter if these are for grownups. Combine the egg, salt and pepper, and heavy cream in a bowl. Spread over the butter. Top with a second slice of bread and cut and crust as desired.

BANANA AND JAM SANDWICHES

White or brown bread   1 cup mashed banana
Sweet butter   Sugar to taste
Sieved jam

Makes 10 to 12 sandwiches

Spread buttered bread with sieved jam, then with the mashed banana sweetened with the sugar. Top with a second slice of bread. Cut and crust as desired.

HONEY SANDWICHES

Use any one of the fruit breads (pages 124 to 132), spread with butter or cream cheese and thick honey (not the clear type).

CREAM CHEESE SANDWICHES

Spread any of the fruit breads (pages 124 to 132) with cream cheese.

BROWN SUGAR AND CHOCOLATE
SANDWICHES

Spread brown bread with a little cream cheese or creamy sweet butter. Sprinkle with a little brown sugar and grated chocolate. Press well with a weight. Cut into pointed soldiers.

Pointed soldiers are what children dip into their boiled eggs!

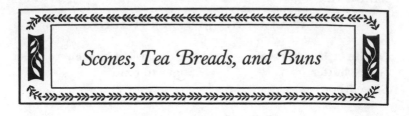

Scones, Tea Breads, and Buns

SCONES

The word *scone*, thought of by many as being Scottish (Celtic), is actually derived from the Dutch word *schoonbrot*, or "beautiful bread."

To Eat a Scone

Traveling on trains in Britain, as I frequently do, I notice, when on those fast expresses running from the West Country counties of Cornwall and Devon to the capital, that American and other foreign visitors, when confronted with scones in the tea car, seem confused as to how to approach this English—or some would say Scottish—phenomenon.

Here's how you go about it.

Take a tea knife and split the scone in half across its girth. Now take a spoonful of jam and a good knob of butter onto your small tea plate. Then spread a little butter on an area of the scone's crumb face, the size you might expect to bite elegantly, top this with as much or as little jam as you wish and eat just that mouthful. Proceed in this manner until there is no scone, butter, or jam left on your plate. The English have an experienced eye for gauging just the right amount so that there are no leftovers. For true English elegance, do not spread the whole half at one time, and most certainly not the whole scone!

When clotted cream is served, as in the West Country manner, this is put on in blobs, *after* the jam (whether you take butter *and* cream is a matter of personal taste and diet consciousness).

This social performance, by the way, is also how the British eat their breakfast toast and, similarly, when taking jam, jelly, or honey with bread and butter at afternoon tea. The bread will be presented in half slices already buttered and crusted. The jam is added with the tip of a tea knife in small amounts as you go along and is not spread over the whole surface in a manner that is considered inelegant in those circles where people know about such matters as tea-table etiquette!

Scones are at their best eaten almost straight from the oven and certainly within an hour or so of baking; however, they do freeze well.

Leftover scones are excellent when split and toasted.

Guidelines for Success

≪← Preheat the oven and the baking sheet to 450°F.

≪← Measure the flour before sifting, then sift twice with the other dry ingredients.

≪← Handle very gently, especially when kneading.

≪← Rub the fats into the flour very thoroughly until the mixture looks like soft bread crumbs or wet sand.

≪← Don't twist the cutter when stamping out the scones or they will bake lopsided.

≪← Always bake immediately after mixing with the liquid ingredients and shaping. To prepare ahead of time, rub in the fat and add the other dry ingredients, such as nuts or fruit, but don't add the liquids until just before baking.

BASIC SCONE RECIPE

Each of the following recipes makes approximately 12 scones, unless otherwise indicated.

2 cups all-purpose flour	5 tablespoons (⅓ cup) sweet
1 tablespoon baking powder	butter
½ teaspoon salt	¼ cup vegetable shortening
	⅓ cup milk

BASIC METHOD

Place the baking sheet in the oven and preheat to 450°F.

Sift the measured flour twice with the baking powder, salt, and other fine ingredients, such as powdered mustard.

Dice the fats into the dry ingredients, then lightly rub in with cool fingertips or a pastry blender until completely blended.

Make a well in the center and stir in the milk. Lightly mix with a fork until the ingredients form a soft dough.

Turn out onto a floured board and knead *very lightly* for about ½ minute to a loose, smooth dough. Roll out with a rolling pin or pat with the hand to approximately ¾ inch thick. Stamp out with a 2-inch cutter or cut into triangles with a sharp knife. Lightly knead together any trimmings and roll and stamp out again. Lift with a spatula onto the *hot* baking sheet, placing 1 inch apart. Brush only the tops with lightly beaten egg or milk.

Bake toward the top of the oven for approximately 10 minutes, or until well risen and golden brown. Lift onto a wire rack with the spatula to cool.

VARIATIONS

CHEESE*

1¾ cups very finely grated   Pinch of dry English mustard
mature Cheddar cheese

SAGE AND WALNUT*

¾ cup finely chopped walnuts   sage OR 1 tablespoon
2 tablespoons chopped fresh   dried

  * Serve savory-flavored scones with potted meats and fish (see pages 244 to 248).

WHOLE WHEAT

Use a mixture of 1½ cups whole wheat and ½ cup white flour. After sifting, tip any bran remaining in the sieve back into the flour you are using.

EXTRA-RICH SCONES

To the basic dry ingredients add 2 tablespoons superfine granulated sugar and use 1 egg beaten with 5 tablespoons milk to mix.

FRUIT SCONES

Sift ¼ teaspoon mixed spice (equal amounts of nutmeg, cinnamon, cloves, allspice, and/or mace) with the flour. Stir in

1 cup golden raisins OR mixed golden raisins and dried currants before adding the liquids.

TREACLE (OR MOLASSES) SCONES

Dissolve 2 tablespoons black treacle or molasses in 2 tablespoons hot water in a measuring cup. Add milk to make ½ cup. Use as the liquid for Whole Wheat Scones.

OLD ENGLISH BUTTERMILK SCONES

3 cups sifted unbleached flour
2 tablespoons baking powder
½ teaspoon baking soda
1 teaspoon salt
2 tablespoons superfine
   granulated sugar

½ cup vegetable shortening
½ cup (1 stick) sweet butter
¾ cup buttermilk
Heavy cream, to glaze

Makes 30 to 40 small scones

Preheat the oven to 400°F. Generously grease a baking sheet but don't preheat it.

Sift all the dry ingredients together into a large bowl. Rub in the two fats until a moist, sandlike texture is reached. Chill, covered, for 30 minutes.

Make a well and pour in the buttermilk. Gather the mixture together with a fork. Turn out onto a lightly floured surface and work together *lightly*. Form into a rectangle.

Roll the dough out into an oblong ¾ inch thick. Cut into 1½-inch squares, but do not separate them entirely. Just move them apart a little.

Brush with heavy cream and bake in the center of the oven for 12 to 15 minutes. Do not overcook. The scones are done when they have risen and are golden brown and firm to the touch.

Serve, split, with clotted cream (Devonshire cream), whipped heavy cream, or butter and jam.

DROP SCONES (OR SCOTCH PANCAKES)
WITH FRUIT

2 cups all-purpose flour
¼ teaspoon salt
½ teaspoon baking soda
1 teaspoon cream of tartar
¼ cup superfine granulated
  sugar
1 large egg, beaten

1 tablespoon corn or maple
  syrup
Milk, to mix
1 teaspoon grated lemon rind
½ cup golden raisins, soaked
  in 1 tablespoon whisky
  (optional)

Makes 18 to 20 scones

Sift all the dry ingredients together into a bowl. Make a well in the center.

Add the egg, syrup, and enough milk to make a thick, heavy pouring batter. Mix in the lemon rind and raisins if used.

Heat a griddle or heavy-based skillet. Grease with a little butter or lard. Drop heaping teaspoonfuls of the mixture from the point of a spoon and bake until set and browned on one side, with bubbles coming to the surface of the batter.

Turn the scones over and bake until the edges are no longer sticky. The scones should be about ⅓ inch thick, so test one before thinning the batter too far. Keep warm in a clean napkin. Serve buttered but *not* split.

DROP SCONES II

These quick and easy teatime treats, also known as Scotch pancakes, are traditionally cooked on a griddle, but will be just as successful made in a heavy-based skillet.

1 cup all-purpose flour
Pinch of salt
2 tablespoons sweet butter

2 teaspoons superfine
  granulated sugar
1 egg, beaten
Approximately ½ cup milk

Makes about 18

Preheat a griddle or heavy-based skillet.

Sift the flour and salt into a large bowl. Rub in the butter with your fingertips or a pastry blender and stir in the sugar.

Make a well in the center of the dry ingredients, add the egg and enough milk to make a thick, smooth batter.

Grease the now-very-hot griddle. Drop about 2 tablespoonsful batter for each scone onto the griddle, spacing them well apart. Cook for 2 to 3 minutes, or until they are slightly puffy and the surface bubbles. Turn over and cook for a further 2 to 3 minutes, or until both sides are golden brown. Let cool between two tea towels on a wire rack while cooking the remaining batter.

Serve freshly cooked and hot, buttered and with preserves if you wish.

VARIATION

Add a few golden raisins, chopped dates, OR dark raisins to the uncooked batter.

GIRDLE SCONES

Popular for tea in Scotland and Wales, where the girdle, or griddle—a round, flat iron sheet with a hooped handle—is used. At one time this would have been suspended from a ratchet over the dying embers of an open fire.

These scones are eaten split and buttered, with or without jam or honey.

2 cups all-purpose flour	Pinch of salt
½ teaspoon baking soda	1 teaspoon sugar
1 teaspoon cream of tartar	½ cup buttermilk OR milk

Makes 6 to 8

Sift all the dry ingredients into a bowl. Add the buttermilk or milk and mix to an elastic dough with the milk.

Turn onto a floured work surface and knead lightly until smooth. Form into a square. Roll out to ½ inch thick. Cut into 6 or 8 squares.

Put onto a greased heated girdle or heavy-bottomed skillet and cook over a low to medium heat until risen and starting to brown. Turn them and continue cooking on the other side, about 8 to 10 minutes in all.

Let cool on a wire rack.

BATCH SCONE

Made in minutes, this very short, light scone needs no rolling or cutting. Serve straight from the oven, cut in wedges, split and buttered.

2 cups all-purpose flour	1 cup golden raisins
1 tablespoon baking powder	1 egg
½ cup (1 stick) sweet butter	3 tablespoons milk
¼ cup vegetable shortening	Extra sugar, to dust the top
¾ cup sugar	

Makes 12 portions

Set the oven to 375°F and place a large baking sheet inside to preheat.

Sift the flour and baking powder together twice, then rub in the two fats with your fingertips or a pastry blender until the mixture looks like bread crumbs. Stir in the sugar and raisins. Beat together the egg and milk and gently blend into the dry ingredients until a soft dough is formed. Tip onto a floured board and knead lightly. Shape into a ball.

Place on the hot baking sheet and flatten slightly to 1½ inches thick. Mark into V wedges with the back of a knife, cutting ¼ inch deep into the dough, and sprinkle well with additional sugar.

Bake for approximately 25 minutes, or until golden brown. Let cool slightly, then cut into 10 or 12 wedges. Split across and butter.

Ideally, serve warm.

SALLY LUNN TEA CAKES

Legend has it that Sally Lunn touted her special Bath buns in the streets of that city. There is reference in 1727 to Lun's cakes, and these were in fact probably made at a baker's shop of that name.

We do know that an enriched bread made with caraway seeds and sprinkled with sugar *was* popular at breakfast time in the eighteenth-century Bath homes and was called *Sol-et-Lune—* literally the Old Norman French for sun and moon, referring to the golden sun color at the egg-glazed top and the whiter, paler under part.

It is said—and not without good reason—that Sally Lunn, when "crying" her wares in the streets, called out, "*Soleilune*." Which came first, we don't really know; the truth lies somewhere between.

What is perhaps even more interesting is that at one time it was traditional to eat "Sally Lunn" with a fork, slicing it horizontally and bathing it with scalded cream!

Today, we eat it thinly sliced and well buttered at afternoon tea or cut somewhat thicker when a day or two old and toasted in front of a roaring fire.

4 tablespoons (½ stick) sweet butter	2 eggs, beaten
¾ cup milk	3 cups white bread flour
1 teaspoon superfine granulated sugar	1 teaspoon salt
1 tablespoon active dry yeast OR ½ ounce fresh	FOR THE GLAZE
	2 tablespoons sugar, mixed with 2 tablespoons water

Makes 10 to 12 slices

Grease two 5-inch cake pans or two 1-pint ovenproof soufflé dishes.

Over low heat, slowly melt the butter in the milk with the sugar. Sprinkle with the yeast and leave for 10 minutes in a warm place until frothy. Beat in the eggs.

Sift the flour and salt together into a large bowl, add the liquid, and mix well. Turn out onto a lightly floured surface and knead for 10 minutes. Shape into 2 balls and place in the prepared pans or soufflé dishes. Place in oiled plastic bags and leave in a warm place for about 1 hour, or until the dough fills the pans.

Preheat the oven to 450°F.

Bake for about 20 minutes, or until golden brown. Turn out onto a wire rack and glaze while still hot. Serve hot, sliced horizontally and buttered.

VARIATION

Add 2 cups dried fruits together with the flour, perhaps mixed golden raisins, dark raisins, dried currants, finely chopped mixed citrus rind, and candied cherries.

CURRANT BREAD

Delicious served thinly sliced and buttered, with the added luxury of homemade jam or honey. If any stays around long enough to lose its freshness—which is doubtful—it is equally good toasted.

1 tablespoon active dry yeast
  OR ½ ounce fresh
1 teaspoon superfine
  granulated sugar
2 cups milk, slightly warm
4 cups white bread flour
2 teaspoons salt
2 tablespoons lard
1½ cups dried currants OR

mixed currants and
  golden raisins
1 tablespoon finely chopped
  mixed candied citrus rind

FOR THE GLAZE
1 tablespoon superfine
  granulated sugar
1 tablespoon milk

Makes two 1-pound loaves

Grease two 1-pound loaf pans.

Mix the yeast and sugar with two-thirds of the milk and leave in a warm place for about 10 minutes, or until frothy.

Sift the flour and salt together into a large bowl; with your fingertips rub in the shortening. Stir in the currants and rind. Stir in the yeast mixture and enough of the remaining milk to form a soft dough.

Turn out onto a lightly floured surface and knead for about 5 minutes, or until the dough feels firm and elastic. Place in an oiled plastic bag and leave in a warm place for about 1 to 1½ hours, or until the dough has doubled in volume.

Preheat the oven to 450°F.

Punch back and knead again for 5 minutes, then divide into two pieces. Fit the dough into the loaf pans. Slip the pans back into the oiled plastic bag and leave to rise for about 20 to 30 minutes, or until the dough has risen to the top of the pans.

Bake for about 15 minutes.

Stir together the milk and sugar for the glaze and brush it over the tops of the loaves.

Reduce the oven temperature to 375° and bake for a further 30 to 40 minutes. Test for doneness by knocking the base of the baked loaf with your knuckle; it should sound hollow.

Turn out onto a wire rack to cool.

TREACLE (MOLASSES) BREAD

4 cups all-purpose flour
1 teaspoon salt
1 teaspoon baking soda
1 teaspoon ginger

¼ cup superfine granulated
   sugar
2 tablespoons molasses
About ¼ cup buttermilk

Makes two 1-pound loaves

Preheat the oven to 450°F.

Sift the dry ingredients together. Mix the molasses with ¼ cup buttermilk and add to the dry ingredients. Add enough additional buttermilk to form a soft dough. Turn out onto a floured board and shape into a round cake. Mark into quarters.

Bake for 30 to 35 minutes. Test for doneness by knocking the base of the baked loaf with your knuckle; it should sound hollow.

Eat, split and buttered, with or without jam or honey.

BANANA BREAD

½ cup (1 stick) sweet butter,
   softened
1 cup sugar
2 large eggs
1½ cups all-purpose flour
1 teaspoon baking soda
1 teaspoon salt

½ teaspoon nutmeg
1 cup mashed ripe bananas
½ cup light cream
1 teaspoon vanilla extract
½ cup crushed toasted
   hazelnuts OR walnuts

Makes one loaf

Preheat the oven to 350°F.

Cream the butter, sugar, and eggs together until light and fluffy. Mix in the bananas. Sift all the dry ingredients together and mix into the first mixture.

Mix in the cream and vanilla extract. Finally stir in the nuts.

Pour into a greased nonstick baking pan (approximately 9 by 5 inches).

Bake for 1 hour. When done, the bread should spring back when lightly pressed with the forefinger.

Invert onto a wire rack and let cool.
Serve thinly sliced and lightly buttered.

HARVO LOAF

Simply mixed together and baked—the simplest of tea breads—this is best kept a day or two before slicing to allow the flavors to mellow. Serve cut ¼ inch thick and buttered. Also good made into sandwiches with a sweet filling, such as cream cheese and chopped dates or bananas.

1 cup milk
1 tablespoon maple syrup
1 cup all-purpose flour
1 cup whole wheat flour
3 teaspoons baking powder
1 cup brown sugar

1 cup mixed golden and dark
   raisins
1 tablespoon granulated sugar
   dissolved in 1 tablespoon
   boiling water to glaze

Makes one 1-pound loaf

Grease and flour a 1-pound loaf pan. Preheat the oven to 350°F.

Gently heat the milk and maple syrup just long enough to melt them together.

Sift the two flours and the baking powder together into a large bowl, tipping in any bran left in the sifter. Stir in the brown sugar and mixed raisins; beat in the milk mixture.

Spoon into the prepared pan and bake for about 45 minutes.

Let cool in the pan, then turn out onto a wire rack. Brush the top of the hot loaf with a little syrup for a shiny, sticky finish.

Let cool completely, then wrap and let mature.

RAISIN AND LEMON TEA CAKE

1 tablespoon active dry yeast
    OR ½ ounce fresh
1 teaspoon honey
1 cup warm water
3 cups white bread flour
1 teaspoon salt
2 tablespoons superfine
    granulated sugar
1 cup golden raisins
Rind of 1 lemon, finely grated

¼ teaspoon nutmeg OR mace
1 egg, beaten

FOR THE ICING
1 cup confectioners' sugar,
    sifted
2 tablespoons lemon juice,
    strained
1 tablespoon honey

Makes two 1-pound loaves

Grease two 1-pound loaf pans.

In a small bowl, mix together the yeast, honey, and ½ cup of the water and leave in a warm place for 10 minutes, or until frothy.

Sift the flour and salt together into a large bowl and mix in the sugar, raisins, lemon rind, and spice.

Add the egg and yeast liquid and enough of the remaining warm water to make a soft dough.

Turn out onto a lightly floured surface and knead for 5 minutes.

Place in an oiled plastic bag and leave in a warm place to rise for about 1 hour, or until doubled in size.

Knead again for 2 to 3 minutes, divide in two, and place in the prepared pans.

Return to the oiled plastic bag and leave to rise again for 40 to 60 minutes.

Preheat the oven to 400°F. and bake for about 30 minutes. Test for doneness by knocking the base of the baked loaf with your knuckle; it should sound hollow.

Turn out onto a wire rack. When cold, mix the confectioners' sugar with enough lemon juice to make a coating consistency. Spoon over the top of the loaves.

Serve fresh, sliced and buttered, with or without honey.

A NOTE ON CUT-AND-COME-AGAIN CAKES

Tea breads with fruit and nuts and made with either white or brown flour are always served already buttered and thinly cut.

The strange title "cut-and-come-again" cake refers to a cake or loaf, sometimes buttered, sometimes not, with a high sugar content, which on baking in the old-fashioned fire- or faggot-heated ovens tended to dry out, the sugar caramelizing to a certain extent due to overbaking. These enriched breads—for this is what they really are—were kept in airtight tins (in country districts they were often wrapped in a blanket and buried outside in the garden) until the crumb matured and the caramel softened—or "came again."

These same rich tea breads are also known by the equally strange title—"cut-and-butter breads," which name is perhaps more self-explanatory. With today's recipes this overbaking doesn't (or shouldn't!) occur, but their comical names persist in many areas. So, if you ever come across one, you will know what to expect!

DATE AND NUT LOAF

This is a very old recipe, dating from c. 1730.

1 cup chopped dates	½ cup sugar
1 cup boiling water	1 egg, beaten
1 teaspoon baking soda	1 cup chopped mixed almonds
4 tablespoons (½ stick) sweet	and walnuts
butter, softened	1 heaping cup all-purpose
¼ cup lard	flour

Makes one 1-pound loaf

Preheat the oven to 400°F.

Cover the dates with the boiling water and leave to cool; drain and reserve liquid. Add the baking soda to the dates. In a separate bowl, cream the butter, lard, and sugar together, and add the egg, nuts, and soaked dates. Stir in the flour, along with the liquid from the dates.

Mix well and put into a well-greased loaf pan. Bake for 1 hour or until firm to the touch and the loaf shrinks from the sides of the pan.

Let cool on a wire rack and serve sliced.

NUT BREAD

2 eggs
1 cup dark brown sugar
4 cups whole wheat flour
4 teaspoons baking powder

½ teaspoon salt
2 cups milk
1 cup finely chopped mixed
    hazelnuts and walnuts

Makes 2 loaves

Preheat the oven to 350°F.

Beat the eggs well and add the brown sugar. Stir the flour, baking powder, and salt together. Add the flour mixture alternately with the milk to the egg mixture.

Stir in the chopped nuts. Divide between two large well-greased bread pans and let stand for 30 minutes before baking.

Bake for 1 hour or until firm to the touch and the loaf shrinks from the sides of the pan.

Let cool on a wire rack.

FREDA MARY LORD'S
DATE AND WALNUT LOAF

Tea breads are halfway between bread and cake; those made without yeast tend more toward the latter. This one is my sister's favorite offering at teatime. Kept for a day or two after making, well wrapped in plastic, the flavor mellows. Serve it sliced and buttered.

1½ cups coarsely chopped
    dates
¾ cup water
1 teaspoon baking soda
2½ cups whole wheat flour
3 teaspoons baking powder

½ teaspoon salt
5 tablespoons sweet butter
1 cup sugar
1 cup coarsely chopped
    walnuts
1 large egg, beaten

Makes one 2-pound loaf

Preheat the oven to 300°F. Grease and flour one 2-pound loaf pan.

Over medium heat, slowly bring the dates and water just

to the boil; remove from the heat, and beat in the baking soda. Let cool.

Sift the flour, baking powder, and salt into a large bowl. Rub in the butter with your fingertips or a pastry blender. Stir in the sugar and nuts.

Add the date mixture and the egg to the dry ingredients and mix together thoroughly.

Spoon into the prepared loaf pan and smooth the top.

Bake in the lower part of the oven for 1½ hours or until firm to the touch and the loaf shrinks from the sides of the pan.

Let cool in the pan before turning out onto a wire rack. When completely cooled, wrap and keep for at least a day before serving.

CHELSEA BUNS

Made of enriched dough stuffed with dried fruit and peel and covered with a sticky glaze, these buns get their name from the Chelsea Bun House in London's now-fashionable residential area, where they were a speciality in the eighteenth century, when Chelsea was a village.

1 tablespoon active dry yeast	FOR THE FILLING
OR ½ ounce fresh	2 tablespoons sweet butter,
¼ teaspoon superfine	melted
granulated sugar	1 cup mixed dried fruit
½ cup warm milk	¼ cup finely chopped mixed
1½ cups white bread flour	candied citrus rind
½ teaspoon salt	⅓ cup brown sugar
1 tablespoon sweet butter	
1 egg, beaten	Honey, to glaze

Makes 9 buns

Grease a 9-inch square cake pan.

Mix the yeast and sugar with the milk in a small bowl and sprinkle it with ¼ cup of the flour. Leave in a warm place for about 15 minutes, or until frothy.

Sift the remaining flour and the salt into a large bowl. Rub in the butter with your fingertips. Add the yeast mixture along with the beaten egg and mix to a soft dough. Turn out onto a lightly floured surface and knead for about 5 minutes, or until smooth.

Place in an oiled plastic bag and leave to rise in a warm place for about 1 to 1½ hours, or until doubled in size. Punch the dough back, knead it, and roll it out to a rectangle 14 inches long by 10 inches wide. Brush with the melted butter and sprinkle with the dried fruit, citrus rind, and brown sugar, but only to within ½ inch of the edges.

Roll up the dough from the longest side and pinch the edges together. Cut the roll into 9 equal slices and place, cut side down, in the greased pan, three in a row.

Slip the pan back into the oiled plastic bag and allow to rise in a warm place for about 30 minutes, or until doubled in size. Meanwhile, preheat the oven to 375°F.

Bake for about 25 to 30 minutes, or until the top has turned a rich golden brown. Turn out onto a wire rack and, while still warm, brush with honey for a shiny, sticky glaze.

Note: *Don't expect Chelsea Buns to be as rich and delicate as Danish pastries, which they closely resemble in appearance. They are more breadlike in texture and intended for the high-tea table, served with butter and jam.*

BATH BUNS

These sweet buns with a crunchy sugar topping were popular with wealthy visitors to the Somerset cathedral city of Bath, famous for its therapeutic "spa" waters, in the eighteenth century. Jane Austen certainly partook of them.

2 tablespoons active dry yeast
    OR 1 ounce fresh
½ cup warm milk
¼ cup warm water
3 cups white bread flour
1 teaspoon salt
⅓ cup superfine granulated
    sugar
4 tablespoons (½ stick) sweet
    butter, melted

2 eggs, beaten
1½ cups golden raisins
½ cup finely chopped mixed
    candied citrus rind

FOR THE TOPPING
Beaten egg
Crushed sugar lumps

Makes 18 buns

Mix the yeast, liquids, and a quarter of the flour in a small bowl and set aside in a warm place for 20 minutes, or until frothy.

Sift the remaining flour with the salt into a large bowl. Add the sugar, butter, eggs, yeast liquid, raisins, and citrus rind, and mix to a soft dough.

Turn out onto a lightly floured surface and knead for 10 minutes, or until smooth. Place in a large oiled plastic bag and leave to rise in a warm place for 1 hour. Knead again for 5 minutes, then divide into 18 pieces. Flour the palms of your hands and roll each piece lightly into a rough bun shape. Place the buns on greased baking sheets. Slip these back into the oiled plastic bag and leave in a warm place for 30 minutes, or until doubled in volume. Meanwhile, preheat the oven to 375°F.

Brush with the beaten egg and sprinkle well with the crushed sugar.

Bake for 15 to 20 minutes, or until golden brown. Let cool on a wire rack.

Serve cool, but freshly baked, split and buttered.

DEVONSHIRE SPLITS

Soft, sweet buns filled with cream and jam—traditionally Devonshire clotted cream and homemade strawberry jam, but whipped cream is almost as good.

1 tablespoon active dry yeast OR ½ ounce fresh	4 tablespoons (½ stick) sweet butter
¼ teaspoon superfine granulated sugar	FOR THE FILLING
1⅓ cups warm milk	Raspberry or strawberry jam
3 cups white bread flour	Whipped cream
1 teaspoon salt	Confectioners' sugar

Makes 18 buns

Mix the yeast and sugar with half of the milk in a small bowl and leave in a warm place for 10 minutes, or until frothy.

Sift the flour and salt into a large bowl. Melt the butter in the remaining milk until lukewarm. Stir this and the yeast liquid into the flour and beat to an elastic dough. Turn out onto a lightly floured surface and knead for 10 minutes, or until smooth.

Slip into a large oiled plastic bag and leave in a warm place for 1 to 1½ hours, or until doubled in volume. Knead again for another 5 minutes. Divide into 18 pieces and shape into round buns. Place on a greased baking sheet, flattening slightly with the palm of your hand.

Return the baking sheet to the oiled plastic bag and leave to rise in a warm place for about 20 minutes. Meanwhile, preheat the oven to 425°F.

Bake for 20 minutes. The buns are done when they have risen and are light brown and firm to the touch. Let cool on a wire rack.

To serve, split the buns almost in half, diagonally if you can, and fill with jam and cream. Dredge with confectioners' sugar.

BRIGHTON ROCKS

¾ cup (1½ sticks) sweet butter	1 cup dried currants
½ cup superfine granulated sugar	1⅓ cups all-purpose flour
½ cup ground almonds	2 eggs, beaten
	1 teaspoon rose water
	Beaten egg, to glaze

Makes 12 to 16

Preheat the oven to 425°F.

Cream the butter and sugar. Work in the ground almonds and the currants. Add the flour with the beaten eggs and rose water. Mix to a stiff dough. Fork into small individual mounds and place on greased baking sheets.

Glaze with a little beaten egg. Bake for about 10 minutes. They are done when golden brown and firm. Let cool on a wire rack.

Serve split and buttered.

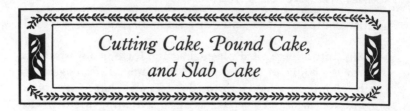

POUND CAKE

This is one of the earliest cakes—in the way we think of cake today—and is unchanged from its original form in the rather extended appendix of the fifth edition of Hannah Glasse's book *The Art of Cookery Made Plain and Easy,* published in 1763. I have translated it into American culinary measures, and to please you, I suggest you use a tube pan (unheard of for cakes in England!). In those days a cake pan or tin was called a hoop.

2 cups sugar	1 teaspoon finely grated lemon
2 cups all-purpose flour	rind
1⅓ cups butter, softened	Brandy or sherry, to make a
5 eggs	spoonable dough

Makes 8 servings

Preheat the oven to 325°F.

This cake can be made by the all-in-one method: Cream the butter and sugar in a food processor or with an electric mixer until pale and fluffy. Gradually beat in the eggs and lemon rind. Add the flour and enough liquor to make a spoonable batter. Allow it to be beaten well for 10 minutes or so.

Bake for one hour, or until the cake is firm to the touch and shrinks from the sides of the pan. Let cool briefly in the pan before turning out onto a wire rack.

POUND CAKE WITH HAZELNUTS

1 cup (2 sticks) sweet butter,
    softened
⅔ cup brown sugar
1 teaspoon vanilla extract
½ teaspoon mace
3 large eggs, separated
1½ cups all-purpose flour

1½ teaspoons baking soda
¼ teaspoon salt
1 cup light cream
2 tablespoons granulated
    sugar
1 cup lightly toasted hazelnuts,
    skins removed, crushed

Makes 8 servings

Butter a 9-inch cake pan and line the bottom with wax paper.

Preheat the oven to 350°F.

Cream together the butter, brown sugar, vanilla extract, and mace until light and fluffy. Beat in the egg yolks.

Sift together onto wax paper the flour, baking soda, and salt. Mix this into the creamed mixture alternately with the light cream.

Beat together the egg whites and granulated sugar until the mixture forms soft peaks. Stir one-third of the beaten whites into the batter. Mix in the crushed hazelnuts, then fold in the remaining egg whites.

Pour into the prepared cake pan. Bake for 40 to 45 minutes, or until the cake is firm to the touch and shrinks from the sides of the pan.

Let cool briefly in the pan before turning out onto a wire rack.

SAND CAKE

1½ cups self-rising flour
1 level teaspoon baking
    powder
⅓ cup rice flour
1 cup (2 sticks) sweet butter,
    softened

½ cup superfine granulated
    sugar
1 teaspoon vanilla extract
3 eggs, beaten
1 tablespoon milk (optional)

Makes 8 generous slices

Liberally butter and sugar a fluted mold or loose-bottomed deep cake pan 7 inches in diameter.

Preheat the oven to 350°F.

Sift the flour and baking powder together. Mix with the rice. Set aside.

Cream the butter, sugar, and vanilla extract until light and fluffy. Beat in the eggs slowly. Gradually beat in the flour mixture, adding a little milk or water until you have a dough of a soft dropping consistency. Turn into the prepared mold or pan and bake for 1 to 1¼ hours, or until the cake is firm to the touch and shrinks from the side of the pan.

Let cool briefly in the pan before turning out onto a wire rack.

SPONGE CAKE

As far as I have been able to discover in my many years of research, Mrs. Elizabeth Raffald gives the first recipe '*To make a Cake without Butter*' in the first (1769) edition of her excellent book of eighteenth-century "receipts," *The Experienced English Housekeeper*, and it is interesting to read her exact directions:

> Beat eight Eggs half an Hour, have ready pounded and sifted a Pound of Loaf sugar, shake it in, and beat it half an Hour more, put to it a quarter of a Pound of Sweat Almonds beat fine, with Orange Flower Water, grate the Rind of a Lemon into the Almonds and squeeze in the Juice of the Lemon, mix them all together, and keep beating them 'till the Oven is ready, and just before you set it in, put to it three quarters of a Pound of warm dry fine Flour; rub your Hoop with Butter, an hour and a half will bake it.

—and all in one sentence with the Old English ∫ for the lower case *s*.

Many people make this type of cake without butter; I find that the tablespoon or so of sweet butter makes it just that little bit more moist.

4 whole eggs, their weight
   (with shells) in superfine
   granulated sugar and in
   self-rising flour

1 teaspoon finely grated
   lemon rind (optional)
1 tablespoon sweet butter,
   melted but cold

Makes 6 servings

Generously butter and dredge with superfine granulated sugar a lightweight 8-inch metal cake pan. Preheat the oven to 375°F.

Beat the eggs and sugar together with the lemon rind until quite stiff and thick. Sift the flour and fold it in, mixing lightly but thoroughly. Pour in the butter, again mixing well.

Spoon the mixture into the prepared pan and bake for 20 to 25 minutes. Serve with jam, cream cheese, and whipped or clotted cream (Devonshire cream).

MADEIRA CAKE

1 cup (2 sticks) sweet butter,
   softened
¾ cup superfine granulated
   sugar
3 eggs, beaten
¾ cup self-rising flour

¾ cup all-purpose flour
Grated rind and juice of 1
   lemon
A little milk if necessary
1 to 2 slices candied citrus rind

Makes 8 servings

Grease and line with wax paper a round 7-inch cake pan. Preheat the oven to 325°F.

Cream the butter and sugar until light and fluffy.

Add the eggs slowly, beating well all the time.

Sift the flours together, fold half into the batter, then add the lemon rind and juice. Fold in the remaining flour.

Add a little milk if necessary to give a dropping consistency.

Pour the mixture into the prepared cake pan. Arrange the citrus rind on top. Bake for 1 to 1¼ hours, or until the cake is firm to the touch and shrinks from the sides of the pan.

Let cool briefly in the pan before turning out onto a wire rack.

LIGHT FRUIT RUM CAKE

1 pound golden raisins
½ pound seedless muscatel
    raisins
1 pound blanched split
    almonds
½ pound glacé cherries
½ pound glacé pineapple
½ pound mixed candied
    citrus rind
Grated rind of 1 lemon and
    1 orange

4 cups all-purpose flour, sifted
    with 2 teaspoons double-
    acting baking powder
    and ½ teaspoon salt
1 cup (2 sticks) sweet butter,
    softened
2 cups sugar
1 cup Jamaica rum
8 egg whites, stiffly beaten

Makes 12 slices

Line the sides and bottoms of two 9-by-5-by-3-inch loaf pans with buttered greaseproof paper. Preheat the oven to 250°F.

Toss all the fruits in 1 cup of the flour mixture until loose and separated.

Cream the butter and sugar together until light and fluffy. Mix in the remaining 3 cups flour alternately with the rum. Fold in the stiffly beaten egg whites. Mix in the fruits. The dough should be of a "soft" dropping consistency.

Bake for 2 to 2½ hours, or until the cake is firm to the touch and shrinks from the sides of the pan. Let cool for 15 minutes and then turn out onto a wire rack.

DUNDEE CAKE

1 cup (2 sticks) butter,
    softened
⅔ cup sugar
4 large eggs, beaten
2½ cups all-purpose flour,
    sifted with 1 teaspoon
    baking powder and ½
    teaspoon salt

1 cup golden or dark raisins
1 cup dried currants
½ cup candied citrus rind
½ cup slivered or flaked
    almonds
¼ cup whisky or rum

FOR THE TOPPING

½ cup glacé cherries, halved

1 cup whole almonds,
    blanched

Makes 12 slices

Line two 8-by-4-inch loaf pans with buttered wax paper. Preheat the oven to 250°F.

Cream the butter and sugar together until fluffy. Dribble in the beaten eggs, beating well and adding a dredge of flour if the batter shows signs of separating.

Mix all the fruits with the flour and almonds. Mix into the cake batter, adding the whisky or rum to give a soft dropping consistency.

Divide the mixture between the two pans. Cover the top of the mixture with the whole almonds and halved cherries.

Bake for 1½ to 1¾ hours, or until the cake is firm to the touch and shrinks from the sides of the pan. Let cool briefly in the pan and then remove to a wire rack.

RAINBOW OR MARBLE CAKE

A marble cake with a difference, as mine has a seam of moist red-currant jelly running through the marbling. This adds an interesting dimension to its overall appearance.

1¼ cups (2½ sticks) sweet butter, softened
1¼ cups superfine granulated sugar
6 eggs
2 cups self-rising flour
2 teaspoons baking powder
¼ cup ground almonds
3 tablespoons milk or water
2 to 3 drops red food coloring

2 teaspoons *essence de framboise* (optional)
1 tablespoon cocoa powder
Grated rind of 1 lemon
1 to 2 drops yellow food coloring
1 teaspoon almond extract
1 to 2 drops green food coloring
2 teaspoons red currant jelly
Confectioners' sugar

Makes 8 servings

Butter and line with wax paper a 12-by-4-by-4-inch oblong cake pan. Preheat the oven to 375°F.

Cream the butter and sugar together thoroughly. Beat the eggs and fold them into the creamed mixture gradually, adding a little of the flour if the batter shows signs of curdling.

Sift together the flour, baking powder, and ground almonds. Fold thoroughly into the batter. Add 2 to 3 tablespoons of milk or water, just enough to create a loose dropping consistency. Divide the batter into three or four equal parts, depending on whether you want three or four colors.

Add to the first part the red food color and the *essence de framboise*. Into the second beat the cocoa powder. To the third add the grated lemon rind and yellow food color. To the fourth add the almond extract and the green food coloring.

To make the cake: Spoon small amounts of different-colored batter along the bottom of the prepared pan. Give the pan a sharp bang on the table or counter to settle things in. Place tiny bits of jelly right down the center. Continue spooning in batter and jelly until both are used up, but do not put jelly on the top.

Bake for 30 minutes, then reduce the oven temperature to 350° and bake 35 to 40 minutes longer, or until a toothpick inserted in the center comes out clean. The cake will also sound quiet if you listen to it with your ear. Let cool on a wire rack and, when completely cool, dust the surface with confectioners' sugar.

TANGY LEMON SPONGE CAKE

For the family, this can be made as two single-layered sticky-topped cakes, in which case you will need 10 extra lemon slices; or, for special occasions, it can be done as one deep, rich, layered cake. This cake can be made by the all-in-one method in a food processor (see page 136).

12 ounces Lemon Cheese
  (page 237)
1 lemon, cut into 10 slices
Sweet butter, equal to the
  weight of the eggs (see
  below), softened
Grated rind of 1 large lemon

Superfine granulated sugar,
  equal to the weight of
  the eggs (see below)
4 large eggs, beaten
1½ cups all-purpose flour
½ cup cornstarch
1 teaspoon baking powder
Lemon juice

Makes 12 to 16 servings

Preheat the oven to 375°F.

Butter and line the bottoms of two 7-inch 1½-inch deep pans with buttered wax paper. Spread the bottom of each with one-third of the Lemon Cheese. Arrange the lemon slices, slightly overlapping, in a circle on top of this.

Cream the butter, lemon rind, and sugar thoroughly. Beat in the eggs a little at a time.

Sift together twice the flour, cornstarch, and baking powder. Mix this into the creamed mixture and, using a little lemon juice, beat until you have a softish dropping consistency. Divide the mixture between the 2 pans, leveling the tops.

Bake for 35 to 40 minutes, or until the cakes are firm to the touch. Turn onto cooling racks. Leave to cool completely.

Divide each cake in half horizontally (or, if you have a good eye and a steady hand, 3 layers makes for a gooier finish). Spread each layer liberally with the remaining Lemon Cheese. Arrange in layers with, obviously, the one decorated with the lemon slices uppermost.

QUEEN'S CAKE

The queen referred to here is Queen Anne, regent of England and, of course, one-time monarch of the American Colonies, too.

I understand this excellent cake enjoys a reputation in the States, particularly in the South; sadly it is not now so known in Britain.

What I think will be of more interest to the reader is that I am the proud owner of *Royal Cookery—or the Complete Court-Cook*, by Patrick Lamb Esquire, "for 50 years Master-Cook to their late Majesties King Charles II, King James II, King William and Mary and to Her Present Majesty Queen Anne." My edition is dated 1710, only four years after Thomas Twining opened his first tea shop. On page 82 the recipe is "To Make a Plum-Cake."

In the first edition of her book, *The Experienced English Housekeeper* (1769), Elizabeth Raffald was already "improving upon" Patrick Lamb's earlier "receipt," giving us twentieth-century cooks license to continue improving matters, so long as we don't lose the spirit of the recipe.

6 eggs, separated
1⅔ cups granulated sugar
1½ cups (3 sticks) sweet
    butter, softened
1 cup brown sugar
1 cup flaked almonds
1 cup dried currants

1 cup glacé cherries, roughly
    chopped
3 cups all-purpose flour
1 tablespoon baking powder
1 teaspoon cinnamon
1 teaspoon ginger
1 cup sherry

Makes 12 servings

Generously butter and line the bottoms of two 8-by-5-inch cake pans with wax paper. Preheat the oven to 275°F.

Beat the egg whites together with ⅔ cup of the granulated sugar until they form peaks.

In a separate bowl, beat the yolks until they are thick.

In another, larger bowl, cream the butter with the rest of the granulated sugar and the brown sugar. Mix the yolks into this.

Toss the currants, cherries, and almonds in 1 cup of the flour to coat them.

Sift the remaining 2 cups flour together with the baking powder and spices and fold into the egg and sugar mixture alternately with the sherry. Mix the fruits and nuts in well. Finally, fold in the egg whites.

Pour into the prepared pans and bake, side by side, for 1¾ hours to 2 hours, or until the cake is firm to the touch and shrinks from the sides of the pan.

Let cool briefly in the pan before turning out onto a wire rack to cool completely.

FEATHER CAKE

As far as I can tell, it is this cake that evolved into America's devil's food cake, although I feel the Devil would have confected—or rather, wrought—something heavier than this delicious confection!

¼ cup vegetable shortening
4 tablespoons (½ stick) sweet butter, softened
1 cup superfine granulated sugar
1 cup brown sugar
3 ounces bittersweet chocolate

½ cup sweet sherry
1 teaspoon vanilla extract
2 large eggs, beaten
2 cups all-purpose flour
1 teaspoon baking powder
¼ teaspoon salt
⅔ cup milk

Makes 12 to 16 servings

Lightly butter two 9-inch cake pans and line them with wax paper—or use two nonstick pans. Preheat the oven to 350°F.

Cream the first four ingredients together until light and fluffy.

Melt the chocolate in the sherry in a bowl over a pan of simmering water. Mix together and allow to cool before adding to the creamed mixture.

Sift the flour with the baking powder and salt, adding the milk gradually as you sift. Divide the mixture between the two prepared pans.

Bake in the oven for 30 minutes or until the cake is springy to the touch. Let cool for 10 minutes, then turn onto a wire rack.

Ice with your favorite frosting, such as chocolate, coffee, or lemon.

SWISS ROLL (Jelly Roll)

About ¾ cup sugar
¾ cup cake flour
¾ teaspoon baking powder
¼ teaspoon salt
4 eggs

1 teaspoon finely grated lemon rind OR 1 teaspoon vanilla extract
About 1 pound jam (optional)

Makes 8 to 10 pieces

Butter and line an 11-by-16-by-½-inch jelly roll pan with wax paper. Preheat the oven to 400°F.

Dampen a kitchen towel with cold water, wring out well, then spread it out on a work surface. On top of this lay a sheet of wax paper approximately 2 inches bigger than the jelly roll pan. Dredge this lightly but evenly with a little of the sugar.

Sift the flour, baking powder, and salt together onto a piece of wax paper. With an electric beater, cream the eggs, lemon or vanilla extract, and ¾ cup of the sugar until thick—the beater will leave a distinct trail. Slowly but thoroughly fold this into the flour.

Pour the mixture into the prepared pan, spreading it into the corners.

Bake for 8 to 10 minutes, or until the center is just firm to the touch.

Allow the roll to cool for a couple of minutes, then invert onto the sugared paper. Remove the pan. Carefully peel off the wax paper.

If you wish to spread the cake with jam, it is done at this stage.

Carefully roll up from the long side, using the damp cloth to aid you, making sure also that you do not trap the wax paper while rolling.

If the cake is to be filled with a cream filling or Lemon Cheese (p. 237), roll it up, and leave covered until ready for filling. Then unroll it, spread the filling over the cake, and reroll it loosely from the narrower end.

Dust the top of the roll with confectioners' sugar. Cut on the diagonal into 2-inch pieces.

CHOCOLATE SWISS ROLL

Substitute ¼ cup cocoa powder for ¼ cup flour in the recipe above before sifting.

CHOCOLATE BUTTER CREAM FILLING
FOR CHOCOLATE SWISS ROLL

2 cups (4 sticks) sweet butter, softened	½ cup cocoa powder
2 cups confectioners' sugar	2 tablespoons brandy, rum, OR sherry

Beat together the butter, sugar, and cocoa until smooth, creamy, and well blended. Beat in the liquor.

Unroll the Chocolate Swiss Roll, spread evenly with the filling, reroll, and dust with confectioners' sugar, as above; or make double the quantity of butter cream and pipe or fork it over the finished roll.

COCONUT KIRSCH ROLL

Light as air with its yummy cream filling laced with kirsch. Nothing a health fiend should even think about, but everything a gourmet should.

FOR THE SPONGE MIXTURE

4 large eggs
½ cup sugar
¼ cup dried coconut

1 scant cup self-rising flour, sifted

FOR THE KIRSCH CREAM FILLING

6 large egg yolks
⅓ cup sugar
1¼ cups light cream
1 teaspoon unflavored gelatin

⅓ cup kirsch
5 tablespoons (⅓ cup) sweet butter, softened

FOR THE TOPPING

1 cup heavy cream
2 tablespoons kirsch

1 tablespoon confectioners' sugar

FOR THE GARNISH

About ½ cup dried coconut, toasted

8 ½-inch pieces glacé or fresh pineapple

Makes 8 to 10 slices

To make the sponge: First butter and line a 14-by-9-inch jelly roll pan with buttered wax paper. Preheat the oven to 375°F.

Using a hand rotary beater or electric hand whisk, cream the eggs and sugar together until the beater leaves a very distinct trail when drawn through the mixture.

Mix the coconut and flour together, then fold this into the egg mixture. Pour into the lined pan and bake for 12 minutes.

Put a clean kitchen towel wrung out in cold water onto a flat surface. Cover with a piece of wax paper at least 18 by 12 inches and dredge this evenly with sugar. When the sponge is ready, invert it onto the prepared paper. Carefully remove the base paper and leave for 30 seconds to allow the steam to escape. Trim the edges.

Gradually and carefully roll up the sponge very loosely,

using the damp cloth to help. Unroll, and reroll it loosely in the paper only. Leave to cool.

To make the filling: In a round-bottomed bowl set over a pan of boiling water, slowly whisk the yolks, sugar, cream, and gelatin until thick and ribboning. Remove from the heat and immediately pour in the kirsch to remove any residual heat.

Put the bowl in a sink of cold water, whisking to cool the mixture. At the same time, whisk in the softened butter bit by bit. Let cool and chill, whisking from time to time to ensure a thick, even-textured consistency—it should be just spreadable. If necessary, add a little more kirsch or light cream to thin it down.

To fill: Unroll the sponge and spread to the edges with the cream filling. Dust with the toasted coconut, then roll up.

To top: Whip the heavy cream, kirsch, and confectioners' sugar to a piping consistency. Pipe a garland down the center of the roll. Dredge with the ½ cup toasted coconut and spike with pieces of pineapple. This should be eaten the day it is made, although it can be frozen.

CHESTNUT CREAM CHEESE AND VANILLA ROLL

3 eggs
6 tablespoons vanilla sugar
1 teaspoon vanilla extract

¾ cup self-rising flour sifted onto paper
2 tablespoons sweet butter, melted but cool

CREAM CHEESE AND CHESTNUT FILLING

One 19-ounce can Faugier *Marrons au Syrop*
One 8-ounce package cream cheese

1 teaspoon confectioners' sugar
1 teaspoon vanilla extract
¾ cup heavy cream

DECORATION

Confectioners' sugar
Whipped cream

1 to 2 drops of vanilla extract

Makes 8 portions

Butter a 14-by-9-inch pan with sweet butter and line the bottom with buttered wax paper. Preheat the oven to 375°F.

Whisk the eggs, vanilla sugar, and vanilla extract until thick and the whisk leaves a very distinct trail. Briskly whisk in the flour and incorporate the cool melted butter at the same time.

Pour into the lined pan. Spread the mixture, paying particular attention to the corners. Bake for 12 minutes.

Have ready a clean tea towel well wrung out in cold water. Invert the sponge onto this and remove the paper. Leave to cool but not go cold, or it won't roll successfully.

To make the filling: Drain and roughly chop the marrons (reserve 4 or 5 for decoration if you like). Beat the cream cheese with the confectioners' sugar and vanilla extract, then fold in the marrons. Whip the cream until it stands in soft peaks and carefully fold it by hand into the cream cheese. (Don't try to do this in a machine or you will end up with a curdled mess.)

Spread the sponge liberally with the filling mixture and roll it gently but firmly, using the towel to hold all together as you roll.

Let cool completely; dust liberally with confectioners' sugar and decorate with extra whipped cream made with half a teaspoon of confectioners sugar and a drop or two of vanilla extract. Decorate, if you like, with marrons.

BATTENBURG CAKE

Named after Prince Henry of Battenburg, this cake is sometimes known in my family as tennis cake because it resembles the four segments of a tennis court.

1½ cups cake flour	¾ cup soft tub margarine
3¼ teaspoons baking powder	4 drops (⅛ teaspoon) of red
3 large eggs	food coloring
3 tablespoons tepid water	8 ounces apricot jam
¾ cup superfine granulated	Almond Paste (page 150)
sugar	

Makes about 8 slices

Use a baking pan approximately 10 by 8 inches by 2 inches deep. Cut a triple thickness of wax or nonstick paper the width of the pan and the length plus 4 inches. Pleat the paper so that when placed in the pan the fold divides it in half across the width. This will enable you to bake both color cakes in the same pan.

Preheat the oven to 375°F.

Sift the flour and baking powder together twice. With an electric mixer or food processor beat together the eggs, water, sugar, and margarine until creamy. Add the flour and continue to beat until the batter is a pale creamy color and looks glossy.

Divide the batter very equally in two and pour one-half into one side of the prepared pan. Beat the food coloring into the second half and spoon into the other part of the pan. Level the tops and bake for approximately 40 minutes.

Leave to cool for 5 minutes, then turn out onto a wire cooling rack, peeling off the paper and separating the two sponges. When quite cold, trim the sponges to make two equal-sized cakes. Cut each in half, top to bottom, lengthwise.

Spread the sides with jam and sandwich together a white and a pink cake side by side, then place the remaining two on top, white over pink, pink over white, to form a checkerboard pattern. Coat the whole of the outside, except for the ends, with jam.

Roll out the almond paste on a lightly sugared board to an oblong the width of the cake and long enough to wrap all the way round it—about 16 by 8 inches. Wrap the paste completely around the cake, pressing the joints together and trimming the edges. Using your thumb and forefinger, pinch the outer edges decoratively—rather like the edge of a pieshell. Score the top with a knife in a crisscross pattern.

ALMOND PASTE

This makes a rich, soft paste made of ground almonds that is traditionally used to top special occasion cakes such as rich fruit cakes for weddings or Christmas, before the white "royal" icing layer is added.

It is also used to wrap the two-colored cake called Battenburg (page 149) and to top the traditional Simnel Cake at Eastertime.

At Christmastime, it can be covered with white icing, to

resemble snow, and decorated with treasured cake ornaments, or it can be topped with layers of jewellike candied fruits.

2 cups confectioners' sugar	1 teaspoon vanilla extract
1¼ cups superfine granulated sugar	2 eggs
	Juice of 1 lemon, strained
4 cups ground blanched almonds	

Makes about 2½ pounds

Sift the confectioners' sugar into a large bowl. Stir in the granulated sugar and the almonds.

In a separate bowl, beat together the eggs, vanilla, and lemon juice. Pour over the dry ingredients and stir together well. Form into a ball—easiest with the hands—and knead on a lightly sugared surface until very smooth and totally blended. Wrap in plastic wrap and chill until required. Almond paste freezes well.

TOFFEE CAKE

4 ounces unsweetened chocolate	2 teaspoons vanilla extract
1 cup (2 sticks) sweet butter, softened	4 eggs, beaten
	1 cup all-purpose flour
1 cup sugar	1 cup crushed walnut halves

Makes 6 portions

Butter a 9-by-12-inch cake pan. Preheat the oven to 325°F.

Melt the chocolate in the top of a double boiler placed over simmering water.

Cream the butter, sugar, and vanilla extract until light and fluffy. Gradually beat in the eggs. Mix in the melted chocolate, then the flour and crushed nuts.

Spoon into the prepared pan and bake for 40 to 45 minutes, or until firm and set. Let cool. Turn onto a wire rack to cool and cut into 3-inch-long fingers before cooling completely.

SPONGE CAKE

4 large eggs
Their weight in both sugar
    and flour

Raspberry jam
Confectioners' sugar

Butter two nonstick 7-by-1½-inch pans. Dust well with flour, shaking away any surplus. Preheat the oven to 375°F.

Arrange a warmed bowl over a pan of barely simmering water. Put in the eggs and sugar and whisk the mixture until light and creamy. The whisk should leave a distinct trail when drawn through the mixture. Remove from the heat.

Sift the flour into the egg mixture, incorporating it by cutting and folding with a pliable balloon whisk. Divide the mixture equally between the two tins.

Bake for 20 minutes, or until firm to the touch. Turn out onto a wire rack to cool.

Spread the top of one cake with plenty of the raspberry jam. Set the second cake on top. Dust with confectioners' sugar.

Eat the same day.

VICTORIA SPONGE CAKE

This very traditional English cake was named after Queen Victoria, though history omits to tell us whether it was actually her favorite cake; one can only assume it was!

It is a very light, melt-in-the-mouth sponge filled simply with jam and dredged in confectioners' sugar.

For a more elaborate filling, whisk Lemon Cheese (page 237) into whipped heavy cream and spoon between the layers.

The traditional recipe involved creaming the fat and sugar together until very fluffy, beating in the eggs one at a time, and then very carefully folding in the flour with a metal spoon. With the development of soft fats and quick-beating electric mixers and processors, the following, far simpler, foolproof method has become very popular. The flavor and texture are as good, if not better, than the traditional method.

While I prefer the flavor of this cake made with butter, the texture is somewhat denser than with margarine.

2 cups cake flour
4½ teaspoons baking powder
4 large eggs
¼ cup warm water

1 cup superfine granulated
    sugar
1 cup soft tub margarine OR
    whipped sweet butter
12 ounces raspberry jam

Makes 8 to 10 slices

Grease, flour, and line with wax paper two 8-inch cake pans. Preheat the oven to 325°F.

Sift together the flour and baking powder twice.

With an electric mixer or a food processor, beat together the eggs, water, sugar, and margarine or butter until very light and creamy. Add the flour and continue to beat until the batter is a pale creamy color and looks glossy. Divide the batter between the two pans.

Bake for 20 minutes, or until the top springs back when pressed with a fingertip. If space doesn't allow both pans on the middle shelf together, place one on the lower shelf and reverse positions halfway through the cooking time.

Stand the cake pans on cooling racks for 5 minutes, then turn the cakes out removing the wax paper. Let cool completely before filling.

TWO-FOUR-SIX-EIGHT CAKE

So called in Britain because 2 eggs, 4 ounces butter, 6 ounces sugar, and 8 ounces flour are used.

For America, I suggest you use different proportions.

3 cups cake flour, sifted
4 teaspoons baking powder
½ teaspoon salt
1 cup (2 sticks) sweet butter,
    softened

2 cups sugar
4 eggs, separated
1 cup milk
1 to 2 teaspoons vanilla
    extract

Makes 8 servings

Preheat the oven to 350°F.
Sift the flour, baking powder, and salt together.

Cream the butter and sugar until light and fluffy. Beat in the egg yolks along with 1 teaspoon of the flour mixture. Beat well. Mix in the remaining flour, the milk, and the vanilla extract.

Beat the egg whites until they stand in peaks. Fold these into the cake mixture.

Divide among three lightly greased 8-inch nonstick cake pans.

Bake for 25 minutes. Let cool a little before turning out onto a wire rack.

Each cake should be split and layered with your favorite butter cream. Then dredge the top with confectioners' sugar.

COCONUT-JAM CAKE

3 cups cake flour
4 teaspoons baking powder
½ teaspoon salt
1 cup dried coconut
1 cup boiling milk
¾ cup (1½ sticks) butter, softened
1½ cups sugar

1 tablespoon kirsch OR 1 teaspoon vanilla extract
4 large egg whites, beaten to soft peaks
12 ounces raspberry OR strawberry jam, sieved, to fill

COCONUT FROSTING

2 cups confectioners' sugar
¼ cup lemon juice
1 teaspoon grated lemon rind

Boiling water, to mix
½ cup dried coconut

Makes 12 servings

Butter and flour two deep 9-inch cake pans. Preheat the oven to 350°F.

Sift together the flour, baking powder, and salt.

Put the coconut into a bowl. Pour the boiling milk over it. Let cool completely, then drain well, reserving the milk.

Cream the butter, sugar, and kirsch or vanilla extract until light and fluffy. Mix in the flour mixture and coconut milk alternately. Mix in the drained coconut. Fold in the beaten egg whites well.

Divide the batter between the two pans and bake for 35 to 40 minutes, or until firm to the touch. Let cool a little. Turn out onto a wire rack.

This can be assembled as one deep cake, or the layers can be split horizontally to make two shallow ones. In either case, fill the cake with the raspberry or strawberry jam.

Mix and beat the sugar, lemon juice, and lemon rind with just enough boiling water to make a spreadable frosting.

Spread a cushion of frosting over the top of each cake. Dust with coconut while the frosting is still soft.

BIBLE CAKE

1 cup (2 sticks) butter (Judges 5:25), softened
1 generous cup sugar (Jeremiah 6:20)
1 tablespoon honey (1 Samuel 14:25)
3 eggs (Jeremiah 17:11)
1½ cups raisins (1 Samuel 30:12)
1½ cups chopped figs (Nahum 3:12)
½ cup almonds, blanched and chopped (Numbers 17:8)
1 pound all-purpose flour (1 Kings 4:22)
Spices, to taste (Chronicles 9)
Pinch of salt (Leviticus 2:13)
1 teaspoon baking powder (Amos 4:5)
3 tablespoons milk (Judges 4:19)

Makes 20 servings

Preheat the oven to 325°F. Grease and line a 2-pound loaf pan.

In a large bowl, cream the butter, sugar, and honey together. (Add the eggs, one at a time, still beating, then the raisins, figs, and almonds, and beat again.

Sift together the flour, spices, salt, and baking powder and add to the batter. Stir in the milk. Bake for 1½ hours, or until a toothpick comes out clean.

Let cool on a wire rack.

Note: *The ingredients for this cake are "hidden" in the Bible. References are to passages in the Authorized Version.*

PLAIN CHRISTMAS CAKE

1½ cups golden raisins
2 cups dark raisins
¾ cup cut mixed candied
 citrus rind
¾ cup glacé cherries, roughly
 chopped
½ cup (1 stick) sweet butter,
 softened

4 ounces lard
1 generous cup superfine
 granulated sugar
4 large eggs, beaten
2 cups all-purpose flour, sifted
½ cup split OR whole
 almonds, blanched

Makes 24 slices

Line two 2-pound cake pans with buttered wax paper.
Preheat the oven to 350°F.

Wash and dry the fruits if necessary. Roughly chop the raisins after washing.

In a large bowl, cream together the fats and sugar until light and fluffy. Beat in the eggs, a little at a time, adding a spoonful of flour if they start to separate. Beat the mixture well until fluffy. Fold in the flour without beating. Fold in the fruits.

Fill the prepared pans two-thirds full with the batter. Top with the almonds. Bake for 1 hour, then lower the temperature to 325° and bake for a further 1 to 1½ hours, or until a toothpick comes out clean.

Let cool on a wire rack.

WEDDING CAKE
(TO ICE OR NOT TO ICE)

27 August 1977 is indelibly printed on my mind. This was the day I was called upon to put into practice what I had endlessly preached to the myriad mothers who had come to me for advice about their daughters' weddings over the many years I was banqueting.

It's all very well telling other people what to do: You can be totally objective, gently persuading the bride's mum that of course there'll be enough food and of course the bridesmaids' frocks will match the wallpaper in the ballroom and of course the church flowers can be got out through the vestry door and appear on the buffet table, rearranged, before the bride and

groom set foot inside the reception rooms (and at no extra cost—
well, at very little extra cost) and no, the soft-iced four-tier cake
that Nanny or Aunt Sophia has made won't topple. (It will, but
I'll have rammed a steel rod through all four tiers in an effort to
eliminate a disaster before the cake cutting! This urge on the
part of relatives to make wedding cakes has its good and bad
points. The balancing act happens to be one of the bad ones.)

When it comes to organizing one's own daughter's wedding,
life suddenly takes on a very different aspect. Suddenly *I* am that
idiot father who can't make up his mind whether to serve all
champagne or a choice of cocktails, with a glass of wine at lunch
and a modest swig of bubbly for the cake cutting. Should the
church flowers and those carried by the girls coordinate with
those in the house or reception rooms? And ought there to be
three courses plus coffee and petits fours? Can one get away
without serving canapés with the reception drinks or will a
couple of packets of twiglets suffice? Then there is the weeding
of the guest list on account of numbers, and all those other
queries, each one causing a sleepless night before it retreats and
another problem supercedes it.

Our family is *not* one of those that lack for ideas. Our
problem was that we all had a headful of ideas, most of them
impractical, and the discussions on them turned into hilarious
"late sittings." My daughter was the calm one. As long as she
could have an old-fashioned bouquet showering down her front
like a flowering waterfall, she was content. I was the jumpy one!
Where will they put all their top hats? Surely they'll leave them
in their cars, but they might not, and is there enough room for
everyone actually to park their cars? Ought there to be an attendant to sort all this out? Perhaps the bridesmaids should stand
in the receiving line? The answer here is a firm no. It only pro-
longs the receiving time, and their job is firstly to help the bride
and secondly to help entertain the guests. Most bridesmaids see
their role as that of man catching, and if they don't have to shake
hands it gives them more time to get on with it!

I only want to talk about the cake, though I will tell you
briefly how I came to terms with, and solved, the problems at
my own Rosie's wedding. (Her real name is Rosanna-Marya but
a more gutsy foreshortening to Rosie has crept in over the years,
except in times of stress!) I'm a cake gobbler—an addict. I will
kill for cake, particularly chocolate cake and rich, moist fruit
cake. Wedding, Christmas, and christening cakes can either be

the best thing ever or abysmal failures. Towering edifices with cherubs and garlands piped everywhere and nerve-racking panels of lace icing to be guarded against shattering for weeks before the nuptials are all very well for the cake-cutting photograph. But to eat?—they're out. The icing on one of these confectioners' masterpieces has to be strong enough to support each tier as it is built up, but it breaks the teeth and makes an unholy mess on the carpet as the groom's sword rasps into it. For me the wedding cake has to be moist, packed indecently with liquor-soaked fruit, topped with crunchy almond paste (another problem, as the oil from such a rich paste stains the virgin icing) and finally a ½-inch layer of soft, lemony, white frosting spread over the top and sides of a large single cake. "But that will look awful" you may rightly say. Maybe, but it will taste fabulous! And it won't look nearly so awful if you follow my instructions for decorating it. The icing is smoothed over as simply as possible, using a palette knife dipped continually into a jug of boiling water to achieve a silky finish to its surface. The cake is then left to dry somewhat, not harden. A garland of flowers around the base and a cushion of roses or whatever is arranged on a board and covers the top completely. Yards of muslin swagged around the cake table, a hired silver stand, further garlands of flowers, and, hey, presto—it will look more bridal than the bride!

I do feel very strongly about making things as easy as possible for one's guests, but this, too, can pose problems, particularly if you don't have a cooperative caterer, so it is all-essential to establish a good relationship with the caterer first. This may mean asking him or her to your home for lunch or dinner if it is to be a home wedding. Even if it is to be in a hotel or suite of reception rooms, I think it pays untold dividends if he is courteously asked to drinks first. Then, having mapped out your idea of things, establish that he understands what you want (and is equipped to do it) and what standards you expect of him. If you cook for him, he already has a yardstick below which he dare not fall. Also, he has, by definition, become involved in your wedding day, and that's a good thing. I know I used to perform better when I had had a chance to get to know the people and we weren't all strangers working at odds with each other.

But as Rosie's wedding was to be in a London restaurant I had designed and established and as the general manager of Walton's was not only a protégé of mine but a close friend, all that was taken care of. However, we did have a major problem: Some 250 people were going to have to get into the place, which meant hiring a furniture van, loading it with excess furniture, parking it around the corner until the event was over, and then putting everything back into place. Any idea of having a large center buffet (which is the ideal situation because guests can circle around it and then get out of the way) was impossible. Guests just could not have fought the "battle of the buffet" in such a confined space. After lots of headaches and discussions, a flash of inspiration came to me in the Museum of Modern Art in New York, no less. I am particularly fond of that museum and had popped into see what was on in their special exhibition room. It was an exhibition of kitsch food paintings! That is how the "platescape" was born. I have used it a lot since. The idea is to treat the food visually so that instead of each guest getting a mixed pile of food, he or she is handed a very attractive and appetizing dinner plate with just four things on it:

« A cheese-pastry tartlet filled with a vegetable mayonnaise

« A circular slice of chicken galantine studded with tongue dice and pistachio nuts

« Spinach and salmon pâté and a little Waldorf salad nestling in a curly lettuce leaf

« A posy of fresh watercress leaves to finish it off

Everything was easily managed with a fork. Tiny triangles of brown bread spread with a lemon-and-herb butter accompanied the 'scape. All the plates were dressed beforehand and stacked, using plate rings. Raspberries and cream were then served, followed by huge silver trays of handmade chocolates and petits fours. These can be bought or, better still, homemade well in advance, using every bit of artistic skill you possess. They are not essential but are one of the touches that can lift an event onto cloud nine. The plate rings can be rented in most large towns, or even borrowed from a school or factory canteen.

Flowers? Here, as with all things, put your eggs into one basket. Having been blessed with the use of Brompton Oratory together with its magnificent choir, we already had a potential bank breaker. The place is ornate and immense. The problem was solved by my designing two 14-foot-high pyramids of feathery gypsophila, the palest of pink hydrangeas, and regal lilies.

They stood on either side of the chancel steps, forming a frame for the bridal party. And Rosie's waterfall? It was of pale pink Carol roses, creamy gardenias, honeysuckle, lilies of the valley, and trails of ribbons falling almost to the ground, each tied with a knob of stephanotis.

ROSIE'S WEDDING CAKE

2 pounds (8 sticks) sweet
   butter, softened
2 pounds (5 cups) brown
   sugar
1 cup molasses or maple
   syrup or honey
24 eggs, separated
Grated rind of 2 lemons and
   2 oranges
Good teaspoon each mace and
   cinnamon
2 teaspoons baking soda
2 pounds (5 cups) all-purpose
   flour
1 pound (4 cups) ground
   almonds or semolina
2 pounds (8 cups) chopped
   stoned muscatel raisins

2 pounds (8 cups) golden
   raisins
1 pound (4 cups) dried
   currants
1 pound (4 cups) roughly
   chopped glacé cherries
¼ pound (1 cup) finely
   chopped candied ginger
¼ pound (1 cup) finely
   chopped candied citrus
   rind
½ bottle (37CL) pale brandy
   (or rum or sherry—use
   the same liquor as in
   the almond paste)
2 cups fresh orange juice

Makes 100 servings

Line the bottom and sides of one 14-inch-diameter cake pan, or one 9-inch and one 6-inch pan (making two tiers) with a double thickness of wax paper. Butter this well with sweet butter. Preheat the oven to 350°F.

In a very large bowl, cream the butter and sugar together until all the granules are totally dissolved. Beat in the molasses. Beat in the egg yolks. Add the lemon and orange rind, the spices, and the baking soda. Beat in the flour and almonds or semolina, using the orange juice when necessary to arrive at a stiffish but soft batter-mix. Add the fruits, ginger, candied rind, and the chosen liqueur. *Stiffly* beat the egg whites and fold in well.

Bake for 1 hour, then reduce the heat to 300° and bake for a further 2 hours.

The cake is done when a toothpick inserted in the center comes out clean.

ALMOND PASTE

This is enough to cover the top and sides of a 14-inch round cake.

2 pounds confectioners' sugar, sifted

3 pounds almonds, ground and rubbed through a coarse sieve

3 eggs well beaten and strained

2 tablespoons medium dry sherry OR rose water OR lemon juice

Extra confectioners' sugar for rolling

In a large bowl mix together the sugar and ground almonds, using a fork. Make a well and add the eggs and sherry. Gather together gradually and form into a paste. (You may find it easier to work with your hands for this large quantity.)

Turn the paste out onto a work surface that has been dredged with confectioners' sugar. Knead the paste until it is quite smooth, about 10 minutes or so.

Divide the paste into two portions. Form one portion into a flat disc. Roll this out to a size ½ inch larger than the cake (use the cake pan as a guide). You can slide a piece of wax paper under the rolled paste to make for easier handling.

Form the second portion of paste into a long oblong.

Cut a long piece of paper the depth and circumference of the cake (you may have to staple two sheets together). Roll the second piece of almond paste out on a work surface that has been dredged with confectioners' sugar until it matches the size of the paper. Use a ruler to cut the edges of the paste neatly.

GLAZE FOR THE CAKE
1½ pounds apricot jam, sieved

Heat the jam in a bowl over a pan of hot water until it is a manageable, brushable consistency. Keep warm and "fluid" until ready to use.

TO COAT THE CAKE WITH THE ALMOND PASTE

If the cake top is not level, you will have to slice off a thin layer, but don't worry too much if the top isn't as smooth as ice. Brush the top of the cake with the jam and invert it onto the rolled-out circle of almond paste, pressing it well onto the circle.

Turn the cake right side up and peel off the wax paper. Using a clean rolling pin, lightly roll the surface to even things off, pressing any overlapping paste down the sides.

Now brush the sides of the cake with jam.

Pick up the cake and roll it on its side onto the long strip of almond paste, pressing it well to make the almond paste adhere. Seal the join and roll the cake gently to smooth everything out.

Stand the cake on a silver cake plate 2 inches larger in diameter larger than the cake.

I prefer my cakes with a plain almond paste coating tied with a huge taffeta bow and decorated with sugar flowers. However, many people like to have a wedding cake covered with Royal Icing.

ROYAL ICING

5 pounds confectioners' sugar, sifted

12 egg whites, lightly beaten

Juice of 1 or 2 small lemons, strained

Sift the confectioners' sugar into a large bowl. Make a well in the center and pour in the egg whites and lemon juice.

Gradually and carefully mix the ingredients together. As soon as they are combined, use an electric mixer and beat the frosting until it is stiff and holds its shape when pulled up into peaks.

Drop a large spoonful or two onto the center of the cake and spread it over the surface using an icing spatula dipped into hot water. (This is easier to achieve, of course, if you have a cake turntable; if not, press on.)

Spread the sides of the cake liberally with the frosting and smooth them.

Using a piping tube fitted with a ¼-inch star nozzle, and two-thirds full of frosting, pipe a collar around the base and the top edge of the cake. Continue to decorate the cake as liberally and fantastically as your skill allows.

Let the iced cake dry for 2 to 3 days.

A cake as rich as this and with a rich coating of almond paste will eventually stain as the natural almond oils seep through. So, while you can cover the cake with almond paste up to two weeks ahead of time, the white frosting should be done only 2 to 3 days ahead.

Wrap a glamorous ribbon of silk or tulle around the waist of the cake and tie a bow, with trailers and white doves tucked in and around.

Decorate the top with dozens of tiny narrow satin ribbon bows or silver leaves, silk flowers, horseshoes, silver balls, or whatever strikes your fancy.

Stand the cake on a handsome silver tray and put it on a cake table covered with layers of stiff white net layered over silver cloth.

OTHELLO LAYER CAKE

FOR THE CAKE BASES

6 eggs

1 cup vanilla sugar (for best results keep a vanilla pod in the sugar jar) OR

1 cup superfine granulated sugar AND 2 teaspoons vanilla extract

1½ cups self-rising flour, sifted

FOR THE CREAM FILLING

2 tablespoons superfine granulated sugar

½ teaspoon cornstarch

3 egg yolks

9 fluid ounces heavy cream, heated just to boiling

Superfine granulated sugar

FOR THE JAM FILLING

½ cup good-quality apricot jam

Superfine granulated sugar

FOR THE CHOCOLATE ICING

4 ounces the very best dark unsweetened chocolate

1 teaspoon flavorless oil

½ cup superfine granulated sugar, dissolved in 2 tablespoons water

Whipped cream   **Chocolate flakes OR squares**
Glacé apricots OR other
fruits

Makes 12 servings

Line two baking sheets with buttered wax paper. With a pencil, draw two circles on each sheet, using a 7-to-8-inch flan ring as your guide. Preheat the oven to 400°F.

To make the cake bases: Beat the eggs and vanilla sugar or sugar and vanilla extract together until white and thick. If you can see the trail left by the beater when it is drawn slowly through the mixture, it is thick enough. Gradually fold in the sifted flour, using a slotted spoon.

Using an icing or palette knife, spread the batter in four equal portions onto the penciled circles. Bake the thin "pancakes" for 10 to 12 minutes, or until they spring back when lightly touched with a fingertip. Turn out onto a wire rack to cool and remove the paper. When cool, use a flan ring or plate as a template to trim the layers.

To make the cream filling: Cream together the sugar, cornstarch, egg yolks, and, for added luxury, a little rum or brandy. Add the heavy cream, then put in the top of a double boiler or set the bowl over a pan of boiling water. Stirring continuously, let the sauce cook for a minute. Allow to cool, sprinkling the surface with a little sugar to prevent a skin from forming. If the finished "cream" or "custard" appears oily, beat in a spoonful or two of hot water.

To make the jam filling: Put the apricot jam into a bowl over hot water until it becomes soft; press through a wire sieve and allow to cool. Sprinkle the surface of the puree with a little superfine granulated sugar to prevent a skin from forming.

To assemble the cake: Spread the jam onto the first base, covering this with the second base, onto which you can then spread the cream filling, covering it with the third base. Spread this with jam and any remaining cream filling and top with the fourth base.

To make the icing: Melt the chocolate and oil in a bowl set over hot water. Boil the sugar syrup to "small thread" on a candy thermometer. If you don't possess one, boil the syrup until it looks thick. Do not stir the mixture or the sugar will crystallize.

Allow to cool a little, then pour into the chocolate, beating until a coating consistency is achieved. If you end up with a solid-looking fudge in your pan, don't panic, all is not lost. Restore to the proper consistency by adding hot water, a tablespoonful at a time, beating well.

Spread the fourth base with the chocolate icing. Pipe whipped cream around the sides, and decorate.

Note: *You will have to work fairly quickly with this icing. An icing knife and a jug of boiling water into which you can frequently dip the knife will facilitate this operation.*

HAZELNUT CAKE

This recipe was adapted by Elisabeth Smith, my wife, for use in the kitchens of my restaurant, Foxhill, in Yorkshire way back in 1955. The original meringue "bases" are from one of Maria Floris's books. At Foxhill, two full cakes were sandwiched together with 8 ounces of fresh (or whole frozen) raspberries topped with 1 cup of whipped heavy cream. The top cake was then dredged heavily with confectioners' sugar.

Malcolm Reid and Colin Long, from the Box Tree Restaurant in Ilkley, enjoyed this so much that they introduced it on the menu at their beautiful restaurant and have, over the years, refined and developed it into a multilayered *gâteau*. However, much as I enjoy theirs, I still hanker after my own rough-hewn and crunchy textured version.

It adds a further note of luxury if you pour 2 tablespoons of kirsch or maraschino liqueur into the cream before whipping it.

5 large egg whites
1⅓ cups superfine granulated
　sugar
1½ cups hazelnuts, toasted
　and finely crushed

2 cups (8 ounces) fresh OR
　whole frozen raspberries
1 cup lightly sweetened
　whipped cream
Confectioners' sugar

Makes 8 servings

Line two 8-inch shallow cake pans with silicone paper. Preheat the oven to 375°F.

Stiffly beat the egg whites as for a meringue, incorporating half the sugar as you beat and the second half toward the end of the beating time as the meringue peaks. Fold in the crushed hazelnuts with a slotted spoon.

Divide the mixture equally between the two pans and bake for 35 to 40 minutes, or until risen and crisp on top.

An hour or so before you want to serve the cake, place the first layer on a piece of wax paper. Cover with the raspberries and pipe over the whipped cream, using a 1-inch star nozzle. Top with the second layer, crusty side up, and dredge heavily with sifted confectioners' sugar. Use a large fish slice to help you lift the cake—which is fragile—onto a nice serving dish.

Note: *The bases can be made days in advance and stored in an airtight tin. However, do not assemble the cakes for serving too far in advance, as the raspberries will make the base cake too soggy.*

SPARTACUS BERNSTEIN'S CHEESECAKE

I first met this extraordinary man from Brooklyn Heights ten years ago in New York City, when I was over there for the Bicentennial. His specialty is, of course, cheesecake, and his shop in Manhattan sold only that and only to the rich and famous, Jacqueline Kennedy Onassis and Princess Lee Radziwill being his most ardent clients.

Spartacus taught me how to make the basic cheesecake in the tiny kitchen of his home on Orange Street in Brooklyn Heights the very first day I met him. It's a cooked cheesecake, which, to my thinking, far outclasses the fluffier gelatin-based type we have become used to, and relates more closely to our own eighteenth-century English "Cheese Pye."

I have made one change, or rather given my preferred alternatives. I use a pastry shell, as given in the eighteenth-century recipe for "Chocolate Pye," in place of the more usual American base of graham cracker crumbs, but here is the Bernstein base.

½ pound plus 2 tablespoons (2¼ sticks) sweet butter

1¼ cups graham cracker crumbs

6 tablespoons light brown sugar

1 cup superfine granulated sugar

4 large eggs, beaten

2 tablespoons all-purpose flour

Grated rind and juice of 1 large or 2 small lemons

½ teaspoon vanilla extract

1½ pounds full-fat cream cheese

¼ cup milk

FOR THE TOPPING

1¾ cups sour cream

Juice of 1 lemon

1 tablespoon confectioners' sugar

Makes 8 to 10 servings

Butter a 10-inch springform mold. Preheat the oven to 375°F.

To make the crumb base: Melt ¼ pound of the butter, then mix in the crumbs and brown sugar. Spread the mixture on the bottom but *not* up the sides of the mold. Stand the form on a piece of foil folded 1 inch or so up around the bottom edge to catch any melting butter that may escape if your mold doesn't fit tightly enough. Bake for 8 to 10 minutes.

Leave this to cool. Reduce the oven temperature to 325° to receive the filled mold.

To make the filling: Beat the remaining butter with the granulated sugar until white and fluffy and add the beaten eggs. Add the flour, mixing in well. Add the lemon rind, lemon juice, and vanilla extract.

Beat the cream cheese in a separate bowl and combine with the milk. *Gradually* incorporate the butter mixture. You will have a soft-flowing mixture that you can pour into the prebaked crumb or pastry shell.

Bake in the center of the oven for 1½ hours. Combine the topping ingredients in a bowl and pour over the top of the cake. Turn the oven up to 375° for a further 10 minutes, or until set. Turn the heat off, leave the door ajar, and let the cheesecake cool in the oven. This eliminates any possibility of a rift or crack appearing on the surface of the cake.

ROMAN CHEESECAKE

This recipe is based on one taken from an early manuscript and is a delicious, easy-to-make sweet. If you have a blender the whole operation can be done in it and then poured into the separately beaten egg whites.

4 tablespoons (½ stick) sweet butter, softened	½ cup light cream
	1 teaspoon vanilla extract
1 heaping cup superfine granulated sugar	5 eggs, separated
	½ cup all-purpose flour, sifted
1 pound (3 cups) cream cheese	
2 tablespoons any good-flavored honey	¼ pound (1 cup) flaked almonds

FOR THE TOPPING

½ cup brown sugar	2 ounces (½ cup) flaked almonds
1 teaspoon cinnamon	
	Confectioners' sugar, sifted

Makes 12 servings

Preheat the oven to 325°F.

In a large bowl, cream the butter and sugar until light and fluffy. Add the cream cheese and beat well. Add the honey, light cream, vanilla extract, egg yolks, and flour and mix well.

In a separate bowl, beat the egg whites to stiff peaks and fold them into the batter together with the flaked almonds.

Pour into a well-buttered 10-inch springform mold and sprinkle evenly with the topping ingredients. (It is not necessary to line the mold with pastry for this recipe, but it is an option.)

Bake for 1 hour, or until set. Then turn off the heat and allow to cool *in the oven* to prevent cracking. Sprinkle with sifted confectioners' sugar before serving.

CHOCOLATE AND RAISIN ROLL

This deliciously rich dessert is more of a mousse than a cake, since it has no flour. Make it the day before you need it.

6 ounces unsweetened
   chocolate
5 eggs, separated
1 scant cup superfine
   granulated sugar

1 cup raisins
½ cup heavy cream
1 tablespoon brandy or
   sherry

Makes 6 to 8 servings

Preheat the oven to 350°F.

Grease and line a 13-by-9-inch jelly roll pan. Break up the chocolate and place in a bowl over hot water until melted.

Place the egg yolks and sugar in a separate bowl over hot water and whisk until the mixture is pale and fluffy, about 5 minutes. Whisk in the chocolate gradually, then stir in half the raisins. Allow to cool for 10 minutes.

In a separate bowl, whisk the egg whites until stiff, then fold carefully into the chocolate mixture, taking care not to knock out the air. Pour into the prepared pan and shake to level the mixture. Bake for 25 minutes, or until firm. Remove from the oven and cover with foil. Leave until completely cold, at least 3 hours.

Whisk the cream until it holds its shape, then stir in the remaining raisins and the brandy or sherry. Turn the roll onto a sheet of sugared paper and spread with the cream. Roll up carefully from a short end and place on a serving plate. The cake will crack slightly as you roll it.

Sprinkle with more sugar and chill until ready to serve.

BUTTERSCOTCH FUDGE CAKE

Commonly known in my family as "naughty cake." It's sticky and gooey and treacherous to the teeth, but very "moreish" and, you don't have to bake it!

1 cup (2 sticks) sweet butter,
   melted
6 tablespoons maple syrup
6 ounces (1½ cups) mixed
   nuts, roughly chopped
4 ounces (1 cup) glacé
   cherries, chopped

8 ounces (2 cups) mixed dried
   fruits (dried currants and
   golden and dark raisins)
8 ounces (2 cups) wheatmeal
   biscuits or graham
   crackers

FOR THE DECORATION

Whipped cream   Glacé cherries

Makes 12 servings

Butter an 8-inch, loose-bottomed cake pan and line it with wax paper.

To make the butterscotch sauce: Stir together the butter and syrup in a heavy-based saucepan. Boil for 2 to 3 minutes, stirring constantly. Let cool for a few minutes.

Place all the nuts and fruit together in a large bowl. Crush half the biscuits and crumble the other half, then add to the fruit and nuts. Pour the butterscotch sauce over all and stir well to coat evenly.

Spoon the mixture into the prepared pan and leave it to set in the refrigerator for 2 to 3 hours. When firm, decorate with the whipped cream and cherries.

ORANGE AND ALMOND LIQUEUR CAKE

2¼ cups self-rising flour
1 teaspoon baking powder
4 ounces ground almonds
1 cup (2 sticks) sweet butter

1 heaping cup superfine
   granulated sugar
2 heaping teaspoons finely
   grated orange rind
4 eggs, beaten

FOR THE SPECIAL BUTTER CREAM

4 egg whites
¾ cup confectioners' sugar
2 drops red food coloring
2 drops yellow food coloring
1 cup (2 sticks) sweet butter,
   very soft

1 teaspoon grated orange rind
2 tablespoons orange liqueur
   (Cointreau, Grand
   Marnier, or curaçao)

FOR THE ICING

¾ cup confectioners' sugar
2 tablespoons orange liqueur
   (as above)
Orange jelly marmalade or
   sliced whole fruit
   (regular) marmalade

Flaked almonds and candied
   orange slices, to decorate
   (optional)

Makes 10 to 12 servings

Butter and line the bases of two 8-inch shallow cake pans. Preheat the oven to 375°F.

Sift together onto a piece of paper, twice, the flour, baking powder, and ground almonds. In a large bowl, cream together the butter, sugar, and orange rind until light and fluffy. Beat in the eggs, then the flour mixture, using a little cold water (about 2 tablespoons) to arrive at a soft dropping consistency.

Divide the mixture equally between the two tins; level the tops and bake for 35 to 40 minutes, or until firm when pressed with a finger.

Turn the cakes out onto a wire rack and let cool completely. Halve each cake horizontally.

To make the butter cream: Stiffly beat the egg whites, then beat in half the confectioners' sugar, adding the food coloring at this stage. Fold in the remaining confectioners' sugar. In a bowl, cream the butter and orange rind very well. Gradually beat in the meringue mixture and liqueur.

To make the icing: Sift the confectioners' sugar into a bowl. Heat the liqueur over a low flame in a metal soup ladle (do not allow it to ignite). Stir, then beat it into the sugar.

Spread this over the uncut bottom side of one of the cake layers, using an icing knife dipped in boiling water to ease the process and to give a smooth finish; set aside.

Spread one-third of the butter cream on the crumb face of one of the layers. Place a second cake on top of this; splash with a little liqueur and spread with some of the remaining butter cream. Spread the next cake with the marmalade, fit it on top of the second layer and spread with some butter cream. Finally, top with the iced layer.

Spread butter cream around the sides of the cake. Press the flaked almonds into this.

Decorate at will with any remaining butter cream piped in blobs and stuck with candied orange.

Cut with a hot, wet knife.

WALNUT AND PINEAPPLE MERINGUE CAKE

Ideal for a special Sunday tea in the garden or as a rich after-dinner dessert. Try sipping a glass of crème de cacao as you munch away.

7 large egg whites
2 cups superfine granulated
    sugar, sifted
2¼ cups crushed walnuts
1 small pineapple
2½ cups heavy cream

2 tablespoons kirsch
    (optional)
1 level tablespoon
    confectioners' sugar
2 pieces glacé pineapple, to
    decorate (optional), cut
    into small pieces

Makes 8 to 10 servings

Butter the bottom and sides of three 8-inch shallow cake pans, and line the bottoms with wax paper (or make the cakes in batches to suit your supply of such pans). Preheat the oven to 375°F.

Beat the egg whites until they stand in peaks. Beat in half the sugar, bringing the mixture back to stiff-peak consistency. Quickly whisk in the remaining sugar and fold in the crushed nuts.

Divide in three parts, pour into the prepared pans and bake for 20 minutes. If, after 20 minutes, there is evidence of scorching, reduce the oven temperature to 350° and add a further 10 minutes to the baking time. These cake bases are quite fragile, so turn them out carefully onto a wire rack, remove the paper, and leave to cool.

To make up the cake: Peel, core, and chop the pineapple. Whip the cream with the kirsch and confectioners' sugar until it stands in peaks.

Place one of the cakes upside down on a serving dish. Pipe around a collar of cream, filling the center with the pineapple. Arrange the second cake on top, right side up. Spread with the remaining cream. Arrange the third cake on top. Dredge with confectioners' sugar, a few blobs of cream, and the glacé pineapple if you wish.

Cut with a serrated knife. Serve the same day.

MUSCATEL BRAN CAKE

The secret of this wholesome cake is in the flavor of the muscatel raisins. These are readily available from most health food shops. The cake is good when sliced and well buttered and served with a mild, crumbly cheese such as Wensleydale or Cheshire. Alternatively, it is delicious toasted for breakfast.

2 cups All-bran (breakfast cereal)	1 cup roughly chopped walnuts
2 cups seedless muscatel raisins	2 teaspoons vanilla extract
1 heaping cup brown sugar	Scant 1 cup milk
	2 cups whole wheat flour
	3 teaspoons baking powder

Makes 16 to 20 servings

Line an 8-inch square cake pan with buttered wax paper. Preheat the oven to 350°F.

Put the All-bran, raisins, sugar, walnuts, and vanilla extract in a bowl. Cover with the milk and mix well. Leave to soak for 2 hours.

Sift the flour and baking powder together. Gradually fold into the mixture. Bake for 1¼ to 1½ hours, or until a toothpick inserted in the center comes out clean.

Let cool on a wire rack.

ORANGE AND GINGER PARKIN

This sticky ginger cake is eaten on Bonfire Night, November 5, a traditional night to celebrate Guy Fawkes day.

½ cup (1 stick) sweet butter	2 eggs
1 pound maple syrup OR old-fashioned brown (not black) molasses	1 tablespoon shredded preserved ginger
1¾ cups superfine granulated sugar	1 tablespoon candied orange rind
¾ cup self-rising flour	3 pieces preserved ginger, cut into thinnest shreds (optional)
Good pinch of salt	Milk, to mix
3½ cups medium oatmeal	
1 tablespoon ginger	

Makes 18 servings

Butter and line with wax paper a 3-pound loaf pan or an 8-inch, loose-bottomed cake pan. Preheat the oven to 350°F.

Melt the butter and syrup or molasses in a nonstick pan over low heat. It should be fully melted, but not hot. In a bowl, mix all the dry ingredients together. Mix in the syrup and butter. Beat the eggs and add these and then the remaining ingredients. Mix to a soft dropping consistency with milk.

Pour into the prepared pan and bake for 1 to 1¼ hours, or until the cake shrinks from the sides of the pan.

The parkin should be left for 2 weeks or more stored in an airtight tin to mature properly.

GRASMERE GINGERBREAD

2¾ cups all-purpose flour	1 cup (2 sticks) margarine
2 teaspoons ginger	OR sweet butter
1 teaspoon baking soda	1 heaping cup brown sugar
1 teaspoon cream of tartar	

Makes 30 pieces

Preheat the oven to 300°F.

Sift together the flour, ginger, baking soda, and cream of tartar. Rub in the fat, then add the sugar and mix well. Grease a 10-by-12-inch flat pan (1-inch deep) and press the mixture into it.

Bake for about 35 to 40 minutes or until cake is firm to the touch and shrinks from the sides of the pan.

Let cool slightly before cutting.

SAFFRON CAKE

Saffron, the dried stigma of the purple flowering crocus, was popular in two parts of England in medieval times. Originating in Arabia, it reached Cornwall in the west of England via Spain. There were also saffron fields in Essex around the town of Saffron Walden, which took its name from the golden-yellow pollen.

Originally used predominantly as a dye and a medicine, it grew in popularity in cooking and was used profusely in Tudor dishes as an aromatic spice and "gilder" of pastry "coffyns."

Saffron Cake is today the only surviving British recipe using this spice.

2 teaspoons active dry yeast	½ teaspoon salt
1 teaspoon sugar	4 tablespoons (½ stick) butter
½ cup warm water	2 tablespoons lard
¼ teaspoon saffron strands	Yellow food coloring
1 tablespoon boiling water	(optional)
1½ pounds white bread flour	1 cup dried currants
1 tablespoon powdered milk	½ cup golden raisins
2 tablespoons superfine	¼ cup candied citrus rind
granulated sugar	

Makes one 2-pound loaf

Put the yeast into a small bowl with the 1 teaspoon sugar. Add the warm water, whisk, and leave to froth for 10 to 15 minutes. Put the saffron strands in a separate cup, add the boiling water, and leave to infuse.

Sift 2 cups of the flour into a bowl, stir in the powdered milk, pour in the frothed yeast, and mix to a batter. Cover the bowl with plastic wrap or a cloth and leave in a warm, draft-free place for 30 minutes (this is the ferment or leaven).

Put the remaining flour into a large mixing bowl, add the sugar and salt, and rub in the fats until the mixture resembles fresh bread crumbs. Pour in the frothed mixture followed by the saffron strands and their soaking water. Beat for 10 minutes by hand (5 minutes in an electric mixer). When ready, the dough should be silky and very elastic. Cover again with plastic wrap and leave in a warm place to rise. It should double in bulk, which usually takes about 1 hour.

Knock back the dough and beat by hand for 5 minutes. Add the yellow food coloring if necessary.

Work in the dried fruits and peel and transfer the dough to a well-greased 2-pound loaf pan. Slip the tin inside a plastic bag, trapping a little air inside so that it balloons up, and tie with a tie-tag. Leave in a warm, draft-free place for about 40 minutes, or until the mixture has risen to the top of the pan.

Meanwhile, preheat the oven to 400°F. Bake for 50 minutes. Turn off the heat, remove the saffron cake from the pan, and return the loaf to lie on one side on the oven rack. Close the door and leave for 5 minutes, then remove and let cool on a wire rack.

RICH DARK PLUM CAKE
(CHRISTMAS CAKE)

This recipe comes to you without Americanization! I urge you to try it. It is heavy with fruit, sticky, and all the things a good Christmas cake should be.

Dare I suggest you try eating fingers of it with a sliver of Wensleydale. Cheshire, or other crumbly English cheese, as we do in my home county of Yorkshire?

3 cups dried currants
3 cups golden raisins
3 cups seedless muscatel
   raisins, chopped
1 cup blanched almonds,
   roughly crushed
1 cup glacé cherries, halved
1 cup glacé apricots, roughly
   chopped
1 cup *prunes fourrés* OR
   pitted prunes, soaked
   overnight in 1 cup rum,
   chopped
6 ounces mixed candied citrus
   rind

3½ cups all-purpose flour,
   sifted with 1 tablespoon
   mixed spice (equal
   portions of mace,
   cinnamon, and/or clove)
¼ teaspoon salt
1¼ cups (2½ sticks) sweet
   butter, softened
10 ounces brown sugar
5 large eggs, beaten
½ cup black molasses
Juice and grated rind of 1
   large lemon
Light rum OR brandy, to mix
   to a soft dropping
   consistency

Makes 30 to 40 servings

In a large bowl, mix together the fruits, nuts, rind, and spiced flour, and salt, coating all the fruits with the flour.

In a second bowl cream the butter and sugar together until quite light in color. Beat in the eggs, then the molasses and lemon juice and rind.

Combine the two mixtures together in one bowl. Mix well, adding enough liquor to arrive at a soft dropping consistency. Preheat the oven to 325°F. Butter and line the bottom and sides of a 10-by-6-inch deep square or round cake pan with double-buttered wax paper. Fill with the mixture, leveling the top. Bake for 1 hour. Reduce the temperature to 275° and bake for a further 2 to 2½ hours. Test for doneness with a toothpick.

Let cool on a wire rack. Store for 1 month to mature. Cover with Almond Paste and Royal Icing (pages 161 and 162).

MY FAVORITE CHOCOLATE CAKE

For me, as for any self-respecting Englishman or -woman, a good chocolate cake was always made with butter, superfine granulated sugar, flour, eggs, and *cocoa*, in a shallow cake pan. A pair of cakes made with this mixture were then sandwiched together with a rich butter cream, made simply by beating butter, superfine granulated sugar (because that left it a little bit crunchy, which was considered to be a desirable texture!) and again *cocoa* with, at Christmas, a drop or two of hooch, in the form of sherry or, if you were daring enough, rum or whisky.

There were two or three different ways of finishing off this rich cake. My mama considered a dredge of superfine sugar over the top quite elaborate enough; my eldest sister made a dark coating of confectioners' sugar and cocoa. My youngest sister carried the center theme onto the top and forked a deep cushion of chocolate butter cream all over; in a fit of excessiveness she has been known to cover the sides as well, and in odd wild moments of total extravagance has then evilly dredged the whole thing with superfine sugar mixed with cocoa—bliss!

Such a chocolate cake cannot be beaten, if you know what I mean (and will forgive the somewhat oblique pun). Also, such a chocolate cake has kept the high reputation of British cakes going.

During the war, when convoys drew up in our village street, en route for "destination unknown," house doors would open, no matter what time of night it was, and curlered and dressing-gowned women would appear with a motley selection of cakes and breads to give the lads a treat and wish them well. Any soldier whose fortune it was to light upon the gates of Bruntcliffe House, my family home in an industrial village near Leeds, would get a neat wedge of chocolate cake straight from the tin, but made to a wartime recipe from beige-colored flour, margarine, molasses, and cocoa (any filling or icing was made from powdered milk, cocoa, and saccharine!). Oddly enough, cocoa was never put on ration—"under the counter" maybe, I don't clearly recall, but not actually rationed by the government. It was at least fifteen years before women were able to return to the glories of a true English chocolate cake.

What has all this got to do with my version of this cake, which bears no resemblance to that delight I have just described? Simply this. My first real memories of chocolate cake were of that very wartime version, complete with an icing the recipe for which came via "sister two," who was a student of the Yorkshire Training College of Housecraft in Leeds (known affectionately in those far-off days as the Y.T.C.H., or, less affectionately, the Dough School).

It wasn't until 1947, when my Liberal-minded father shipped me off to foreign parts, in fact to the École Hotelière in Lausanne, that I realized cooks actually used butter, sugar, and *real* block chocolate in their cooking. It was there I learned the mysteries of a *pâte à génoise* (cake mix with butter in it—and *melted* butter, *poured* in, to boot!) and a *pâte Savoie* (without butter— jelly roll or sponge cake mix to me in those days). Chocolate went into cakes and icings, butter creams, and sweet sauces in the form of melted chocolate no less.

I still cannot decide which chocolate cake I like best, the good old English version or my new version: Three Nut Chocolate Layer Cake.

It's good. It's very rich. It's expensive. But my goodness it's more-ish!

THREE-NUT CHOCOLATE LAYER CAKE

SPONGE

½ cup walnuts	¾ cup self-rising flour, sieved
6 large eggs	twice with 1 teaspoon
Scant cup superfine	baking powder and ½
granulated sugar	cup cocoa powder

APRICOT PUREE

12 ounces apricot jam	1 tablespoon kirsch, gin, or
	Scotch whisky

HAZELNUT CHOCOLATE BUTTER

2 cups hazelnuts
1½ cups confectioners' sugar
3 tablespoons cocoa powder

1 cup (2 sticks) sweet butter, softened
1 tablespoon kirsch, gin, or Scotch whisky

GANACHE

10 ounces unsweetened chocolate

10 fluid ounces light cream

TOPPING

12 marrons glacé

4 ounces chocolate-coated almonds (optional)

Makes 12 to14 servings

To make the sponge. Roughly crush the walnuts, spread them on a baking tray and toast in a preheated oven at 400°F for 4 to 6 minutes. Watch carefully and shake the tray gently several times to prevent them from burning or scorching at the edges, but make sure they are toasted thoroughly.

Using a hand rotary beater or electric whisk, whisk the eggs and sugar until they are light and fluffy and the whisk leaves a distinct trail.

Mix the toasted walnuts with the flour, baking powder, and cocoa powder, then fold into the egg mixture.

Pour the mixture into a round, lined 10-inch-by-4-inch-deep nonstick baking pan. Bake on the middle shelf of the oven at 400°F for 50 minutes to 1 hour, or until the cake begins to leave the sides of the pan and is firm to the touch.

Allow to cool for a few minutes, then turn onto a wire rack and remove the lining paper.

To make the apricot puree: Warm the apricot jam, then press through a fine meshed sieve. Cool slightly, then cover with plastic wrap to prevent a skin from forming. Just before using, whisk in the kirsch, gin, or whisky to make the puree.

To make the hazelnut chocolate butter: Toast and finely crush the hazelnuts as for walnuts in the sponge mixture, making sure to rub away the skins first. Sift the confectioners' sugar with the cocoa powder, and beat into the butter. Add the toasted hazelnuts and mix well. Just before spreading, whisk in the kirsch, gin, or whisky.

To make the ganache: Break up the chocolate and melt it gently with the cream in a double boiler over boiling water. Just as the mixture is about to set, whisk until it is light in color and pipeable.

To make up cake: When the sponge is completely cool, cut it into three equal layers. If the top layer of the sponge is not even, carefully shave off a little until it is level. Turn it onto a cake board and spread with half the apricot puree. Then spread half the hazelnut chocolate butter on top of this and repeat the process with the second layer of sponge, using the rest of the apricot puree and hazelnut chocolate butter. Using two icing knives, carefully lift the second layer of sponge and place it on top of the first.

Put the third sponge layer on top. Spread two-thirds of the ganache over the top and sides, using the last third to pipe a collar around the edge of the cake. Decorate the top with marrons glacé and split chocolate-coated almonds.

Serve at room temperature so that the butter cream is soft and the sponge moist.

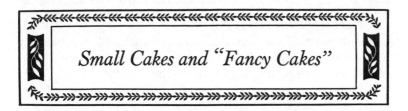

Small Cakes and "Fancy Cakes"

COCONUT MACAROONS

Almond macaroons (page 198) have been popular sweetmeats in England since medieval times. Coconut macaroons are a Victorian version of the original recipe using dried coconut in place of ground almonds. Made this way, children love them! Top with a sliver of candied cherry or tint them the palest pink with a drop or two of red food coloring.

Rice paper

2 egg whites

1 cup confectioners' sugar
3 cups dried coconut
Glacé cherries, sliced

Makes 12

Lay the rice paper on an ungreased baking sheet with the smooth side uppermost. Preheat the oven to 325°F.

Whisk the egg whites until stiff. Whisk in the sugar, then fold in the coconut. Pile the mixture in twelve pyramid shapes on the rice paper. Top each pyramid with a small slice of cherry.

Bake for 20 to 30 minutes, or until a pale golden brown.

Leave on the baking sheet until cold. Tear around the rice paper to separate.

COVENTRY GODCAKES

Long ago in Coventry, godparents gave their godchildren these cakes for good luck in the New Year.

One 12-ounce package frozen
    puff pastry, thawed

8 ounces mincemeat
Sugar, to sprinkle

Makes 12 cakes

Preheat the oven to 425°F.

Roll out half the pastry to a 12-by-8-inch oblong, then cut into 4-inch squares. Repeat with the other piece of pastry, then cut all the squares in half to form triangles.

Place a teaspoonful of mincemeat in the center of half the triangles. Dampen the edges of the pastry and place the remaining triangles on top, pressing to seal the edges.

Brush the tops of the triangles with water and sprinkle with sugar. Make 3 slits in the top of each. Bake on dampened baking sheets for 15 to 20 minutes, or until the cakes have risen and are golden brown. Let cool on a wire rack.

MERINGUES

The first reference to meringues is revealed to us under a different guise, where *"To Make Cream Cakes"* appears as a "receipt" on page 250 of Elizabeth Raffald's *The Experienced English Housekeeper* (1769 edition)—an indication that meringues were popular in Britain over two hundred years ago.

In the original recipe, the reader is bidden to "beat the whites of nine eggs to a stiff froth" before "shaking in softly" double-refined sugar. The meringues were then sandwiched together with a puree of fresh raspberries and whipped cream.

Today the meringue is still the most popular of the fancy cakes presented at teatime.

Light as air, crisp outside and aerated inside, meringues form the basis for many delicious cakes and desserts. Piped into cones or baskets or simply spooned onto lined baking sheets, they literally "dry out" in a very low oven. After cooking, meringues will keep almost indefinitely in an airtight container.

Serve filled with whipped cream and, if you like, fruit.

Here are some guidelines for success:

⋘ The whisk, or beaters, and the bowl must be absolutely clean, free of any grease, and dry.

⋘ Ideally, use egg whites from 2- to 3-day-old eggs, which should be at room temperature.

⋘ Be very careful when separating the eggs to avoid even the slightest trace of yolk in the whites.

≪← Use superfine sugar or equal quantities of superfine and confectioners' sugar.

≪← Line the baking sheet with wax or nonstick paper.

2 large egg whites   **2 to 3 cups superfine**
                                     granulated sugar

Makes 6 to 8 whole meringues (pairs)

Line a baking sheet. Preheat the oven to 250°F.

In a large bowl, whisk the egg whites until stiff. Sprinkle with half the sugar and continue to whisk until the texture is smooth and close and the whites stand in stiff peaks when the whisk is lifted out. Lightly fold in the remaining sugar with a metal spoon.

Using a metal spoon and a spatula, spoon into ovals on the baking sheet. Alternatively, spoon the meringue into a fabric icing bag fitted with a large star nozzle and pipe into cone shapes.

Bake for 3 to 4 hours, or until dry. Let cool completely on a wire rack before storing in an airtight container.

To serve, sandwich together with whipped cream shortly before serving.

CRISPY JAM HEARTS

Heart-shaped, sugar-encrusted flaky pastries sandwiched in pairs with whipped cream (vanilla-flavored) and homemade raspberry jam.

Makes about 16 to 18 hearts

Place a chilled 1-pound block of puff pastry with the fold toward you. Cut vertically into 3 portions. Wrap and return 2 to the refrigerator.

Keeping the fold toward you, lightly roll out the pastry to a 20-by-5-inch strip. Sprinkle generously with superfine granulated sugar. Fold the ends to the center and press down firmly. Sprinkle with more sugar and again fold the ends to the center.

Press and sprinkle with sugar again. Place the two folded portions together and press.

With a sharp knife, cut into ¼-inch slices across the folds of pastry—about 12 slices. Place the pastry well spaced on a moistened baking sheet and open them up *slightly*.

Preheat the oven to 425°F.

Bake for 10 minutes, then turn the cakes over and bake for a further 4 to 5 minutes. They are done when brown and crisp. Let cool on a wire rack.

Repeat with the remaining two-thirds of the pastry. When cooled, spread one with a spoonful of raspberry or strawberry jam, sandwich with whipped cream flavored with vanilla extract or vanilla sugar.

BRANDY SNAPS

½ cup (1 stick) sweet butter
   OR margarine
½ cup sugar
½ cup maple syrup
⅔ cup all-purpose flour

½ teaspoon mixed spice
   (equal amounts of
   nutmeg, cinnamon,
   cloves, allspice, and/or
   mace), optional
½ teaspoon ginger

Makes 20 to 30 snaps

Line two baking sheets with nonstick parchment. Preheat the oven to 350°F.

Put the butter, sugar, and syrup into a pan and heat gently until melted; remove from the heat.

Sift the flour, spice, and ginger together, then add to the melted mixture. Mix well and drop by teaspoonfuls onto the lined sheets, allowing plenty of room for the mixture to spread.

Bake for 7 to 10 minutes, or until bubbly and golden brown. Remove from the oven and as the mixture begins to firm up, roll each brandy snap quickly around a greased wooden spoon handle. Leave until set, then twist slightly and remove to a wire rack to cool.

If you like, these may be filled with whipped cream.

RASPBERRY-COCONUT SLICE

PASTRY

1½ cups flour   2 tablespoons butter
¼ pound lard

FILLING

1 cup (2 sticks) sweet butter,   3 large eggs, lightly beaten
    softened   1 tablespoon all-purpose flour
1 cup superfine granulated   1½ cups dried coconut
    sugar   12 ounces raspberry jam
Finely grated rind of 1 lemon

Makes 16 to 20 squares

Make up the pastry (see page 205). This will be sufficient to
line a jelly roll pan of approximately 14 by 9 inches and leave
enough pastry to make lattice strips to decorate the top of the
slice.

Preheat the oven to 375°F.

Cream the butter and sugar with the lemon rind. Beat in
the eggs slowly, then the flour. Mix in the coconut.

Spread the jam evenly over the bottom of the pastry-lined
tin. Spoon over the coconut mixture, spreading evenly. Arrange
lattice strips of pastry over the top.

Bake for 35 to 40 minutes. Let cool.

Cut into squares or fingers and store in layers in an airtight
tin with wax paper between the layers.

ALMOND AND QUINCE SLICES

PÂTE FROLLÉ

1½ cups all-purpose flour   1 teaspoon grated lemon rind
½ cup (1 stick) sweet butter,   1 egg
    slightly chilled   ¼ cup ground almonds, sifted
½ cup superfine granulated   2 to 3 tablespoons quince OR
    sugar   apricot jam

FRANGIPANE

½ cup (1 stick) sweet butter,   1 cup ground almonds
   softened   1 tablespoon all-purpose flour
1 scant cup superfine   ½ cup flaked blanched
   granulated sugar   almonds
2 eggs, at room temperature

FLAVORING

1 tablespoon dark rum   1 heaping teaspoon grated
1 tablespoon triple-strength   orange rind
   orange-flower water, or   1 tablespoon lemon juice or to
   to taste   taste
                               1 teaspoon lemon rind

Makes 16 to 18 pieces

Sift the flour onto the work surface. Make a well in the center and add the butter in small lumps, the sugar, lemon rind, and egg. Sprinkle the almonds over the top. Pinch the ingredients between your fingers to combine to a smooth paste. Chill well before using to line a rectangular 12-by-8-by-½-inch pan. Chill again before spreading on the quince or apricot jam.

Preheat the oven to 350°F.

To make the frangipane: Cream the butter and sugar together. Lightly beat the eggs, then beat into the creamed mixture by degrees. Add flavoring, or leave it plain, and fold in the ground almonds and the flour. Spread evenly over the jam base and sprinkle thickly with the flaked almonds.

Bake in the center of the oven for 45 minutes. Let cool in the pan on a wire rack. When cool cut into squares.

LADYFINGERS

3 large eggs, separated   Pinch of salt
1 teaspoon vanilla extract   ⅔ cup sifted cake flour
½ cup plus 1 tablespoon   Confectioners' sugar
   superfine granulated
   sugar

Makes about 36

Preheat the oven to 300°F.

Beat the egg yolks, vanilla, and ½ cup of sugar with a balloon whisk until the mixture ribbons or leaves a distinct trail when the whisk is drawn through the mixture.

In a separate bowl, beat the egg whites with the salt and the remaining tablespoon of sugar until they peak.

Mix the flour into the yolk mixture. Fold in the beaten egg whites. The mixture should be airy.

Fit a pastry bag with a plain ½-inch nozzle. Pipe four-inch lengths of the mixture onto lightly but evenly buttered and flour-dredged baking sheets.

Dust lightly with confectioners' sugar, brushing away any surplus on the sheet with a dry pastry brush.

Bake for 15 to 20 minutes. Remove with a spatula to a wire rack to cool. Dust with extra confectioners' sugar.

VARIATION

Take two ladyfingers and spread the first generously with sieved homemade raspberry or apricot jam.

Pipe on a column of sweetened whipped cream.

Lay the second biscuit on top.

ORANGE-BLOSSOM CAKES

¾ pound (3 sticks) sweet butter, softened

1¾ cups sugar

6 large eggs, beaten

2½ cups self-rising flour, sifted with 2 teaspoons baking powder

1 cup rice flour

4 teaspoons finely grated orange rind

½ cup fresh orange juice, strained

FOR THE BUTTER CREAM
(OR use sieved apricot jam OR marmalade)

½ cup (1 stick) sweet butter, softened

½ cup confectioners' sugar, sifted

2 tablespoons any orange-flavored liqueur, such as Cointreau or Grand Marnier

FOR THE MARZIPAN TOPPING

Jam OR jelly, sieved

1 pound marzipan

Confectioners' sugar

SCENTED FROSTING

Boiling water	1 teaspoon glycerine
½ cup confectioners' sugar,	2 teaspoons triple-strength
sifted into a bowl	orange-flavor water OR
1 drop of orange food coloring	orange liqueur

Makes 16 to 20

Preheat the oven to 325°F.

Butter an oblong baking pan approximately 10 by 8 by 3 inches) and line the bottom with buttered wax paper. Preheat the oven to 325°F.

Cream the butter and sugar together until light and fluffy. Beat in eggs gradually, adding a sprinkling of flour to prevent curdling.

Beat in the orange rind and a little of the juice.

Fold in the flours. Mix to a soft dropping consistency with more juice or cold water. Spoon into the prepared baking pan, leveling the top. Bake for 1¼ to 1½ hours, or until the cake is springy to the touch and shrinks from the sides of the pan.

Let cool in the pan for 10 minutes, then invert onto a wire rack. Remove the paper carefully. When cool, trim the browned sides off, and cut in half horizontally.

To make the butter cream: Beat all the ingredients to a smooth paste.

To assemble the cakes: Spread butter cream on the cut surface of the split cake. Cover with the other layer.

Cut the cake into 1½- to 2-inch squares, or, using a small circular template, cut into rounds with a long pointed knife. (Use all remains to make cake crumbs for some other dish.)

To cover with marzipan: Put the sieved jam in a bowl set in a pan of simmering water to warm and melt somewhat.

Knead the blocks of marzipan until completely pliable, working on a surface well dredged with confectioners' sugar. Use the heel of your hand to do this; it takes quite a bit of strength initially. Form into a rectangular block. Press and roll out into a sheet ⅛ inch thick.

Make a template of paper ⅛ inch deeper than the cut cakes and ⅛ inch longer than the circumference. Using the template and a ruler as a guide, cut out the same number of strips as you have cakes and trim them to size. Using the same template you used to cut the cakes, cut out the required number of circles.

Brush one side of the marzipan strips with jam or jelly. Wrap one around each cake. Brush one side of each circle and fit it inside the top, jam side down. Crimp the edges together. Dust with confectioners' sugar. Fill the indentation with a good teaspoon of scented frosting. Decorate with a nut or sugared flower.

To make the scented frosting: Add boiling water to mix all the ingredients to a smooth paste, using 1 tablespoonful to begin with. The final mixture should *just* flow.

BROWNIES

There are many different recipes for brownies, some more "cakey" than others. I prefer mine to be chewy, so that is what this recipe produces. They are also quite sweet, and all the better for that, too.

4 ounces unsweetened chocolate	1 teaspoon vanilla extract
¾ cup (1½ sticks) sweet butter	2 eggs, lightly beaten
1¾ cups superfine granulated sugar	⅔ cup self-rising flour, sifted with ½ teaspoon salt
	1½ cups roughly crushed walnuts

Makes about 16

Butter and line an 8-inch square cake pan. Preheat the oven to 350°F.

Soften the chocolate in a bowl set over hot water. Beat in the butter away from the heat. Beat in the sugar and vanilla extract. Beat in the eggs a little at a time. Quickly stir in the flour and salt. Fold in the nuts.

Spoon and spread evenly into the cake pan. Bake for 35 to 40 minutes or until firm to the touch. Allow to cool slightly and cut into squares. Store in an airtight tin. The brownies can also be frozen.

GOBBET CAKES

So called by me because they illustrate perfectly that eighteenth-century word for "a mouthful." Flavored with lemon and ginger, these little cakes, served with coffee after dinner, make a tasty and lightweight conclusion to a meal.

½ cup (1 stick) sweet butter, softened
½ cup superfine granulated sugar
Finely grated rind and juice of 1 lemon

¾ cup all-purpose flour
2 teaspoons baking powder
2 eggs
About 4 pieces preserved ginger

Makes 20 to 24

Preheat the oven to 375°F.

Cream the butter and sugar with the lemon rind. Sift the flour and baking powder together. Beat the eggs and gradually fold into the creamed mixture. Add the sifted flour, using a little lemon juice to arrive at a dropping consistency.

Butter tartlet pans well. (Use mini-tartlet tins if you have them.) Put teaspoonfuls of the mixture into the pans with a slice of ginger on top. Bake for 12 to 15 minutes, or until firm when pressed with a fingertip.

MAID-OF-HONOR TARTS

These famous cheesecakes, a specialty of Kew, Surrey, are made from a sixteenth-century recipe. This one is from Hampton Court Palace. They were said to have been a favorite delicacy of Anne Boleyn, the name being given to them by Henry VIII when he saw her eating them while she was a maid of honor to Catherine of Aragon, Henry's first wife.

2½ cups raw milk (not pasteurized)
1 teaspoon rennet
Pinch of salt
½ cup (1 stick) sweet butter
2 egg yolks
2 teaspoons brandy
1 tablespoon slivered almonds

A little sugar
A little cinnamon
Grated rind and juice of ½ lemon
8 ounces Puff Pastry (see page 205)
Dried currants, to decorate

Makes 12 to 16

Preheat the oven to 425°F.

Warm the milk to body temperature. Add the rennet and the salt. When the curds have set, strain through a fine muslin overnight. Rub the curds through a sieve along with the butter. Beat the egg yolks to a froth with the brandy. Add to the curds.

Blanch the almonds and add them to the curds along with a little sugar and cinnamon. Add the lemon rind and juice.

Line tart pans with the puff pastry. Fill them with the mixture and sprinkle with the currants. Bake for 20 to 25 minutes, or until well risen and golden brown. Remove from the pans and cool on a wire rack. Serve warm rather than cold.

BAKEWELL TART

In the Derbyshire village of Bakewell—hard by Chatsworth House, the palatial country seat of the duke and duchess of Devonshire—these are made small and are referred to as Bakewell puddings. Whatever you call them, they are delicious cut into slim slices for afternoon tea.

¾ cup (1½ sticks) butter,
    softened
¾ cup sugar
Fincly grated rind and
    strained juice of 4 lemons
4 eggs

2½ cups fresh white bread
    crumbs
1 prebaked Rich Short-crust
    Pieshell (page 192)
Confectioners' sugar, to
    dredge
Whipped cream (optional)

Serves 6 to 8

Preheat the oven to 350°F.

Beat together the butter and sugar until soft and fluffy. Beat in the lemon rind, then the eggs, one at a time. Gradually beat in the lemon juice and fold in the bread crumbs. The mixture will be quite soft.

Spoon into the prebaked pieshell and smooth the top. Stand on a baking sheet to cope with possible spillage when cooking. Bake for about 1 hour, or until the filling is firm and a rich golden brown.

Serve at room temperature, well dredged with confectioners' sugar and with whipped cream if you like.

PRE-BAKED PIESHELLS
1 recipe of Rich Short-Crust Pastry (page 205)

Two 9-inch pieshells

Chill for 30 minutes after rolling out and lining the pie plates. Line with wax paper and fill with baking beans (or crushed foil). Preheat the oven to 425°F for 10 minutes. Reduce oven temperature to 375° and remove beans and paper. Continue baking for about 20 minutes, or until the pastry looks dry and starts to brown.

Let cool before filling.

Baked shells freeze well. Defrost before adding filling.

CHERRY WHIRLS

1 cup (2 sticks) sweet butter, softened	1 teaspoon vanilla extract
⅓ cup confectioners' sugar, sifted	1 cup all-purpose flour, sifted
	8 to 9 glacé cherries, halved

Makes 16 to 18

Preheat the oven to 325°F.

Cream the butter until it is light and soft. Add the confectioners' sugar and vanilla and beat until smooth, then stir in the flour.

Transfer the mixture to a large piping bag fitted with a large star nozzle. Pipe 16 to 18 fairly small whirls onto two greased baking sheets and top each one with half a cherry. Bake in the center of the oven for 20 minutes, or until they have turned a pale gold.

Leave on the baking sheet for 5 minutes before transferring carefully to a wire rack. Store in an airtight container when cold.

CHOCOLATE ÉCLAIRS

1 recipe Choux Pastry (page 206)

Pipe into 3-inch-long "tubes." Bake as instructed. Let cool.

Split open and fill with either of the following creams and frostings.

Makes 12 to 16 éclairs

CREAM FILLING I

2½ cups heavy cream   ⅓ cup liqueur of your choice
⅓ cup sugar   OR 2 teaspoons vanilla
        extract

Whip all the ingredients together to piping consistency. Transfer the cream to a pastry bag fitted with a ½-inch star nozzle. Pipe a thick band of cream on the base of the split éclair. Dip each top into frosting and place on top of the cream.

CREAM FILLING II (ENGLISH CUSTARD CREAM)

6 large egg yolks   2 cups whole milk OR half
½ cup sugar   and half
2 teaspoons vanilla extract   4 tablespoons (½ stick) sweet
½ cup sifted all-purpose flour   butter, softened

In a bowl, cream the egg yolks and sugar until light and fluffy. Add the vanilla extract. Gradually beat in the flour.

Bring the milk or half and half to a boil, and pour gradually over the creamed mixture, stirring, slowly at first, with a wire balloon whisk. As you add the milk, change to a more rapid whisking movement and whisk until smooth.

Return the pan to low heat and, whisking all the time, allow the custard cream to boil. It should be thick enough to pipe, but not stiff. Beat in the butter.

Let cool; it will thicken further.

Cover with plastic wrap to prevent a skin from forming. When cold, pipe onto éclairs or choux pastry buns.

CHOCOLATE ICING OR FROSTING (I)

6 ounces semisweet chocolate,   ¾ cup heavy cream
    broken up

Melt the chocolate along with the cream in a bowl over simmering water, whisking until smooth.

CHOCOLATE FROSTING (II)

¾ cup confectioners' sugar   A little boiling water
¼ cup cocoa powder   2 drops vanilla extract

Sift the two dry ingredients into a bowl. Add spoonfuls of boiling water until you have a spreadable consistency, beating well after each addition. Stir in the vanilla.

CREAM PUFFS

Makes 16 to 20

Allow 3 to 4 inches between each piped-out mound of Choux Pastry (page 206).

Lightly butter a 2½-inch individual brioche mold and place over each mound. Bake as instructed. Do not be tempted to lift the mold for the first 25 minutes of baking.

The puffs should be quite dried out. They will have crazed tops. Let cool on a wire rack.

Split and fill each puff with plenty of lightly sweetened, liqueur-flavored whipped cream.

Dust well with confectioners' sugar.

RICH ECCLES CAKES

Eccles cakes should always be served warm with clotted cream or rum butter. And that is advice from a man from the north of England! If you have great patience, as with mince pies, Eccles cakes are extra special when made in miniature, 2 inches in diameter when finished.

FILLING

1 cup seedless muscatel raisins, roughly chopped	⅓ cup sweet butter, softened
1 cup dried currants	⅓ cup light brown sugar
3 tablespoons rum OR whisky	Grated rind and juice of 1 lemon
⅓ cup ground almonds	½ teaspoon cinnamon

SUGAR GLAZE

2 tablespoons water	⅓ cup superfine granulated sugar

PASTRY
1 pound Puff Pastry (page 205)

Makes 10 to 14

Soak the raisins and currants in the rum or whisky over-night. Mix with the rest of the filling ingredients.

Make the sugar glaze by bringing the water and sugar to a boil. Let cool. (The syrup should be clear and sticky, not wet.)

Preheat the oven to 425°F.

Roll out the pastry evenly into one large sheet. Using a saucer as a template, cut out 4-to-5-inch circles. Just how many you get will depend on how thin you roll the pastry.

Put a spoonful of the filling mixture into the center of each circle. Gather the pastry over the mixture and pinch together to seal the edges.

Invert the cakes onto a buttered baking sheet. Lightly press them flat, but don't squash them totally. Brush with a little of the sugar glaze.

Bake for 15 minutes. Reduce the oven temperature to 350°F and bake 20 minutes longer, or until crisp and browned. Cool on a wire rack.

Brush the finished cakes with more syrup to glaze.

GINGER COOKIES

3¼ cups all-purpose flour
½ teaspoon baking soda
1 tablespoon ginger
½ teaspoon salt

1 cup molasses
¼ cup vegetable shortening
4 tablespoons (½ stick) sweet
    butter

Makes 30 to 40

Lightly butter a baking sheet. Preheat the oven to 350°F. Sift the dry ingredients together.

In a saucepan, heat the syrup or molasses until hot and runny. Add the fats and mix until melted. Scrape into a bowl. Mix in the dry ingredients to form a dough. Chill in the refrigerator for 1 hour.

Roll out in manageable batches to ¼ inch thick. Cut out with a round cookie cutter.

Bake for 8 to 10 minutes.

Let the cookies cool on a wire rack.

ORANGE COOKIES

½ cup (1 stick) butter,
    softened
1 cup sugar
2 egg yolks
1 tablespoon orange juice
Grated rind of ½ orange

1½ cups all-purpose flour
¼ teaspoon salt
1 teaspoon baking powder
1 tablespoon sweet butter,
    melted

Makes 20 to 24

Preheat the oven to 375°F.

Cream the butter. Beat in the sugar, egg yolks, orange juice, and grated rind. Sift together the flour, salt, and baking powder and add to the butter mixture; mix well. Chill in refrigerator for 3 or 4 hours.

Roll by teaspoonsful into small balls. Place on a greased baking sheet, flatten slightly, and bake for 8 to 10 minutes. Cool on a wire rack and brush lightly with melted butter while the cookies are still warm.

AVOLA STICKS

Avola, in southern Sicily, produces the best almonds, hence the name of these cookies.

1¼ cups (2½ sticks) sweet butter
1½ cups all-purpose flour
1¾ cups ground almonds, sifted

1 generous cup granulated sugar
2 eggs, lightly beaten

Makes 30 to 40

Preheat the oven to 325°F.

Rub the butter into the flour. Toss in the ground almonds and sugar, mixing thoroughly.

Mix in the eggs and gather to a soft paste.

Butter a baking sheet. Fit an 8-point "rope" nozzle or a plain ½-inch nozzle into a pastry bag. Pipe out "sticks" about 3 inches long (quite hard work for a small hand, so drag in the men!).

Bake for 30 minutes, or until golden brown. Let cool on a wire rack.

ALMOND PETTICOAT TAILS

These crisp shortbread biscuits take their name from the paneled hoops of ladies' skirts.

1 heaping cup all-purpose flour	½ cup (1 stick) sweet butter
4 tablespoons rice flour	1 egg white, beaten
4 tablespoons superfine granulated sugar plus more for dusting	2 tablespoons flaked or slivered almonds

Makes 8 segments

Preheat the oven to 300°F.

Sift the flour, rice flour, and sugar together onto a work surface.

Cut the butter into cubes and rub it in. Knead lightly and form into a ball. Flatten and roll lightly into an 8-inch circle. Place on a buttered baking sheet.

Using a knife, divide the circle into 8 even segments without cutting all the way through. Brush with the beaten egg white. Sprinkle with a little sugar and the almonds. Press lightly with the palm of your hand.

Bake for 40 to 45 minutes. Let cool for a little while before cutting through to separate the cookies.

Store, as with other cookies and macaroons, in an airtight tin. If you want to freeze the shortbread, do so before it is baked.

ALMOND MACAROONS

1 generous cup superfine granulated sugar	2 egg whites
1 cup ground almonds, sifted	Rice paper
2 heaping teaspoons rice flour	Split almonds, to decorate

Makes 18 to 20

Preheat the oven to 325°F.

Mix together the sugar, ground almonds, and rice flour. Stir in the *unbeaten* egg whites.

Line a baking sheet with rice paper, then either spoon or pipe the mixture onto the paper. Place a split almond in the center of each macaroon.

Bake for 20 to 25 minutes, or until golden brown. Let cool on a wire rack.

FLAPJACKS

⅔ cup (1¾ sticks) sweet
   butter
¼ cup sugar

2½ tablespoons molasses
2 cups rolled oats
Pinch of salt

Makes about 16 to 20 flapjacks

Grease an 8-inch square baking pan. Preheat the oven to 375°F.

Beat the butter and sugar together until smooth. Heat the syrup or molasses in a saucepan; stir into the butter and sugar, then add the oats and salt and mix well.

Spread the mixture into the prepared pan, pressing well into the corners and flattening the top.

Bake for 30 to 40 minutes, or until crisp and golden brown. Mark into bars immediately upon removal from the oven.

Leave in the pan to cool before removing and breaking into bars.

TILE COOKIES

⅓ cup sweet butter
⅓ cup superfine granulated
   sugar
2 egg whites

½ cup all-purpose flour
Pinch of salt
Grated rind of ½ lemon OR
   1 teaspoon vanilla extract

Makes 16 to 20 cookies

Line 2 baking sheets with nonstick parchment paper. Preheat the oven to 375°F.

Soften the butter in a bowl over hot water but do not let it get oily. Beat lightly with a fork, gradually adding the sugar, until very light and fluffy. Beat in the egg whites a little at a time.

Sift the flour and salt into a bowl and fold gently into the batter. Flavor with lemon rind or vanilla extract.

Put into a pastry bag fitted with a ½-inch nozzle and pipe 2-inch lengths onto the prepared baking sheets, allowing room for the cookies to spread. Bake for 10 minutes, or until golden brown around the edges.

While the tiles are still warm, carefully remove from the baking sheets and lay over a greased rolling pin or wine bottle to make them curl. Leave until cold.

RICH SHORTBREAD

1½ cups all-purpose flour	5 to 6 tablespoons sugar
½ cup (1 stick) sweet butter, cubed	1 large egg yolk, lightly beaten

Makes 36

Lightly butter an 8-inch square nonstick baking pan.
Preheat the oven to 350°F.
Rub the flour into the butter until sandlike in texture. Toss in 4 tablespoons of the sugar, mixing well.
With a fork, mix in the yolk to form a rough, dryish paste.
Press the mixture evenly into the pan. Prick all over in rows at ¼-inch intervals.
Sprinkle with the remaining 1 to 2 tablespoons sugar.
Bake for 20 minutes. Reduce the oven temperature to 200° and continue baking for 50 minutes to 1 hour, or until golden brown.
Cut into 1-by-2-inch fingers while still warm. Leave to cool completely in the pan.
Shortbread stores well in an airtight tin; it also freezes for up to 6 months.

APRICOT SHORTCAKES

1½ cups all-purpose flour	About ⅓ cup superfine granulated sugar
¾ cup (1½ sticks) sweet butter	About 5 tablespoons apricot jam
⅓ cup rice flour	Extra jam to decorate

Makes about 20 to 30 shortcakes

Preheat the oven to 375°F.
Sift the flour into a bowl and rub in the butter until the

mixture resembles fine bread crumbs. Add the rice flour and ⅓ cup sugar and mix together. Put 5 tablespoons jam in the center of the mixture and work into a smooth dough.

Roll out on a floured board to about ¾ inch thick. Cut into fancy shapes. Place on 1 large or 2 small greased baking sheets. Make a small hollow in the center of each biscuit with a thimble and put a little more jam in each hole.

Bake for about 20 minutes. Let cool on a wire rack and, when the shortcakes are cold, dust with additional sugar.

COCONUT COOKIES

⅓ cup sweet butter, softened
½ cup superfine granulated
   sugar

1 egg
¾ cup all-purpose flour
⅓ cup dried coconut

Makes 20 to 24

Preheat the oven to 325°F.

Cream the butter and sugar together until light and fluffy. Beat in the egg, then fold in the flour and coconut. Drop by the teaspoonful onto greased baking sheets and bake for 10 to 15 minutes. Let cool on a wire rack.

WALNUT SHORTBREAD

This pastry is soft and must be handled with care. It can be made in a food processor using the all-in-one method.

2¼ cups cake flour
1 cup finely crushed walnuts
1½ cups (3 sticks) sweet
   butter, softened

Generous ½ cup
   confectioners' sugar
2 small egg yolks
1 teaspoon vanilla extract

Makes 16 to 20

Preheat the oven to 400°F.

Sift the flour and crushed nuts together into a bowl. Make a well in the center. Mix the butter to a paste with the sugar and egg yolks and place in the well. Gradually draw the flour

into the center and mix into the butter, forming a dough. Roll
out to ⅛ inch. Cut into 2-inch circles or squares.

Bake for 8 to 10 minutes in a heavy square or oblong pan.
Let cool on a wire rack. Cut into square biscuits.

PALM COOKIES

Traditionally served on Palm Sunday.

1 pound Puff Pastry,   **Sugar**
    commercial brand or
    homemade (page 205)

Makes 24 to 30

Roll the pastry into an oblong 8 inches wide and no more
than ⅛ inch thick. Trim to an even shape.

Dredge the pastry evenly and well with a $\frac{1}{16}$-inch coating
of sugar. Fold each long side to the center, that is, left to middle;
right to middle. Press well together. Cut crosswise into ⅜-inch
slices.

Wet a baking sheet.

Arrange the biscuits 3 to 4 inches apart, cut side up. Chill
in the refrigerator for 1 hour.

Preheat the oven to 450°F.

Bake for 5 to 6 minutes. Turn the cookies over, sprinkle
with more sugar, and return to the oven for 5 to 6 minutes more,
or until they have caramelized.

Remove immediately to a wire rack to cool.

Note: *Do not be tempted to touch the sticky, hot caramel with
your fingers. Work with a metal spatula and a dinner fork. If
the cookies stick—and you have to work quickly when turning
them—return the sheet to the oven for a minute or so.*

SAND COOKIES

Known in France as *sablés*.

¾ cup (1½ sticks) sweet   2 egg yolks
    butter, softened   1 teaspoon vanilla extract
⅔ cup sugar   2 cups cake flour

FOR THE GLAZE
1 egg yolk, mixed with 2 teaspoons cold water

Makes 24 to 30

In a food processor or with an electric mixer, cream the butter and sugar. Add the egg yolks and vanilla extract, and mix well. Add half the flour and mix in. Add the remaining flour, stopping the machine as soon as it is incorporated.

Lightly flour a sheet of nonstick plastic wrap. Form the dough into one or two 3-inch pipes, rolling it to an even shape.

Chill in the refrigerator for one hour. Preheat the oven to 350°F.

Cut the dough into ⅛ inch disks and arrange on well buttered baking sheets. Brush each cookie with a little of the glaze and bake for 8 to 10 minutes; or until firm and light golden brown.

Remove to a wire rack to cool.

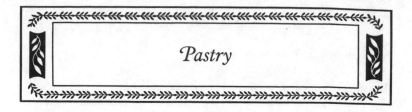

Pastry

English cookery embraces many different types of pastries, from the simplest short crust through rich melt-in-the-mouth sweetened flan pastry and the more complicated flaky varieties.

Basic short-crust pastry is the most widely used as a base for both sweet and savory recipes. Rich short-crust pastry has a higher proportion of fat to flour with sugar included, and eggs are used as the liquid ingredient. Roll slightly thicker than basic short-crust pastry. Puff pastry is the richest, takes longer to make, and also takes a little practice to get perfect. It rises spectacularly into lots of flaky layers and is used for such recipes as vol-au-vents or mille-feuilles.

Choux pastry uses a completely different method, first cooking on the stove before shaping and baking it. It is used for such cakes as éclairs and profiteroles.

Here are some guidelines for success

⫷ Always make the pastry in a cool, dry atmosphere.

⫷ Handle the pastry as little as possible. Use only the fingertips if rubbing in by hand, or use a pastry blender or processor.

⫷ Use ice water for mixing.

⫷ If making in a food processor, do use the specified amount of water.

⫷ Use very little flour to roll out on. Use a pastry cloth and a stockinette cover on the rolling pin.

⫷ Roll the pastry lightly, rotating it regularly to keep an even shape.

⫷ Avoid stretching the pastry unnecessarily, as it will only shrink back while baking, thus spoiling the finished shape.

⫷ If possible, chill the pastry between mixing and rolling out. This allows the gluten content of the flour to relax.

SHORT-CRUST PASTRY

2 cups all-purpose flour   4 tablespoons (½ stick) butter
½ teaspoon salt   3 tablespoons water
¼ cup lard

Sift the flour and salt together into a large bowl. With your fingertips or a pastry blender, rub in the fats until the mixture resembles fine bread crumbs.

Sprinkle the water over the flour and stir together with a fork. Gather into a ball with floured fingertips and knead lightly for a few seconds, to give a firm, smooth dough. Slip into a plastic bag and chill in the refrigerator for at least 30 minutes.

Roll out on a lightly floured board, rolling evenly in one direction only, turning the pastry around occasionally but not turning it over. Avoid unnecessary pulling or stretching.

Roll to about ⅛ inch thickness.

RICH SHORT-CRUST PASTRY

2 cups all-purpose flour   ¾ cup (1½ sticks) sweet
3 tablespoons superfine   butter
    granulated sugar   1 egg plus 1 egg yolk
½ teaspoon salt

Sift the flour, sugar and salt together into a large bowl.

With your fingertips or a pastry blender, rub in the butter until the mixture resembles fine bread crumbs.

Beat together the egg and the yolk, then stir into the mixture with a fork. With floured fingers, collect into a ball and knead lightly and briefly to give a smooth, firm dough.

Slip the pastry into a floured plastic bag and chill in the refrigerator for 30 minutes.

Lightly dredge a work surface with flour and roll the pastry out to the desired shape and thickness.

PUFF PASTRY

2 cups all-purpose flour   ½ cup water
1 teaspoon salt   1 tablespoon lemon juice
1 cup (2 sticks) sweet butter

Mix the flour and salt.

Soften the butter on a plate with an icing knife, then rub 2 tablespoons into the flour. Mix to a soft, pliable dough with the water and lemon juice. Turn out onto a floured board and knead lightly until smooth.

Shape the remaining butter into a 6-by-3-inch oblong. Roll the pastry into a 6-inch square. Place the butter on one side, folding over the pastry to enclose it. Press the edges to seal.

Turn the pastry so that the fold is to the side, then roll out to a 5-by-15-inch rectangle. Fold the bottom third up and the top third down and seal the edges by pressing lightly with the rolling pin.

Slip into a plastic bag and refrigerate for 20 minutes. Place the pastry with the fold to one side and repeat the above sequence, including chilling. Repeat 5 times.

After the final chilling, shape the pastry as required and continue with the individual recipe.

CHOUX PASTRY

This is a light, crisp pastry that trebles in size when cooked due to the air trapped inside. Following are some guidelines for success:

≪ Add all the flour at once.

≪ Beat the mixture over the heat until it leaves the sides of the pan cleanly and forms a ball.

≪ Add the eggs gradually and beat very thoroughly until the mixture has a sheen.

≪ Chill the mixture in the piping bag for about 30 minutes to make it handle more easily.

≪ Dampen the baking sheets before piping to help to prevent sticking.

≪ Do not open the oven door during baking.

≪ Split open the baked pastry to let out any steam.

½ cup (1 stick) sweet butter   ½ cup all-purpose flour, sifted
½ cup water   2 eggs, beaten

Put the butter and water into a medium-size pan and heat gently until the butter has melted, then bring to a boil. Remove from the heat.

Tip in all the flour. Beat thoroughly. Return the pan to the heat and beat until the mixture forms a ball.

Remove from the heat and let cool for a minute or two. Gradually beat in the eggs to give a piping consistency. Beat vigorously to trap as much air as possible; beat until the mixture is shiny.

Spoon the dough into a piping bag fitted with a ½-inch icing pipe. Chill in the refrigerator for 30 minutes.

JAM TARTS

1 recipe Rich Short-Crust   12 to 16 ounces raspberry jam
  Pastry (page 205)

Makes about 30 individual tarts

Butter 30 individual shallow tart pans. Preheat the oven to 400°F.

Roll out the pastry on a lightly floured board to approximately ¼ inch thick.

Using a 2¾-inch fluted cutter, cut the pastry into circles and place in the prepared tart pans.

Spoon two-thirds full with jam or Lemon Cheese (page 237).

Bake for approximately 15 minutes, or until pastry is a pale golden brown.

Let cool on a wire rack.

FRUIT TURNOVERS

1 recipe Rich Short-Crust   16 ounces apple pie filling oʀ
  Pastry (page 205)   mincemeat

Makes about 20

Preheat the oven to 400°F.

Cut the pastry into circles about 3 inches in diameter, using a coffee saucer as a template.

Spoon fruit pie filling or mincemeat onto one side of each circle. Brush the edges with lightly beaten egg and fold over. Pinch the edges together and place on a baking sheet.

Brush with egg and sprinkle with sugar. Slash the tops 2 or 3 times with a sharp knife to allow steam to escape.

Bake for about 20 to 25 minutes, or until the pastry is a rich golden brown. Serve warm or cold.

APPLE PASTY

1½ pounds cooking apples,
   peeled, cored, and sliced
5 tablespoons sugar
1 tablespoon sweet butter

1 teaspoon grated lemon rind
3 to 4 tablespoons water
1 pound Short-Crust Pastry
   (page 205)

Makes 12 to 16

Put the apples, 4 tablespoons of the sugar, butter, lemon rind, and water in a saucepan. Cook, covered, over low heat until soft. Mash to a puree with a fork while still warm. Let cool. Preheat the oven to 400°F.

Roll out the pastry on a lightly floured work surface to a 12-inch square.

Spread the apple puree to within ½ inch of the edge of half the pastry. Brush the exposed edges of the pastry with cold water and then fold the pastry over the filling and pinch the edges together.

Slide the pastry onto a greased baking sheet. Brush the top with cold water and cut two or three 1-inch slits in the top of the pastry. Sprinkle with the remaining tablespoon of sugar.

Bake for 20 to 25 minutes, or until golden brown. Let cool on a wire rack. Then cut into fingers.

JAM PASTY

1 pound Rich Short-Crust
   Pastry (page 205)

1 pound raspberry or
   strawberry jam

Makes 12 to 16

Follow the directions for Apple Pasty, but bake for only about 20 minutes.

CURRANT AND MINT PASTY

1 pound Short-Crust Pastry
    (page 205)
1½ cups dried currants,
    soaked in ¼ cup Scotch
    whisky

¼ cup plus 1 tablespoon
    sugar
4 tablespoons (½ stick) sweet
    butter
12 mint leaves, shredded

Makes 12 to 16

Roll out the pastry on a lightly floured work surface to a 12-inch square. Preheat the oven to 400°F.

Spread the currants to within ½ inch of the edge of half the pastry. Sprinkle with the ¼ cup sugar. Put dabs of the butter over the currants and sprinkle the mint leaves over all.

Brush the exposed edges of the pastry with cold water and then fold the pastry over the filling and pinch the edges together.

Slide the pastry onto a greased baking sheet. Brush the top with cold water and cut two or three 1-inch slits in the top of the pastry. Sprinkle with the remaining tablespoon of sugar.

Bake for 20 to 25 minutes, or until golden brown. Let cool on a wire rack. Then cut into fingers.

CHESHIRE SOULING CAKE

Souling cake was traditionally made for the custom of Hodening, which took place on All Souls' Day, 2 or 3 November. A band went through the streets, accompanied by the "Soulers," and children went from house to house singing this song:

> Soul! Soul! for a Soul Cake!
> I pray you good missis, a Soul Cake,
> An apple, a plum, a pear or cherry,
> Or any good thing to make us all merry.
> One for Peter and two for Paul,
> Three for Him that made us all.

3 cups all-purpose flour	1 cup (2 sticks) margarine OR
½ teaspoon cinnamon	sweet butter
½ teaspoon allspice	1 egg
Pinch of nutmeg	1½ teaspoons red wine
1 cup sugar	vinegar

Preheat the oven to 350°F.

Mix the dry ingredients. Rub in the fat. Drop in the egg and add the vinegar. Knead until soft. Roll out to ¼ inch thick, cut into rounds with a 3-inch round or fluted cookie cutter, bake for 15 to 20 minutes, or until golden brown.

Let cool on a wire rack.

LARDY CAKE

"Shaley cake," as it is known in Wiltshire, is a flaky, rich, spicy, fruited cake that can also be eaten hot as a pudding. If it has lost its freshness, refresh in a medium oven for 10 minutes. Hampshire and Wiltshire are renowned for their lardy cakes, as are Yorkshire and Lancashire.

1 tablespoon active dry yeast	4 tablespoons (½ stick) sweet
OR ½ ounce fresh	butter, flaked
1 tablespoon sugar	¾ cup superfine granulated
1⅓ cups warm water	sugar
3 cups white bread flour	1 teaspoon allspice
2 teaspoons salt	½ cup yellow raisins OR
Vegetable oil	dried currants
	4 tablespoons lard

Makes 8 to 12 slices

Grease a 10-by-8-inch cake pan.

Mix the yeast, sugar, and the warm water in a small bowl and leave in a warm place for 10 minutes, or until frothy.

Sift the flour and salt together into a large bowl. Stir in the yeast liquid and 1 tablespoon of the oil. Mix to a soft dough. Knead on a lightly floured surface for 5 minutes.

Place in a lightly oiled plastic bag and leave in a warm place for 1 to 1½ hours, or until doubled in size. Knead again for 5 minutes.

Roll out to an oblong ¼ inch thick. Cover two-thirds of the dough with the butter flakes and sprinkle with 3 tablespoons superfine sugar, half the allspice and the raisins or currants. Fold and roll out as for Puff Pastry (see page 205); repeat with the lard, 3 more tablespoons superfine sugar, and the remaining mixed spice and fruit.

Fold and roll again. Fold and place in the prepared pan. Return to the oiled plastic bag and leave to rise in a warm place until doubled in size, about 1 hour. Preheat the oven to 425°F.

Brush with a little of the oil and sprinkle with the remaining superfine sugar. With a sharp knife, mark a crisscross pattern on top. Bake for about 30 minutes, or until a rich golden brown.

Turn out onto a wire rack and let cool. Serve either warm or cold.

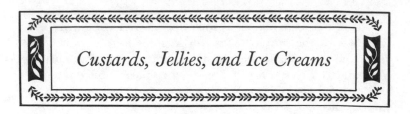

Custards, Jellies, and Ice Creams

STRAWBERRIES AND CREAM

Where else in the world do you get such fine, luscious piquant strawberries than in England?

Strawberries and cream are *de rigueur* at Wimbledon, Glyndebourne, Ascot, Stratford, Putney, and Henley. They appear at every tea party in the land, from church social to that "cuppa" snatched in your own backyard.

There are endless arguments as to what is served with them. Let us take the "original" way first.

Unhulled strawberries are presented on a silver-plated strawberry dish, each leafy hull pointing outward. Along with this is passed a jug of thick, thick, yellow, buttery cream as can only be found in the English countryside.

A woven silver basket lined in blue Bristol glass contains the "castor" sugar (which name was given in the eighteenth century to the fine-grained sugar, grated from the sugar loaf and filled into a silver sugar dredger or "caster" with an elegant domed pierced top).

Strawberries, a blob of cream alongside, and a spoonful of sugar are served onto small glass plates.

Each person then takes hold of a strawberry by the hull, dips it first into the rich, thick cream, then into the sugar, before popping it, whole, into the mouth, where, with the help of the fingers, the hull is pulled away and discarded to the side of the plate. There you have it!

I can assure you this is the most sensual way of eating strawberries and cream.

For those who are unsure whether they can pull this off with elegant aplomb, small crystal bowls are the next best thing, using a fine dessertspoon and fork as the means of transporting fruit, sugar, and cream to their resting-place in the mouth with some semblance of dignity!

Then there are those who like pepper on strawberries and

212

no cream. Try it. The complement is wonderful, particularly with a squeeze of lemon juice.

Or again, some strange people take a little salt; but, to each his own!

An exotic and pretty wonderful way of serving strawberries on a hot summer's afternoon, while sipping a glass of champagne, perhaps on the lawns at Glyndebourne—England's opera in a hayfield—is to serve them halved or quartered, their cut faces bathed in kirsch before masking them in a fresh, tangy Raspberry Sauce (below).

RASPBERRY SAUCE

1 pint (2 cups) fresh
    raspberries

¼ cup confectioners' sugar
Juice of ½ lemon

Makes about 6 servings

Mix all these together, then press and rub the fruit through a fine meshed sieve. Chill well.

STRAWBERRY CHAMPAGNE CUP FOR GLYNDEBOURNE (OR TANGLEWOOD!)

1 bottle pink champagne, well
    chilled
1 sugar cube per glass, rubbed
    over an orange to absorb
    the oil
1 drop per glass of Angostura
    bitters
1 small tot per glass curaçao
Small twists of orange zest

1 strawberry per glass,
    quartered
1 well-shaped strawberry per
    glass, nicked with a knife
    and slipped over the rim
    of the glass
Extra unhulled strawberries,
    to dunk!

Makes 6 servings

RASPBERRIES AND CREAM

At one time these had a very short season, and many people still rate them above strawberries for excellence of flavor. Today in Britain they are available for much longer periods from the raspberry gardens in Scotland. They also freeze well.

For their first appearance, they must be served traditionally with fresh cream and sugar. Then you can ring the changes, either by complementing them with their own sauce (page 213) or with the following Red-Currant-Liqueur Sauce. Whichever way you choose, the option is yours as to whether you serve cool heavy cream—which is such an excellent complement—or not.

RASPBERRIES WITH
RED-CURRANT-LIQUEUR SAUCE

4 piled cups raspberries
(frozen ones are *almost*
perfect)
2 cups red currants, picked
over

2 tablespoons sugar
2 tablespoons water
2 tablespoons kirsch or
eau de vie de framboise
½ cup flaked (shaved)
blanched almonds

Makes 4 to 6 servings

Do *not* rinse the raspberries! Just pick them over.

Put the currants, sugar, and water into a heavy-bottomed saucepan. Shake and stir over low heat until the juices draw. Simmer until tender. Let cool somewhat before pressing and rubbing through a fine-meshed sieve. Stir in the liqueur.

Chill well.

Dribble the sauce over the raspberries 1 hour before serving. Serve well chilled, garnished with the flaked almonds.

CUSTARDS, JELLIES AND CREAMS

It was customary in Georgian England to go to the Assembly Rooms, not only in the evenings when possibly a "Rout"* was taking place, but also in the morning after visiting your milliner, haberdasher, or glove maker.

People went there to parade, promenade, and pirouette; to see and be seen and indulge in that wonderful eighteenth-century social habit—gossip!

"Subtleties," and "conceited" dishes, such as creams, jellies, and ices, would be served.

Special glasses were blown to receive these delicacies: the V-shaped syllabub glass, the handleless jelly glass, and the miniature custard cup with its tiny looped handle. All would be displayed on flat, broad, round, single-footed glass stands or tazzas, sometimes today mistaken for cakestands when, in fact, they were, and still are when you can find one, syllabub stands.

The delightful habit crossed the century, and even in late Victorian times these dishes were still being presented—but now at the afternoon tea table.

Sherry or small wineglasses or christening cups make perfect substitutes for "the real thing." Present a selection of these delicacies on a silver salver or a glass platter.

* A "rout" was an assembly or party, derived from the word *root*, "to dig out (of bed or of the house)."

CUSTARD CUPS

Custard, which even the French have the grace to call crème à l'anglaise, or English cream, is as old as the Conqueror!—and makes a delightful "subtlety" (as such confections were called in seventeenth- and eighteenth-century England) at teatime. Custards were usually aromatized delicately with rose- or orange-flower water, cowslips, or violets!

8 large egg yolks	2 tablespoons orange- OR
1 teaspoon cornstarch	rose-flower water OR
4 tablespoons sugar	brandy
1 cup heavy cream	Confectioners' sugar
1½ cups light cream	(optional)
	Sugar Rose Petals (page 222)

Makes 8 to 10

Cream the egg yolks, cornstarch, and sugar together until light and fluffy.

In a nonstick saucepan bring the two creams to the boil.

Using a balloon whisk, beat the hot cream into the egg mixture.

Return to the pan, set over very low heat and stir well until the custard has thickened, about 10 to 15 minutes. Remove from the heat.

Have an ice cube ready to pop into the mixture to remove any residual heat that might curdle the custard. Keep on stirring briskly while you pour in the flower water or brandy. Let cool.

Pour into individual custard cups (or coffee cans) and chill in the refrigerator.

Sprinkle the tops with confectioners' sugar or cover with plastic wrap to prevent a skin from forming.

Decorate each cup with a Sugar Rose Petal.

SACK CREAMS

Sack was an old English word for sherry.

Proceed as for Custard Cups (page 215), substituting cream sherry for ½ cup of the light cream. Omit the flower waters.

ORANGE JELLIES

6 to 8 oranges
1½ teaspoons unflavored
   gelatin
¼ cup curaçao

2 dashes Angostura bitters
   (optional)
Extra orange segments to
   decorate

Makes 6 to 8

With a vegetable peeler, pare the rind off 2 of the oranges. Squeeze and strain the juice—you should have 2½ cups. Put the pared rind along with the juice into a pan and bring to a boil slowly in order to extract the oils from the rind. Turn off the heat.

Sprinkle the gelatin over the juice and stir until fully dissolved. Let cool completely. Add the liqueur and bitters.

Strain into individual glasses and chill to set in the refrigerator, covered with plastic wrap. Before serving, decorate each glass with 2 orange segments.

WINE OR CLARET JELLY

The English word for red Bordeaux wines used to be *clairette*—hence the word *claret*.

The very word *jelly* smacks of nursery food and school

meals, but a wine jelly is a long step from this type of food, and it makes a most refreshing finish to any meal. For those with endless patience in their kitchens it can be made with 1 cup of fresh black-currant juice, when these berries are in season, but the following recipe using a package of gelatin is a very good substitute and will convert many jelly loathers!

Rind of 1 orange (pared with a potato peeler to eliminate bitter white pith)	1 package black-currant or other dark or red fruit flavored gelatin
2 heaping tablespoons sugar	2½ cups claret-type wine
	1 cup heavy cream, whipped, to decorate

Makes 6 to 8 servings

Finely shred the orange rind and place in a bowl together with the sugar and the gelatin.

Bring the claret to just below boiling and pour it into the bowl, stirring until all the powder is dissolved. Let cool, then pour into a glass bowl or individual glasses, and put to set in the refrigerator.

Decorate with lots of unsweetened whipped cream.

SYLLABUB (SILEBUBE)

Syllabub is England's answer to the Italian zabaglione and the French sabayon and was something people ate or drank both at home and in the Assembly Rooms.

The name is, in fact, derived from the Old French name for champagne: *sille*. The Tudors and Hanoverians must have actually *drunk* it, and what we class as syllabub today is actually a first cousin of the frothing affair served in its own glass and elegantly placed on its own glass syllabub stand.

"Receipts" abound in old cookery books for "A Sillebub to last a Week," as well as for "A Syllabube under the cow." For this latter one, the instructions are to pour the warm milk "from a great height" when "no cow was to hand"!

This is one of England's great sweets. It has made a return to favor, and already there are many versions. It slots ideally into an afternoon-tea menu when the occasion is special.

1 orange   1¼ cups heavy cream
4 tablespoons superfine   Pieces of candied fruit
   granulated sugar   (optional)
⅓ cup medium dry Madeira
   (Sercial) OR
   Amontillado-type sherry

Finely grate the rind from the orange and squeeze the juice. Put the juice, rind, sugar, and Madeira or sherry into a bowl. Cover and leave for a few hours to let the oils from the rind impregnate the liquor.

Strain the liquid into a clean bowl and stir in the cream, gradually beating until it "ribbons" and nearly stands in peaks. (Only take it to "peak" stage if you want to serve the syllabubs immediately.)

Pour into the most attractive glasses you have—use custard cups or, if you are lucky, real syllabub glasses. Chill overnight and decorate, if you like, with striplets of candied fruits.

ICE CREAMS

Delicious ices are often served at afternoon tea, particularly when the occasion is an extra-special one, such as an afternoon wedding or a christening.

Here I give you some traditional creams plus one or two new ones.

BASIC VANILLA ICE CREAM (CUSTARD ICE CREAM)

5 eggs, beaten   5 cups half and half
1¼ cups vanilla sugar, OR   5 cups heavy cream
   plain sugar plus 1 vanilla
   pod or ½ tablespoon
   vanilla extract

Makes 3 quarts

Cream the eggs and vanilla sugar together until white and fluffy. In a nonstick saucepan, bring the half and half to boiling point (with the vanilla pod, if used). Pour over the egg mixture (remove the pod), stirring all the time.

Return the pan to low heat and stir with a wooden straight-edged spatula until the mixture thickens enough to coat the back of the spatula and leaves an obvious trail when a finger is drawn across the coated spatula. *Do not allow to boil.*

Let cool, then chill for 30 minutes.

Whip the cream to soft peaks and fold into the custard.

Pour into an ice-cream maker to freeze, following the directions that pertain to your particular machine.

BROWN-BREAD ICE CREAM

For each quart of Basic Vanilla Ice Cream (page 218) add the following:

5 tablespoons (⅓ cup) sweet butter	½ cup sugar
	1 teaspoon vanilla extract
1 cup torn soft white bread crumbs	½ cup sweet Madeira or sherry

Melt the butter in a wide skillet without browning.

Stir in the bread crumbs, sprinkle with the sugar and vanilla, and allow the whole mass to caramelize and crisp up over low heat for 15 to 20 minutes, stirring the crumbs around all the while to prevent scorching and promote even coloring.

When ready, tip onto a baking sheet to let cool.

Crush with the butt of a rolling pin.

Add to the ice cream with the Madeira while churning.

GINGER ICE CREAM

For each quart of Basic Vanilla Ice Cream (page 218) add:

2 teaspoons ground ginger to the eggs and sugar	6 pieces preserved ginger, finely shredded, while churning

GOOSEBERRY AND ROSEMARY ICE CREAM

1 pound gooseberries, rinsed
    and trimmed
¼ cup cold water
½ cup sugar
Rind of ½ lemon (pared
    with a potato peeler)

1 good sprig dried rosemary
    OR 1 teaspoon ground
    rosemary
1¼ cups heavy cream,
    half-whipped

Put the first five ingredients into a saucepan, cover, and simmer over low heat until the fruit has pulped.

Let the fruit cool, then puree it in a blender or food processor. Rub the puree through a fine-meshed sieve.

Fold in the half-whipped cream.

Churn and freeze.

FRUIT-SALAD ICE CREAM

This ice cream, which can be made with or without the heavy cream, is tangy and very refreshing. It can be served either molded or scooped.

2 cups Stock Syrup (page 221)
1 cup strained fresh lemon
    juice (approximately 5
    lemons)

½ small egg white, slightly
    beaten
½ cup heavy cream, whipped
    to soft peaks

FOR THE FRUIT SALAD

½ fresh pineapple, peeled,
    cored, and cut into small
    cubes
2 kiwi fruits, peeled and diced
1 orange, peeled, segmented
    and cut into 1-inch pieces
¼ pound seedless grapes,
    halved

¼ pound small wine grapes
    OR black grapes, halved
    and seeded
6 strawberries, quartered
Rind of 1 orange and ½
    lemon

MARINATED IN

3 tablespoons kirsch or
    Cointreau

3 tablespoons lemon juice

Mix the first four ingredients together and pour into an ice-cream maker. As soon as the mixture gets to the ribbon stage, where the paddles are leaving a distinct trail, add half the fruit-salad mixture. Continue churning until frozen to your liking. Serve the remaining fruit as an accompaniment.

STOCK SYRUP

Use this mixture for sweetening fruit salads, ices, iced tea, punches, etc.

2 cups cold water
2 cups superfine granulated
    sugar

Rind of 1 lemon

Bring all the ingredients to a boil in a saucepan. Reduce the heat and simmer for 10 minutes. Cool and then strain. Store in the refrigerator in a covered glass jar or plastic container.

APPLE AND ROSE-PETAL ICE CREAM

This creamy ice is evocative of an English garden; it would be perfect served at an afternoon wedding reception.

1¾ cups Stock Syrup (recipe above), made without lemon rind
1¾ cups concentrated apple juice
½ egg white, lightly beaten

3 teaspoons triple-strength rose-flower water
3 drops of red food coloring
1 cup heavy cream, whipped to soft peaks

FOR THE GARNISH
Sugared rose petals (see below)

Makes 6 to 8 servings

Put all the first five ingredients into an ice-cream maker. When the ice cream is ribboning, spoon in the half-whipped cream and churn until you reach a soft set.

Store in the freezer or spoon into ice glasses and serve freshly churned.

Decorate with sugared rose petals.

Note: To Sugar Rose Petals:
Pick old-fashioned, scented, blowsy red or pink roses. Use only perfect petals.

Beat an egg white until light and frothy.

With a paintbrush, brush each petal, completely on both sides with egg white. Arrange the petals on a sheet of wax paper laid on a tray. Dredge on both sides with superfine granulated sugar and leave to dry overnight or for as long as it takes. Store in an airtight container. Any bald patches will go moldy, so take care to cover each petal meticulously.

Where the atmosphere is very humid, you may have difficulty drying them. In England, we do this in what is called the airing cupboard which is above the hot-water tank, where sheets and towels are kept "aired."

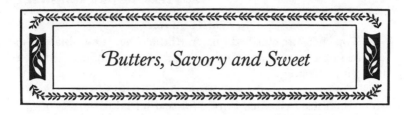

Butters, Savory and Sweet

Any sandwich is improved by a generous amount of well-flavored butter spread on the bread. Butters can be either sweet or savory and are made up in flavors to complement the particular filling used. As well as enriching the sandwich, butter keeps the bread moist and at the same time prevents any wetness in the filling from making it soggy. So make sure you "spread-to-the-edge," a motto that should be engraved on your cutting board! Decrusting can be done before making the sandwiches so that there is no waste, but for a neater finish to the cut edge, it is best done after the filling has been added.

Instead of butter, other spreads, such as flavored cream cheese or herb-tinted and lemon-spiked mayonnaise, can be used—or even vegetable purees, such as mushroom, celeriac, carrot, or pea. For example, you might enjoy spreading the bread with a cushion of cold, well-seasoned creamed celeriac when you make a chicken sandwich; similarly a fine puree of mushroom has a place in a crisp bacon "sarnie"—that's Cockney for *sandwich*! There are absolutely no rules as to what to put with what.

Unsalted butter is called for in all my recipes and certainly for all sweet recipes. You can add salt, but you cannot take it out.

I also advise all young cooks who come under my wing to practice melting butter. This may sound prosaic, but butter is used not only for its fat content, to enrich foods, but also to impart flavor to them. One of these flavors is that delicious almondy aroma emanating from "nut" butter, that is, butter melted carefully and evenly—by tilting and turning the pan over moderate heat so that the butter melts and colors without burning at the edges. The "nut" stage is reached when the butter, after sizzling and spluttering a little, goes quiet, has a delicate tan color, and gives off an exotic almond smell.

To Clarify Butter

Top chefs use clarified butter all the time. It eliminates the salt in salted butter and any excess moisture (important when using it for frying).

The amateur cook may not wish to use it all the time, but you would need clarified butter for sealing potted meats or fish and for panfried bananas or pineapple, where any sediments would be unsightly.

There is little reason to clarify unsalted butter, but margarine fanatics might like to clarify this, as margarine contains a lot of water, almost one-third of the content in some brands, and is improved when clarified.

The easiest way to proceed is to cut ½ pound cold butter or margarine into cubes and bring it to a boil in 1 cup water. Let cool and allow it to set. Lift off the set fat and scrape off any sediment from the undersurface before patting it dry. Remelt over low heat and pass it through fine muslin before use.

To Soften and Cream Butter

In certain recipes where butter is used for enriching and supporting other ingredients, such as in some savory mousses and pâtés, it is essential, in order to obtain a velvety texture to the finished dish, that the butter be properly softened and creamed.

Ideally, start with the butter at room temperature. If you have forgotten to take it from the refrigerator, cut it into squares, put it into a bowl, and stand this in a microwave or regular oven at 150°F for a minute or so, taking care it doesn't oil, until it is soft enough to beat. Using a spatula, beat the butter until it is lump-free, white, and light-textured.

An alternate method is to turn the butter onto a clean work surface and cut and squash it with a spatula before transferring it back to the bowl for creaming as above.

Note: *Any soup or sauce recipe intended for serving either cold or chilled should use a flavorless soy or vegetable oil instead of butter, as melted butter goes "grainy" when set.*

As a general guide, 2 cups (1 pound) butter is enough to spread twenty to twenty-four 4-inch-square slices of bread.

Note: *All these butters can be used as an accompaniment to grilled fish, chicken, and meat, should you have any left over. Simply form into a small roll, wrap in foil or freezer wrap, and store in the freezer.*

SAVORY BUTTERS

TOMATO CURRY AND ORANGE BUTTER

2 cups (4 sticks) sweet butter,
    softened
1 teaspoon salt
2 tablespoons good tomato
    puree

1 teaspoon finely grated
    orange rind
1 heaping teaspoon mild
    Madras curry powder

Mix all the ingredients together in a blender. Rub through a fine-meshed sieve. Put into wax or plastic containers and chill until needed in either the freezer or the refrigerator. Before using, allow the butter to come to room temperature.

LEMON BUTTER

2 cups (4 sticks) butter,
    softened
1 teaspoon salt

Freshly ground white pepper
Finely grated rind and juice
    of 1 lemon

Make a paste of all the ingredients in a blender. Rub through a fine-meshed sieve. Pack and store as above.

LEMON-AND-PARSLEY BUTTER

Make up one recipe Lemon Butter. After sieving, add 1 cup very finely chopped parsley.

FOIE GRAS AND ARTICHOKE BUTTER

One 4-ounce can artichoke
    bottoms, drained, rinsed,
    and drained again
1 cup (2 sticks), sweet butter,
    softened

One 4-ounce can mousse de
    foie gras
1 teaspoon salt
Freshly ground white pepper
2 teaspoons orange juice

Cut the artichoke bottoms into very fine dice. In a blender, make a fine puree of all the remaining ingredients. Scrape into a bowl. Mix in the diced artichoke. Pack and store as above.

MINT BUTTER

2 cups (4 sticks) sweet butter,   2 teaspoons lemon juice
   softened   1 teaspoon salt
1 packed cup mint leaves,   1 teaspoon sugar
   picked over and rinsed

Make a fine puree of all the ingredients in a blender. Rub through a fine-meshed sieve. Pack and store as above.

GARLIC BUTTER

8 large cloves garlic, peeled   1 teaspoon salt
2 cups (4 sticks) sweet butter,   2 teaspoons lemon juice
   softened

For sandwiches, the garlic aroma must be soft and gentle. So, blanch the garlic in boiling water for 2 minutes first; drain and let cool. Put through a garlic press and beat into the softened butter along with the salt and lemon juice. Pack and store as above.

MIXED HERB BUTTER

½ cup of each of the following   2 cups (4 sticks) sweet butter,
   fresh herbs: parsley,   softened
   fennel leaves, chervil,   ½ clove garlic, crushed
   and chives or basil; OR   1 teaspoon lemon juice
   tarragon, chives, and   1 teaspoon salt
   flat-leaf parsley   Freshly ground pepper, to
                                     taste

Chop the herbs, leaving some texture, and mix into the softened butter along with the last four ingredients. Pack and store as above.

BASIL BUTTER

2 cups (4 sticks) sweet butter,
    softened
1 tablespoon tomato puree
1 teaspoon lemon juice
1 teaspoon sugar

1 teaspoon salt
1 packed cup freshly
    shredded or chopped
    basil leaves

Make a fine puree of the first five ingredients, adding the basil leaves toward the end so that some texture is left. Pack and store as above.

TARRAGON BUTTER

2 cups (4 sticks) sweet butter,
    softened
1 packed cup torn and rinsed
    fresh tarragon leaves

1 tablespoon tarragon
    vinegar, warmed
1 teaspoon salt
Freshly ground pepper, to
    taste

In a blender make a fine puree of the ingredients (the warm vinegar is to help the mixture emulsify in cold weather). Rub through a fine-meshed sieve.

Pack and store as above.

CHIVE BUTTER

2 cups (4 sticks) sweet butter,
    softened
1 teaspoon lemon juice

Freshly ground white pepper,
    to taste
½ cup finely snipped chives

Beat the butter with the lemon juice and pepper. Mix in the snipped chives. Pack and store as above.

WATERCRESS BUTTER

2 bundles crisp dark-leaf
    watercress
1 cup (2 sticks) sweet butter,
    softened

1 teaspoon sugar
1 teaspoon salt

Pick all the leaves from the watercress. Drop them into a pan of boiling, lightly salted water for 1 minute only. Drain, rinse under cold water, and drain again. Squeeze out any excess water. In a blender, puree the watercress with the butter, sugar and salt. Pack and store as above.

TOMATO BUTTER

2 cups (4 sticks) sweet butter, softened
½ cup tomato puree
½ teaspoon mace OR rosemary OR nutmeg
1 teaspoon brown sugar
1 teaspoon salt
¼ teaspoon freshly ground black pepper
1 tablespoon dry sherry, warmed

In a blender, make a fine puree of all the ingredients. Pack and store as above.

ANCHOVY BUTTER

1 cup (2 sticks) sweet butter, softened
1 clove garlic, crushed
12 anchovy fillets
1 teaspoon lemon juice
1/16 teaspoon cayenne OR 3 to 4 dashes Tabasco
¼ teaspoon freshly ground black pepper

In a blender, make a puree of all the ingredients, then rub the mixture through a fine-meshed sieve. Pack and store as above.

MUSTARD BUTTER

2 cups (4 sticks) sweet butter, softened
¼ cup mild French mustard
1 tablespoon lemon juice

Beat everything to a smooth paste. Pack and store as above.

HORSERADISH BUTTER

2 cups (4 sticks) sweet butter,
   softened
2 tablespoons finely grated
   freshly scraped
   horseradish root

2 teaspoons lemon juice
2 teaspoons sugar
Salt, to taste

In a blender, make a puree of all the ingredients. Pack and store as above.

SWEET BUTTERS

HAZELNUT BUTTER

2 cups (4 sticks) sweet butter,
   softened
2 teaspoons brown sugar
¼ teaspoon cinnamon

1 tablespoon brandy
¾ cup hazelnuts, toasted and
   skins rubbed off

In a blender, make a puree of all the ingredients, adding the nuts a few at a time in order to leave some nutty texture. Pack and store as above.

CINNAMON BUTTER

2 cups (4 sticks) sweet butter,
   softened

1 cup brown sugar
2 teaspoons cinnamon

In a blender, make a fine puree of all the ingredients. Pack and store as above.

CUMBERLAND RUM BUTTER

2 cups (4 sticks) sweet butter
1 cup dark brown sugar

½ teaspoon nutmeg
½ cup light rum, warmed

In a blender, make a puree of all the ingredients, dribbling in the warm rum so that the mixture emulsifies. Pack and store as above.

BRANDY BUTTER

2 cups (4 sticks) sweet butter,   Juice of ½ small lemon,
   softened   strained
1½ cups confectioners' sugar   ½ cup brandy, warmed
1 teaspoon grated lemon rind

    In a blender, make a puree of all the ingredients, dribbling
in the warmed brandy, so that the mixture emulsifies. Pack and
store as above.

HONEY BUTTER

2 cups (4 sticks) sweet butter,   acacia, or orange
   softened   blossom)
4 tablespoons flower-scented   1 tablespoon rose-flower water
   honey (Hymettian,   (optional)

    In a blender, make a fine puree of all the ingredients. Pack
and store as above.

WALNUT BUTTER

2 cups (4 sticks) sweet butter,   ¼ teaspoon nutmeg
   softened   2 teaspoons lemon juice
2 teaspoons brown sugar   1 cup finely ground walnuts
1 tablespoon brandy

    Make a puree of the first five ingredients. Fold in the ground
walnuts. Pack and store as above.

ORANGE BUTTER

2 cups (4 sticks) sweet butter,   2 teaspoons finely grated
   softened   orange rind
                                    ¼ teaspoon mace

    In a blender, make a fine puree of all the ingredients. Pack
and store as above.

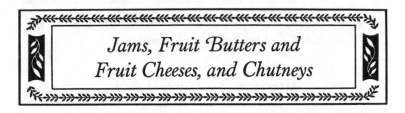

Jams, Fruit Butters and Fruit Cheeses, and Chutneys

JAMS

I cannot think of many jams popular here in England that are not in common use in the United States; and our best commercial products, such as Tiptree and Elsenham, are readily available in better American food stores.

However, here are a few that may have escaped attention, most of them from my own Edwardian mother's recipe book!

MARROW AND GINGER JAM

6 pounds prepared* squash
Juice and grated rind of 4
    lemons

3 ounces fresh ginger
6 pounds granulated sugar

Makes approximately 12 pounds

Cut squash into ½-inch cubes, and steam in batches (if necessary) over boiling water until tender.

Put the cooked squash into a bowl with the lemon rind and juice.

Peel the ginger, slice it roughly, and bruise it with the butt of a rolling pin. Tie loosely in a piece of muslin cloth with a string long enough to attach it to the handle of the jam pan.

Mix in the sugar and add the ginger, cover, and leave in a cool place overnight.

The next day, put everything into a pan and stir over medium heat until the sugar is quite dissolved. Continue cooking gently until the squash is transparent and the syrup thick. Remove the ginger and drain by pressing with a wooden spoon against the side of the pan. Discard it.

* Peel, seed, and remove the pith from the squash before weighing the flesh. Several smaller squash will yield a better texture than a few huge, coarse ones.

231

Pour into sterilized jam jars. Seal with a thin layer of paraffin, cover, label, and store in a cool place.

ENGLISH SUMMER JAM WITH ROSE PETALS

As with summer pudding—one of our national dishes—this jam can only be made during that short time when the fruits are all available simultaneously.

Only "blowsy," velvety, heavily scented, old-fashioned roses should be used.

1 pound black currants	½ cup water
1 pound red currants	1 pound raspberries
1 pound strawberries	4 pounds granulated sugar
Petals of 1 large unsprayed	
blowsy red rose	

Makes about 8 pounds

Rinse and pick over the currants with the tines of a large dinner fork.

Rinse, hull, and quarter the strawberries.

Rinse the rose petals, discarding the "green" inner ones.

Simmer the black currants in the water until tender. Add all the remaining fruits and simmer until they, too, are tender.

Add the sugar and cool, stirring, until the sugar has dissolved. During the final 10 minutes stir in the rose petals.

Boil hard to setting point (220°F. on a candy thermometer).

Pour into sterilized jam jars. Seal with a thin layer of paraffin, cover, label, and store in a cool place.

RHUBARB AND RASPBERRY JAM

3 pounds raspberries	1¼ cups water
3 pounds rhubarb	6 pounds granulated sugar

Makes about 12 pounds

Pick over the raspberries and rinse them with a water spray. Trim, wash, and cut the rhubarb into 1-inch pieces.

Over low heat, simmer the rhubarb in the water until soft. Add the raspberries, stir, and continue cooking until they, too, are soft.

Add the sugar and cook over high heat, stirring, until the sugar has dissolved.

Boil hard to setting point (220°F. on a candy thermometer).

Pour into sterilized jam jars. Seal with a thin layer of paraffin, cover, label, and store in a cool place.

APRICOT JAM

6 pounds fresh apricots
Juice of 1 lemon
2 scant cups water

1 teaspoon vanilla extract
6 pounds granulated sugar

Makes about 12 pounds

Wash, split, and pit the apricots. Crack the pits, take out the kernels, and blanch these in boiling water for 2 to 3 minutes. Rinse, let cool, and roughly crush them.

Meanwhile, cook the apricots with the lemon juice and vanilla and the 2 cups water until quite soft, about 15 to 20 minutes. Add the kernels when they are ready. Add the sugar and cook over high heat, stirring, until the sugar has dissolved.

Boil hard to setting point (220°F. on a candy thermometer).

Pour into sterilized jam jars. Seal with a thin layer of paraffin, cover, label, and store in a cool place.

GOOSEBERRY AND ELDER FLOWER JAM

These two strange English flavors make a very good marriage, particularly when spread on toasted Crumpets (page 93) or spread as a layer in Chocolate Cake (page 177).

6 pounds underripe
    gooseberries
10 heads of elderberry flowers

5 cups water
6 pounds granulated sugar

Makes approximately 12 pounds

Wash and trim the gooseberries.

Pick the elderberry flowers off their stalks. Discard the stalks; roughly chop the flowers.

Simmer the fruit and flowers in the water until the gooseberries have pulped; mash them as they cook.

Add the sugar and cook over high heat, stirring, until the sugar has dissolved. Boil briskly to setting point (220°F. on a candy thermometer).

Pour into sterilized jam jars. Seal with a thin layer of paraffin, cover, label, and store in a cool place.

Note: *Fast boiling produces a green jam. Prolonged boiling yields a darker, almost red one.*

BLACK CURRANT JAM

4 pounds black currants   6 pounds granulated sugar
2 quarts water

Makes about 10 pounds

Rinse the berries and remove them from their stalks.

Put into a jam pan with the water and simmer until soft; about 10 to 15 minutes.

Add the sugar and cook over medium heat, stirring until it dissolves. Then boil hard to setting point (220°F. on a candy thermometer).

Pour into sterilized jam jars. Seal with a thin layer of paraffin, cover, label, and store in a cool place.

GREENGAGE JAM

6 pounds greengage plums   6 pounds granulated sugar
2½ cups water

Makes about 12 pounds

Wash the greengages and cut them in half, removing the pits.

Crack the pits and remove the kernels. Blanch the kernels

for 2 minutes in boiling water and split or cut them in half.

Put the greengages, kernels, and the 2½ cups water in a jam pan and simmer until soft, about 20 to 25 minutes.

Stir in the sugar and boil hard to setting point (220°F. on a candy thermometer).

Pour into sterilized jam jars. Seal with a thin layer of paraffin, cover, label, and store in a cool place.

DAMSON JAM

Damson plums, with their deep crimson color, are not readily available in America. However, there may be garden enthusiasts who grow these trees—their blossom is so pretty—if not, use beach plums. At home my mother never removed the stones, telling us children to make up a game by counting them on our plate edge! It was her way of getting us to eat this jam.

3 pounds damson plums   3 pounds (preserving) sugar
2 cups water

Makes about 6 pounds

Wash the plums. Simmer them in the water until soft, skimming off any stones that come to the surface.

Mix in the sugar and boil over high heat to setting point (220°F. on a candy thermometer).

Pour into sterilized jam jars. Seal with a thin layer of paraffin, cover, label, and store in a cool place.

FRUIT BUTTER AND FRUIT CHEESE

The difference between a fruit butter and a fruit cheese is in the consistency. Both are an old-fashioned—and still very desirable—way of preserving fruits.

Fruit butter is soft and spreadable on crumpets, muffins, or just plain buttered brown toast, whereas fruit cheese is set in straight-sided jars, turned out, and cut into slices.

In the eighteenth century it was eaten—alone—with a fork or served with cold meats rather as you would serve cranberry sauce. Today it is a novelty to serve at teatime.

BLACKBERRY CHEESE

This is wonderful served spread on buttered whole meal bread with a mature Cheddar cheese or a crumbly Wensleydale.

4 pounds blackberries   Sugar, as needed
2 teaspoons tartaric acid

Makes about 6 to 8 pounds

Pick over and rinse the fruit. Put into a pan with the tartaric acid and barely enough water to cover. Simmer until the fruit is soft. Press and rub through a fine-meshed sieve. Weigh the pulp.

Add 1 pound sugar for each pound of pulp. Stir over low heat until dissolved.

Boil gently until very thick, stirring almost continuously. (So have a book at your side to read!)

Pour into sterilized small straight-sided containers. Cover and seal as for jam (page 232).

To serve: Run a hot knife around the sides of the jars. Turn out and slice with a hot knife.

APPLE AND PLUM BUTTER

3 pounds apples, peeled,   ½ cup water
    cored, and roughly cut up   Juice of 1 lemon, strained
1 pound red plums, stoned   Sugar, as needed
    and cut up

Makes about 6 to 8 pounds

Over low heat, cook both fruits in the water until pulped. Add the lemon juice. Stir well during this process.

Pass through a food processor and rub the fruit pulp through a fine-meshed sieve.

Weigh the pulp, put into a clean pan, and add 1¾ cups sugar for each pound of pulp. Stir the mixture until the sugar is dissolved.

Boil over medium heat until thick.

Pour into sterilized jars. Seal as for jam (page 232).

LEMON CHEESE

In some parts of England this is called lemon curd. Use it in tarts, as a spread on tea breads, or as an accompaniment to ice cream.

4 large lemons

¾ cup (1½ sticks) sweet butter, softened

2¼ cups sugar

4 large eggs, well beaten

Makes approximately 2 to 3 pounds

Grate just the rind from the lemons, avoiding the bitter white pith. Squeeze the juice and strain it, pressing well.

In a double boiler, or in a heatproof bowl set over a pan of simmering water, melt the butter. Add the lemon juice, rind, and sugar and stir with a wire balloon whisk until the sugar is dissolved.

Gradually incorporate the well-beaten eggs and stir slowly but thoroughly until the mixture is thick and "ribbons" or "trails" well when the whisk is drawn through.

Pour into smallish sterilized jars.

CHUTNEY

Chutney has its roots in imperial India. The word derives from the Hindu *chatni* and is an integral part of Indian meals.

In Britain—during and following the Raj—chutney became popular as an accompaniment to cold cuts. The belly-burning curries so sought after today as a result of the rise in popularity of ethnic restaurants were not known in England before the Second World War. However, chutney was and is an excellent addition to many sandwich fillings.

English-made chutneys, I think, are milder and often more subtle than their "mother" chutneys.

I give you my three favorites to try as an introduction, though in better food stores you will find good commercial brands, such as Sarsons, Tiptree, and Elsenham.

TOMATO CHUTNEY

1 pound ripe tomatoes,
    skinned and chopped
2 eating (dessert) apples,
    cored and chopped
½ pound onions, peeled and
    finely chopped
1 pound golden raisins
1 cup brown sugar

2½ cups malt or red wine
    vinegar
2 teaspoons salt
1 tablespoon mustard seed,
    tied in a bag
2 teaspoons ginger
Tip of a teaspoon of cayenne
    OR ¼ teaspoon Tabasco

Makes about 4 to 5 pounds

Put all the ingredients into a preserving pan. Bring to a boil and simmer, stirring from time to time, until the mixture is thick and has a good reddish brown color, about 1 hour.

Pour into sterilized jars. Seal as for jam (page 232).

APPLE CHUTNEY

2½ cups malt or red wine
    vinegar
1 tablespoon salt
2½ cups light brown sugar
1 tablespoon ginger
3 chilies OR 1 tablespoon
    mustard seed
5 pounds eating apples,
    peeled, cored, and diced

2 cups peeled and finely
    chopped onions
2 cups muscatel raisins,
    chopped
2 cups golden raisins
Grated rind and juice of
    1 lemon

Makes about 7 to 8 pounds

In a preserving pan bring to a boil the vinegar, salt, sugar, and chilies or mustard seed. Add all the remaining ingredients and simmer for 1 hour or more.

The type of apples used will determine how much juice they yield and how soft the chutney will be.

The chutney should be boiled until it is of a jam-like consistency. Stir from time to time to prevent scorching.

Pour into sterilized jars. Seal as for jam (page 232).

GOOSEBERRY CHUTNEY

3 pounds green gooseberries	2 teaspoons salt
4 cups brown sugar	2 heaping teaspoons mustard
2 cups muscatel raisins	seed, tied in a muslin bag
1 pound Bermuda onions,	¼ teaspoon cayenne
peeled and finely chopped	3½ cups red wine vinegar

Makes about 7 to 8 pounds

Put all ingredients into a preserving pan. Bring to a boil, reduce the heat, and simmer gently for 1¾ to 2 hours, stirring from time to time to prevent scorching.

The chutney should be well cohered and the consistency of jam.

Pour into sterilized jars and seal as for jam (page 232).

CHRISTMAS MINCEMEAT WITH RUM

While any spirit can be used (it is to preserve and mature the ingredients), rum is perhaps most associated with Christmas in England. Make the mincemeat at least a month in advance so that it will have time to mature properly. Store in a cool place.

2 pounds green cooking apples	Juice and grated rind of 1
3 cups muscatel raisins	large lemon
2 cups golden raisins	Juice and grated rind of 1
3 cups dried currants	orange
3 cups shredded or ground	1 teaspoon cinnamon
beef suet (commercial	1 teaspoon mace
brand)	½ teaspoon nutmeg
2 cups finely chopped mixed	4 cups brown sugar
candied citrus rind	1 teaspoon salt
	1½ cups dark rum or brandy

Makes 8 to 10 pounds

Core, seed, and grind the unpeeled apples (or use the coarse side of a grater). Roughly chop all the dried fruits; resist the temptation to grind these, as a rough texture is preferable.

With your hands, mix all the ingredients very well in a large bowl. Leave for 24 hours in a cool place, covered with plastic wrap.

Stir well again, when all the juices should be absorbed. Pack into cold jars. Seal with plastic wrap or old-fashioned screw-top lids with rubber ring seals. Leave to mature in a cool place for at least a month.

Other Savory Items

PATTIES

This is the English name for a small (1-inch) vol-au-vent and is not to be confused with the French *pâté*. Rather, the word *patty* is cognate with the word *pastry*, which (of course!) came from the French *pâté*, or "paste," the circumflex indicating the missing *s*. Patties are an essential item on an afternoon-tea menu when it is a party occasion and are served warm with a variety of fillings based on a creamy white sauce (béchamel).

Fill them cold and then warm through in the oven at a low temperature.

MUSHROOM PATTIES

To each 2½ cups of cold Rich Cream Sauce (see page 243) add:

2 cups finely chopped   1 teaspoon mild French
    white-cap mushrooms   mustard
½ cup dry Madeira

Makes enough for 24 to 30 patties, depending on their size

Simmer and toss the mushrooms in the Madeira. Strain and reduce the liqueur to 2 tablespoonsful. Mix in the mustard. Then mix the whole lot into the white sauce.

SHRIMP PATTIES

To each 2½ cups of cold Rich Cream Sauce (see page 243) add:

1½ cups finely chopped   1 teaspoon each paprika, salt,
   cooked shrimp   and freshly ground
A good squeeze of lemon juice   pepper

Makes enough for 24 to 30 patties, depending on their size

CHICKEN PATTIES

To each 2½ cups cold Rich Cream Sauce (see page 243), add:

1 tablespoon sweet butter   1 teaspoon mace
2 small raw chicken breasts   ¼ cup dry sherry
   cut into ¼-inch dice

Makes enough for 24 to 30 patties, depending on their size

Melt the butter in a heavy skillet. Over high heat, seal and fry the diced chicken, seasoning with the mace as you go along.

Pour in the sherry and bubble until syrupy, when the chicken will be cooked but still moist, about 2 minutes.

Let cool before stirring into the sauce.

SALMON PATTIES

To each 2½ cups cold Rich Cream Sauce (see page 243), add:

1 cup cold poached salmon,   Salt and freshly ground
   flaked or ground   pepper, to taste
A good squeeze of lemon juice

Makes enough for 24 to 30 patties, depending on their size

PATTY CASES (PATTY SHELLS OR BOUCHEES)

1 pound Puff Pastry (page   Beaten egg, to glaze
   205)

Makes 20 to 24

Use two cutters, one 1½ inches in diameter and a center cutter 1 inch in diameter. Preheat the oven to 450°F.

Roll out the puff pastry evenly to ⅓ inch thick. Cut all the way through the pastry with the larger cutter. Do not twist as you cut or this will seal the edges and impede the rising of the pastry. Cut halfway through the pastry with the smaller cutter.

With a spatula, lift the patties to a wetted baking sheet, placing them 1 inch apart. Brush the tops with the beaten egg, being careful not to get any on the cut edges.

Bake for 10 minutes, then reduce the heat to 350° and bake for a further 7 to 10 minutes, or until the shells are risen, golden brown, and crisp. Remove from the oven and let cool.

With a pointed knife, carefully cut around and remove the center ring; this will reveal some soft dough in the cavity. Using the rounded end of a teaspoon handle, or something similar, carefully scrape as much of this out as will readily come without piercing the base.

Either reheat the shells and lids and fill with hot cream filling (see pages 241 to 242) or leave to cool, fill with cold filling, put on the lids, and reheat as instructed on page 244.

For variety, the patties can be cut 1½ inches square.

HEAVY, RICH CREAM SAUCE FOR PATTIES

5 tablespoons (⅓ cup) sweet
    butter
2 tablespoons all-purpose flour
1¼ cups milk
¼ cup light cream

1 teaspoon salt
¼ teaspoon mace
A little freshly ground pepper
1 teaspoon lemon juice

Enough for 24 to 30 small patties

In a nonstick saucepan, melt the butter and stir in the flour.

Using a wire balloon whisk, beat in the milk and, stirring, let the sauce come to a boil. Reduce the heat, and simmer for 2 minutes. Stir in the cream, seasonings, and lemon juice.

Cover with a buttered circle of paper to prevent a skin from forming. Let cool.

When ready for use, stir in the chosen filling (see pages 241 to 242), spoon into the empty patty (vol-au-vent) cases and set these on a baking sheet. Heat through in a preheated 300°F. oven for 20 minutes.

Serve the patties on a silver dish lined with a folded white napkin.

POTTED MEATS AND FISH

Potting has been used as a means of preserving foods throughout Europe for hundreds of years. It is a method whereby cooked flesh is sealed under a thick layer of butter or lard, giving it an extended storage life.

Originally these coarse-textured potted meats, fish, and game were eaten at breakfast time or as part of the high tea still served in the Midlands, the counties in the North of England, Wales, Ulster, and Scotland. They preserve the natural flavors of the food, and it is therefore understandable that they have stayed popular in the English repertory. Potted foods moved gradually toward the tea table in the nineteenth century, becoming more refined as they did so and joining the repertoire of sandwich fillings.

Today, potted foods are regaining their popularity as an alternative—and often a better one—to the ubiquitous pâtés. In most country towns, potted beef and salmon "paste" can be purchased at any good family grocer. They are excellent spread on small crackers at cocktail time and better still if attractively displayed in their own handsome "pot" for guests themselves to spread onto mini-muffins or biscuits.

Potted foods make excellent starters for a lunch or dinner party, served, again, in their pot and eaten with crusty bread, dry brown toast, or fingers of buttered hot toast.

Some people like to spread a film of clarified butter on their toast first; others do not choose to add to their cholesterol intake! For added interest, I sometimes add a smidge of mace, nutmeg, or thyme and a little grated lemon rind to the clarified butter before spooning it over the food to be potted.

The all-essential ingredient is, of course, the sealing butter. Today, clarified butter is used, as it is free of any sediment that might otherwise allow the fat to become rancid. Clarifying also drives out the air from the butter, giving it a "hard" set.

When the pots have been prepared, they can be kept in the refrigerator for up to 2 weeks, and they freeze well for up to 6 months. Always allow the potted product to come to room temperature before serving. This will bring out the flavor.

POTTED MEAT

1 pound lean boneless stewing
  beef
½ cup medium dry Madeira
  wine OR sherry
1 teaspoon salt

1 teaspoon mace
1 teaspoon freshly ground
  pepper
½ cup clarified butter (page
  224)

Makes about 1½ pounds

Trim the meat of all skin and fat and cut into ½-inch cubes. Place in a small heatproof bowl or casserole and add the wine and seasonings. Cover tightly with foil and/or a well-fitting lid.

Stand the bowl in a medium saucepan and add boiling water to two-thirds the depth of the casserole. Cover the casserole and simmer for 2½ to 3 hours, or until the meat is tender. Top up the boiling water if it evaporates. Remove from the heat and allow to cool.

Transfer the meat to a food processor and process at top speed until you have a fine puree. With the machine running, gradually add three-quarters of the cool clarified butter. Continue to process until well blended. Adjust the seasoning if necessary.

Spoon into one large or several individual pots or ramekins. Spoon over a thin film of the remaining butter, being sure to completely cover the meat. Store in the refrigerator.

Allow to come to room temperature before serving with hot buttered toast, buttered crumpets, or as a sandwich filling.

POTTED SALMON

One 1-pound piece fresh
  salmon
1 teaspoon mace
1 slice lemon
¼ teaspoon ground clove
  OR 2 whole cloves
¼ teaspoon ground bay OR

1 bay leaf, broken into
  bits
Salt and freshly ground
  pepper, to taste
½ cup (1 stick) sweet butter
⅓ cup clarified butter (see
  page 224)

6 to 8 servings

Preheat the oven to 400°F.

Skin and slice the salmon into thinnish pieces. Put into an earthenware pot just large enough to contain it, seasoning well with the herbs and spices as you arrange the pieces and dispersing the ½ cup butter among the fish pieces.

Cover the pot and stand this in a pan of hot water.

Bake until the fish is cooked, about 45 minutes. Let cool completely.

Puree in a food processor or blender. Adjust the seasoning if necessary and pack the puree into an attractive china container. Chill well.

Pour cool clarified butter over the chilled salmon puree and return the dish to the refrigerator to set again.

Serve like a pâté.

POTTED SMOKED TROUT

10 ounces smoked trout, skinned and boned
4 tablespoons (½ stick) sweet butter
½ cup cream cheese
2 tablespoons sour cream
Juice of ½ small lemon

2 to 3 dashes Tabasco
½ teaspoon mace
Salt and freshly ground pepper, to taste
¼ cup clarified butter (see page 224)

Makes about ¾ pound

Puree the fish in a blender or food processor.

Mix in all the remaining ingredients except the clarified butter.

Spoon into a pretty pot or dish. Pour over a thin film of clarified butter. Refrigerate to set.

Remove from the refrigerator 1 hour before serving.

POTTED KIPPERS

Smoked haddock can be used as an alternative, but it is not so robust and smoky as a good Loch Fine or Manx kipper.

½ pound cooked kipper OR
    smoked haddock
4 tablespoons (½ stick) sweet
    butter
4 ounces cream cheese
2 tablespoons heavy cream

Freshly ground pepper, to
    taste
1 tablespoon whisky or
    bourbon
Clarified butter (page 224)

6 servings

Puree the kipper or haddock in a blender.

Mix in the remaining ingredients (except the clarified butter) in short, sharp bursts.

Spoon into a pretty pot or dish and pour over a film of clarified butter. Refrigerate to set.

Take out of the refrigerator at least 1 hour before serving. Serve with hot, dry brown toast.

POTTED TONGUE

⅓ to ½ pound cooked beef
    OR lamb's tongue
5 tablespoons (⅓ cup) butter
1 tablespoon dark rum
1 teaspoon mild French
    mustard

An extra ¼-inch slice of beef
    tongue, diced
½ cup clarified butter (see
    page 224)

Makes about ½ pound

Put the first four ingredients into a blender or food processor and make a fine paste. Scrape into a bowl and mix in the diced tongue.

Transfer to a dish or individual ramekins. Spoon over a thin film of clarified butter. Refrigerate until ready for use.

POTTED DEVILED HAM

½ pound cooked lean smoked
    ham, rind removed,
    diced, including any fat
½ cup (1 stick) sweet butter
1 good teaspoon mild French
    mustard
3 to 4 dashes Tabasco

2 to 3 pinches cayenne
Salt (optional)
1 tablespoon Worcestershire
    sauce
⅓ cup clarified butter (see
    page 224)

Makes about ½ pound

In a food processor or blender, make a fine puree of all the ingredients except the clarified butter.

Transfer to a pot or pots. Spoon over a thin film of clarified butter.

Allow to set in the refrigerator.

RICH POTTED CRAB

2 tablespoons Amontillado
  sherry
Strained juice and grated rind
  of 1 small orange
½ cup (1 stick) lightly salted
  butter, softened

½ pound dressed crab meat
  (use both dark and light
  meat)
¼ teaspoon salt
¼ teaspoon pepper
2 to 3 dashes Tabasco
Clarified Butter (page 224)

Makes about ¾ pound

Bring the sherry, orange juice, and orange rind to a boil in a small saucepan. Reduce to 1 tablespoon over high heat. Strain and then cool. When cool, beat into the softened butter.

Combine the butter with the crab meat and beat until smooth. Season with the salt, pepper, and Tabasco.

Spoon the mixture into a serving bowl, cover, and refrigerate for 30 minutes. Seal with clarified butter and refrigerate again.

SAUSAGE ROLLS

These little meat-filled pastry rolls have done much to earn Britain a bad name; they appear everywhere, from station buffets and tea shops to school lunch boxes and vending machines in factory canteens.

Yet there was a time when to have afternoon tea without a sausage roll was unthinkable. They were made small, with a melt-in-the-mouth crust and a tasty sausage-meat filling.

I urged you to try my recipe with its filling of homemade sausage; I think you'll agree that sausage rolls deserve to regain their good reputation.

3 cups all-purpose flour	2 tablespoons light cream
1 teaspoon salt	OR milk
1 cup (2 sticks) butter	Chicken and pork fillings
½ cup lard or vegetable	(see below)
shortening	1 egg, beaten with 1
1 egg	tablespoon milk, to glaze
1 egg yolk	

Makes about 30 small rolls of each filling

Sift the flour and salt into a large bowl. With your fingertips or a pastry blender, rub in the butter and shortening until you have a moist, sandlike texture.

Whisk together the egg, egg yolk, and cream or milk. Using a fork, mix this into the dry ingredients to form a soft dough. With your fingers, draw the dough into a ball, wrap in plastic, and refrigerate for at least 1 hour.

Preheat the oven to 375°F.

Cut the chilled pastry in two. Roll one half into a 20-by-10-inch rectangle. Cut in half lengthwise to give two 20-by-5-inch oblongs. Place a roll of chicken filling down the center of each pastry oblong, brush the edges with egg wash and fold over to enclose the filling. Press and pinch the edges together. Cut each roll in half and place all four rolls on a lightly greased baking sheet. Brush all over with egg wash and make cuts three-quarters of the way through each roll at approximately 1-inch intervals.

Repeat with the other half of the pastry, using the pork filling this time.

Bake for 20 to 25 minutes, or until golden brown. Let cool slightly before completely cutting through.

These freeze well; simply thaw and gently reheat. They may also be frozen shaped but unbaked: Thaw and cook as above, brushing with egg wash *after* thawing.

Sausage Rolls are always eaten hot or warm.

CHICKEN FILLING

1 pound raw, boned chicken
   breast, skinned and diced
½ pound raw pork (from the
   leg)
¼ pound bacon
½ cup fresh white bread
   crumbs
1 teaspoon mace

1 teaspoon salt
1 teaspoon freshly ground
   pepper
1 egg, beaten with 4
   tablespoons heavy cream
4 tablespoons finely chopped
   parsley

Makes about two pounds

In a food processor, blend the chicken, ham, and bacon until fine. Add the bread crumbs, seasonings, and the egg mixture. Blend thoroughly. Finally add the parsley quickly.

Turn out onto a floured board. Divide the mixture in half and shape each half into a sausage shape approximately 20 inches long.

PORK FILLING

1¼ pounds boneless pork
   loin, diced
1 eating apple, quartered and
   peeled
1 cup fresh white bread
   crumbs

2 teaspoons rubbed sage
½ teaspoon mace
1 teaspoon each salt and
   freshly ground pepper
1 egg, beaten with 1
   tablespoon heavy cream

Makes about two pounds

In a food processor, blend the pork until finely ground. Slice in the apple and blend for 1 minute. Add the remaining ingredients and continue to process just to blend well together.

Turn out onto a floured board. Divide the mixture in half and shape each half into a sausage shape approximately 20 inches long.

PATUM PEPERIUM
(GENTLEMAN'S RELISH)

This extraordinary and uniquely English food is sold in flat white china pots, not unlike pomade jars. It is a very strong pâté with a heavy anchovy base—anyone who has ever tasted Tapénade when in the south of France, will be thinking on the right lines!

It is spread on Bath Oliver biscuits or fingers of hot buttered toast and certainly induces a thirst! Its name was first used in the Gentlemen's Clubs of St. James.

A sophisticated hostess would always have a pot to hand at afternoon tea for any gentlemen present, the minuscule sandwiches being considered too effete for the visiting country squire or clubland gentleman.

Note: *Elsenham produces it, and it is probably available from specialty food shops such as Dean & DeLuca or the Silver Palate in New York City—for those of you inquisitive enough and with a strong nerve!*

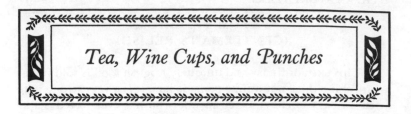

Tea, Wine Cups, and Punches

ICED TEA

For a good clear liquid, it is better to use a cold infusion, although Keemun tea does give an effective brew when made hot. You might like to try Twinings black currant tea, which I am told is highly popular in the United States among the cognoscenti.

4 teaspoons tea (Darjeeling, orange pekoe, OR Yunnan)
2 cups cold water

3 teaspoons sugar, or to taste, OR use Sugar Syrup (page 253)

Makes 4 servings

Put all the ingredients into a glass jug. Stir well and refrigerate for 12 hours or overnight.

Stir well before going to bed, and when you get up again! Some leaves will sink, other will float.

Strain, first through a fine sieve, then through a sieve lined with paper or clean muslin.

Chill again.

TEA PUNCHES

For best results, infuse the leaves of a good-quality tea, such as Ceylon, Yunnan, Darjeeling, or Keemun, overnight in the refrigerator: You will get a crystal-clear liquid (see previous recipe). A hot infusion, while quicker, often produces a cloudy liquid.

It is also easier to use a sugar syrup for sweetening cold teas: this can be prepared and stored indefinitely in the refrigerator.

SUGAR SYRUP

2¼ cups superfine granulated   2 cups cold water
    sugar   Pared rind of 1 lemon

Makes 4 servings

Combine all the ingredients in a saucepan and bring to a boil slowly over medium heat. Simmer for 10 minutes, or until clear.

Let cool. Store refrigerated in a screw-top glass jar. It will keep indefinitely.

CHAMPAGNE TEA FIZZ

2 cups Yunnan, Darjeeling,   Curls of pared orange rind
    or Keemun tea (made   (1 for each glass)
    with 2 tablespoons tea   1 "stick" pineapple for each
    leaves), chilled   glass
1 bottle inexpensive domestic   1 tablespoon Cointreau for
    champagne, well chilled   each glass
Sugar Syrup (above), to taste
    (about 1 teaspoon per
    glass)

Makes 8 large servings

Have ready chilled glasses, containing the syrup, orange rind, pineapple stick, and Cointreau. Half-fill these with the chilled tea. Top up with champagne as they are served.

SIMPLE CHILLED TEA PUNCH

Keemun or Ceylon tea   Cold water

Infuse the tea as described on page 252. Serve in elegant small glasses over cracked ice, with sprigs of bruised apple-mint, a slice of lemon, and sugar syrup to taste.

HOT TEA PUNCH

This punch is excellent served chilled with the addition of cucumber sticks and the odd borage flower.

4 cups hot tea
Sugar Syrup (page 253), to
   taste

2 cups freshly squeezed orange
   juice, strained
½ cup freshly squeezed lemon
   juice, strained

Makes about 8 servings

Serve with slices of lemon and orange in heatproof tea glasses.

TEA TODDY

2 cups hot Lapsang souchong
   tea
Juice of 2 lemons, strained
Pared rind of 1 small lemon

Sugar Syrup (page 253), to
   taste
½ cup Irish whiskey

Makes about 6 servings

Pour a little whiskey into each of 6 glasses. Add an equal amount of lemon juice and a piece of lemon rind to each glass. Pour in the hot tea and sweeten to taste.

ICED STRAWBERRY TEA PUNCH

2 strawberries, quartered, per
   glass
2 bruised mint leaves per glass
2 cups Earl Grey tea, chilled

Crushed ice or ice cubes
Grenadine or Sugar Syrup
   (page 253), to taste

Makes 6 to 8 servings

Cool glasses containing the fruit and mint in the refrigerator.
Pour in the chilled tea. Add a little ice. Sweeten to taste with grenadine or Sugar Syrup.

RUM TEA PUNCH

2 cups hot Yunnan,
    Darjeeling, or Ceylon
    tea (made with 2
    tablespoons tea leaves)
1 stick cinnamon, broken up

Rind of 1 large orange
Sugar Syrup (page 253), to
    taste
½ cup dark rum

Makes 8 to 10 servings

Infuse the tea with the cinnamon and orange rind. Sweeten to taste with the sugar syrup. Strain into a warm punch bowl and add the rum. Serve with a cinnamon stick in each toddy glass. Serve in small quantities!

AFTERNOON CUPS

On special occasions, and particularly when gentlemen are to be present at an afternoon reception, a wine cup should be served.

CLARET CUP

This is a very simple and effective afternoon drink. Pour equal quantities of any claret-type wine and dry ginger ale over crushed ice. Add a sprig of mint to each glass.

PIMM'S CUP

This is a very English drink made with a base mixture to which is added lemon soda. If you cannot buy the basic Pimm's No. 1 mixture, the following recipe makes a good near miss!

1 cup London gin
1 cup sweet vermouth

¼ pint 1 part dry vermouth
4 dashes Angostura bitters

Makes 8 to 10 servings

Pimm's cups are traditionally served chilled in silver, pewter, or glass tankards, into each of which should be put:

Ice cubes
1 stick peeled cucumber
1 wedge eating apple
½ slice orange

½ slice lemon
1 maraschino cherry on a stick
1 sprig of mint

Top up with chilled lemon soda. Just how much of the base mixture you use depends very much on how strong you like your drinks. I suggest you start with ¼ cup per tankard or glass.

PIMM'S ROYALE CUP

Follow the recipe for Pimm's Cup (above), but use champagne in place of lemonade.

BUCK'S FIZZ

A combination of chilled champagne and chilled orange juice in proportion of 2 to 1.

STRAWBERRY CHAMPAGNE CUP

Into each glass put a sugar cube, over which pour 1 tablespoon of framboise, a quartered strawberry, and top up with chilled champagne.

SPARKLING CIDER CUP

⅓ cup Sugar Syrup (page 253)
⅓ cup brandy
⅓ cup curaçao
2 cups weak China tea (made with 2 tablespoons

Yunnan tea leaves)
Juice of 2 oranges, strained
1 large bottle sparkling cider
Slices of fruit, to garnish

Makes 8 to 10 servings

Put ice cubes into a punch bowl or jug. Pour over all the ingredients, adding the sparkling cider just before you serve the cup.

FRESHLY MADE LEMONADE

6 large lemons   6 cups boiling water
1 cup sugar

Makes 7 to 8 servings

Cut the lemons in half, squeeze, and strain the juice.

Put the squeezed lemons into a china jug, add the sugar, pour over the boiling water, stir well. Leave to cool, then chill overnight.

Strain the liquid off, squeezing the lemon skins well. Add the lemon juice to the liquid. Chill again until ready for use.

Serve topped up with sparkling water, such as Perrier.

CLARET CUP FOR A WINTER'S DAY

1 bottle claret   Pared rind of 1 lemon and
½ cup dry sherry   1 orange
¼ cup brandy   Sugar Syrup (page 253) to
¼ cup maraschino liqueur   taste

Makes 6 to 8 servings

While this is served cold, it should be presented in small tots, as it is fairly potent!

An alternative is to serve it in larger glasses and top it up with soda water to taste.

WEDDING CHAMPAGNE PUNCH

Ice cubes   ¼ bottle Cointreau, chilled
1 bottle dry champagne,   Slices of orange
   chilled   Slivers of orange rind
1 bottle Sauternes, chilled

Makes 14 to 16 servings

Half-fill a punch bowl with ice cubes (crushed ice melts too quickly.) Pour over all the liquid ingredients. Float orange slices in the punch bowl and twists of orange rind in each glass.

When orange blossoms are in season, it is pretty to scatter a few of the scented blooms in the punch bowl.

BADMINTON CUP

This is a Victorian red wine "spritz" or "seltz."

1 bottle red burgundy OR	Pared rind of 1 lemon
Beaujolais	½ cup curaçao
Pared rind of 1 orange	2 large bottles soda water

Makes 6 to 8 servings

Put all the ingredients except the soda water into a punch bowl or glass jug. Chill very well.

Serve in small glasses, topped up with soda water—about ⅓ wine to ⅔ soda.

WHITE WINE "SELTZ"

This drink was considered elegant, refreshing, and quite proper for ladies to partake of in the afternoon without getting tipsy!

1 bottle dry Moselle OR	Twist of lemon rind
Rhine wine, chilled	Soda water, chilled

Makes 6 servings

Fill each glass one-third with wine, top up with soda water, and squeeze a twist of lemon oil over the surface.

LOVING CUP

To serve as a toast at weddings.

1 cup sugar cubes	1 bottle champagne
2 lemons	3 cups soda water
½ bottle Madeira	Sprigs of apple-mint, to
¼ bottle brandy	garnish

Makes 12 servings

Rub the sugar cubes over the lemon rind until saturated with the lemon oils. Remove the lemon peel and slice the lemons thinly.

Put all the ingredients except the champagne, soda water, and apple-mint into a punch bowl. Chill well.

When ready to serve, stir until the sugar is dissolved. Fill up with the champagne and soda water and garnish.

MOSELLE CUP

1 bottle Moselle	¼ cup sugar, or to taste
½ cup curaçao	Soda water
Strained juice and thinly	
pared rind of 1 lemon	

Makes 6 to 8 servings

Chill the first 4 ingredients well. Half-fill each glass and top up with soda or other sparkling water.

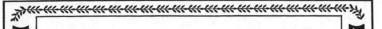

Index

MICHAEL SMITH is a champion of English food and cookery. His early training at the International Hotel Schools in Lausanne and Paris only helped to strengthen his belief in the quality and value of his native cuisine, and he is now held to be the acknowledged authority on, and advocate for, English cookery.

Hailed by the *New York Times* as "the doyen of English Cookery," his writing, broadcasting, and lecturing on all aspects of food preparation, presentation, and enjoyment reach an enormous audience, including viewers of B.B.C. T.V.'s "Pebble-Mill-at-One" and readers of *Homes and Gardens* and recently the *Daily Telegraph*.

Michael Smith believes that a glamorous dish deserves a glamorous setting and has demonstrated his unerring eye for color and line in the interior decoration of Walton's and several other leading restaurants.

Using his expertise as a food historian, he has served as a consultant on such well-loved television series as "Upstairs, Downstairs" and "The Duchess of Duke Street."

Professional cooks use his books for reference; amateurs turn to them for inspiration. The infectious enthusiasm conveyed in his writing reaches out to anyone who enjoys good food, good drink, and good company.